COMPUTED SYNCHRONIZATION FOR MULTIMEDIA APPLICATIONS

THE KLUWER INTERNATIONAL SERIES
IN ENGINEERING AND COMPUTER SCIENCE

MULTIMEDIA SYSTEMS AND APPLICATIONS

Consulting Editor

Borko Furht
Florida Atlantic University

Recently Published Titles:

STILL IMAGE COMPRESSION ON PARALLEL COMPUTER ARCHITECTURES, by Savitri Bevinakoppa
    ISBN: 0-7923-8322-2
INTERACTIVE VIDEO-ON-DEMAND SYSTEMS: *Resource Management and Scheduling Strategies*, by T. P. Jimmy To and Babak Hamidzadeh
    ISBN: 0-7923-8320-6
MULTIMEDIA TECHNOLOGIES AND APPLICATIONS FOR THE 21st CENTURY: *Visions of World Experts*, by Borko Furht
    ISBN: 0-7923-8074-6
 INTELLIGENT IMAGE DATABASES: *Towards Advanced Image Retrieval,* by Yihong Gong
    ISBN: 0-7923-8015-0
BUFFERING TECHNIQUES FOR DELIVERY OF COMPRESSED VIDEO IN VIDEO-ON-DEMAND SYSTEMS, by Wu-chi Feng
    ISBN: 0-7923-9998-6
HUMAN FACE RECOGNITION USING THIRD-ORDER SYNTHETIC NEURAL NETWORKS, by Okechukwu A. Uwechue, and Abhijit S. Pandya
    ISBN: 0-7923-9957-9
MULTIMEDIA INFORMATION SYSTEMS, by Marios C. Angelides and Schahram Dustdar
    ISBN: 0-7923-9915-3
MOTION ESTIMATION ALGORITHMS FOR VIDEO COMPRESSION, by Borko Furht, Joshua Greenberg and Raymond Westwater
    ISBN: 0-7923-9793-2
VIDEO DATA COMPRESSION FOR MULTIMEDIA COMPUTING, edited by Hua Harry Li, Shan Sun, Haluk Derin
    ISBN: 0-7923-9790-8
REAL-TIME VIDEO COMPRESSION: *Techniques and Algorithms*, by Raymond Westwater and Borko Furht
    ISBN: 0-7923-9787-8
MULTIMEDIA DATABASE MANAGEMENT SYSTEMS, by B. Prabhakaran
    ISBN: 0-7923-9784-3
MULTIMEDIA TOOLS AND APPLICATIONS, edited by Borko Furht
    ISBN: 0-7923-9721-5

COMPUTED SYNCHRONIZATION FOR MULTIMEDIA APPLICATIONS

by

Charles B. Owen
Michigan State University

Fillia Makedon
Dartmouth College

KLUWER ACADEMIC PUBLISHERS
Boston / Dordrecht / London

Distributors for North, Central and South America:
Kluwer Academic Publishers
101 Philip Drive
Assinippi Park
Norwell, Massachusetts 02061 USA
Telephone (781) 871-6600
Fax (781) 871-6528
E-Mail <kluwer@wkap.com>

Distributors for all other countries:
Kluwer Academic Publishers Group
Distribution Centre
Post Office Box 322
3300 AH Dordrecht, THE NETHERLANDS
Telephone 31 78 6392 392
Fax 31 78 6546 474
E-Mail <orderdept@wkap.nl>

 Electronic Services <http://www.wkap.nl>

Library of Congress Cataloging-in-Publication Data

Owen, Charles B.
   Computed synchronization for multimedia applications / by Charles
B. Owen, Fillia Makedon.
    p. cm. -- (The Kluwer international series in engineering and
computer science ; SECS 513)
   Includes bibliographical references.
   ISBN 978-1-4419-5093-2
   1. Multimedia systems. 2. Synchronization. I. Makedon, F.
(Fillia) II. Title. III. Series.
QA76.575.O92   1999
006.7--dc21   99-27711
                                              CIP

Printed on acid-free paper.

Printed in the United States of America

Contents

List of Figures

List of Tables

Preface

The analysis of images, audio, video, and other multimedia data is an exciting field that has been active for several years. Content-based retrieval systems, improved compression methods, and multimedia data servers are just some of the applications this analysis has made possible. However, the vast bulk of this work seeks to index, analyze, compress, or in other ways study one media data type at a time. Even common joint media presentations such as video and audio are studied in isolation. Admittedly, this is significant and difficult work. This book examines these same media as well, but in combination. This new concept, the joint analysis of multiple media components, leads to powerful tools in many application areas such as compression and content-based retrieval. The focus of this research is computed synchronization, correlations among multiple media streams that are not explicitly defined in the data type but are, rather, discovered by analysis techniques such as those described in this book.

This book is the outgrowth of research conducted at the Dartmouth Experimental Visualization Laboratory in the Dartmouth College Department of Computer Science during the years 1993-1998. This volume presents this work in a form suitable for study and further development. Chapters 1 and 2 develop the general concept of multimedia data and are basic introductions to this topic. These chapters also introduce a new discrete data representation for media data, the media representation graph. Chapter 3 introduces multiple media correlation, the underlying concept behind computed synchronization. Chapter 4 introduces a basic algorithm for computing synchronization data among streams that is applicable to a wide variety of media combinations. This algorithm has several variations that are more efficient in specific applications. Chapters 5 and 6 illustrate the use of these algorithms in two disparate applications. Parallel text alignment seeks to compute an alignment between multiple translations of the same base content. This alignment can be used to compare translations or to augment retrieval technologies. Text-to-speech alignment computes an alignment between a textual document and a vocal presentation of that document. This technology can be used for automatic closed-captioning, fine-grain retrieval, or synchronized presentation. Chapter 7 introduces the Xtrieve cross-modal information retrieval system. Xtrieve brings together the concepts of computed synchronization and cross-modal retrieval so as to demonstrate the use of these technologies in a multimedia information retrieval system. This system can locate content in Homeric translations using terms that do not even exist in the document and can locate broadcast television news content using simple text queries, presenting the retrieved result with precise starting and ending locations. Chapter 8 then discusses the future of our work in this field and additional applications that are possible.

This book is an introduction to the new field of computed synchronization. It does not claim to present the fastest, most efficient algorithms, nor the absolute best analysis methodologies. That will, of course, be a natural outgrowth of this work. It is our hope that this work will provide the seeds for a larger group of researchers to expand on this work and make multiple media techniques a common tool.

Acknowledgments

Most of all, I would like to thank my wife Mary for her support through the years we have been together. Also, thanks to my children: Crissa, Neil, Patricia, and Noel.

Charles B. Owen
Michigan State University

Many thanks to my Parents, Vasilios and Calliope Makedon and to Otmar Foelsche and my daughter Calliope who tolerated long working days.

Fillia Makedon
Dartmouth College

Chapter 1

INTRODUCTION

This monograph introduces the concept of *computed synchronization* for multimedia applications. Computed synchronization seeks to discover hidden relationships among multiple media data objects. These relationships may be due to similar sources, adaptation over time, or related content categories. This text illustrates methods for discovering these relationships and demonstrates uses for the computed synchronization data, particularly in the area of information retrieval.

The analysis of *multimedia* is based on the analysis of *media objects*. "Media" is a very general term used to describe virtually any means of transmitting data, though the work described herein is almost always concerned with data types representing information easily comprehended by humans. A media object is a physical instantiation of a media type. Examples of media types include text, audio, and video. *Multimedia* extends the root with the prefix "multi-", implying many. Indeed, a good definition of multimedia is the simultaneous processing and delivery of two or more discrete media objects.

Most common approaches to media data analysis can be better described as "monomedia" approaches in that they focus on a single media object such as a video clip, audio track, or textual document. Content-based browsing of digital video ignores contributions from the audio track [7]. Speech-based retrieval systems do not take advantage of any known transcript data [16]. That work is important and involves complicated solutions. However, many applications can benefit from the simultaneous analysis of multiple media objects. In such applications it is the *relationship between media objects* that is important as opposed to the relationship between a query and a single object. Indeed, in many cases the relationship between the objects can simplify the relationship between a query and an object.

Multiple media analysis, multiple media correlation, and *cross-modal information retrieval* are new terms proposed in this volume. These new concepts categorize work in multiple media analysis.

Multiple media analysis is the analysis of multiple media objects in order to derive new or hidden information. As a general analysis category, multiple media analysis includes any analysis methodology that accepts multiple media objects as input. A query-based information retrieval (IR) system that must combine results of single-media queries is a simple example of multiple media analysis.

Multiple media correlation is a specific category of multiple media analysis. Multiple media correlation is the derivation of relationships between two or more media objects. An example is the correlation of lip motion in video data to words in speech audio — the audio provides clues as to the motion of the lips. If the *spatial* synchronization between the two media objects can be determined, (moving lips located within a frame), the audio can be used to predict the lip motion, allowing joint audio-video data compression [20], or the speaker can be physically located in the image sequence, providing locality cues for speaker recognition and robotic navigation. The result of multiple media correlation is referred to as *computed synchronization*, the automatically determined relationships among media objects.

1.   MOTIVATION

Multimedia databases are accumulating at a massive rate. Yet, locating specific content in multimedia data is often very difficult. Many media types, such as audio, images, and video, contain large amounts of redundancy, are suffused with noise, and contain information which is not well understood computationally. However, some other media types are relatively easy to query. Methods for indexing and searching text have existed for hundreds of years and electronic indexing and querying of text databases is a mature technology. Also, some media have annotation information which is easy to comprehend and search. Such an example might be the slides used in a presentation. The order and content of the slides is known in advance of the presentation and is easy to browse and search. Locating the video segment of a presentation that discusses a particular slide is not so simple. Speech-based audio is also very difficult to query. Locating words in audio media objects is prone to all of the problems of open vocabulary word spotting and, therefore, requires relatively new technologies which often quote accuracy numbers in the 60% range [17].

For a large class of multimedia data, varying degrees of redundancy exist between the component media and can be exploited by multiple media correlation. Video of human speakers contains mouth motions highly correlated to the speech audio, for example, and closed-captioned video has text information which presents what is spoken in the audio redundantly (and provides cues to sound effects and music). Any application where a script or transcription exists (court testimony, dramatic productions, or broadcasting, for example) has a large amount of redundancy between the transcript and the audio. Often this redundancy represents identical information in more than one media object, one of which is easy to query, while the other is difficult. Locating specific content in a text transcript is easy. Locating the same content in speech audio is difficult. However, it is often the complicated media result that is desired and more useful.

It would be advantageous to query the easier media object and present the result in the other one. In court cases an attorney typically wishes to play a video segment of testimony rather than reading it, if possible, a task typically performed now by shuttling videotape to locate the appropriate testimony, even though its exact location in the transcript is known.

Many computed synchronization applications exist. The need for quality synchronization data is illustrated by how often it is manually produced. Video captions are aligned by hand [109]. Content is manually located in video tapes and the location of the content saved as annotations to simplify future searching. Slides are manually aligned to lectures in order to build high quality multimedia presentations [71]. In each of these applications and many more, computed synchronization can both replace manual operations and permit analysis of a much larger quantity of content.

A major new multimedia retrieval technology made possible by multiple media correlation is *cross-modal information retrieval*. Cross-modal information retrieval is the querying of one media object for results in another. The underlying requirement for cross-modal information retrieval is the existence of synchronization information which allows the location of the desired result in a target media object given its location in a query media object. If a textual transcription for recorded speech and its temporal alignment to the speech audio are available, a query into the transcript can be used to locate a desired speech segment, thus achieving text-to-speech information retrieval. Multiple media correlation computes the alignment between these objects.

2.   RELATED WORK

As a research field, multimedia is very much an integrating area. Tools are needed to integrate diverse representations of different media types. This book describes a new tool in the form of computed synchronization. The subject of this book, multiple media correlation, is a technology that applies to many different media formats including conventional multimedia data types such as audio, images, and video, but also text, medical imagery, and composite multimedia presentations. Hence, a large body of previous work has been drawn on in this research. The following chapters present many diverse topics, so related work specific to the chapter content is included in each chapter and briefly summarized here. This section also describes work related to the general concepts of this topic and work that has been published by the author in this area. It also indicates an important distinction with the conventional multimedia topic of synchronization (the synchronized presentation of content with existing explicit correlations).

2.1   MEDIA AND SYNCHRONIZATION MODELS

This text develops models for media data which are closely related to those of Gibbs, Breiteneder, and Tsichritzis[45, 46]. In the Gibbs et al. model, media objects consist of media data (frames, samples, etc.) combined with a discrete time system, a mapping from media object indices to moments in time, a specific temporal requirement. A major goal of the Gibbs et al. temporal media representations is synchronized presentation, not analysis or correlation. Multimedia composition models have been developed to model the combination of component media objects into presentations. Common composition models include spatio-temporal composition [65], Object Composition Petri nets [69], and time-line models [51]. Synchronization data models have focused on the synchronized delivery and presentation of multimedia content and are presented by many authors [10, 99, 69].

Much of the work on media models is an extension of textual data models developed by Salton and others [111]. Structured text, as evidenced by SGML and related standards [5, 116], is the foundation for hierarchical media models.

2.2   MULTIPLE MEDIA ANALYSIS AND CORRELATION

Multiple media analysis is a relatively new area. Some early projects included alignment of newly recorded voice audio to degraded voice audio, a technique used in motion picture dubbing (the replacement of an existing soundtrack with a new one in a studio). This work is described along with several other unsolved application areas by Chen et al. [21] and by Bloom [14]. The ViewStation project included cross-modal retrieval of close-captioned video, which falls into the *script-tight* category described in this book [68]. Chen, Graf, and Wang [20] and Rao and Chen [103] illustrate joint audio-video coding based on audio prediction of lip motion in order to achieve higher compression levels. Cross-modal compression technologies are a major potential application area for the techniques developed in this text.

2.3   PARALLEL TEXT ALIGNMENT

One of the applications presented in detail in this book is the alignment of intra-language parallel texts, documents in the same language which are based on underlying original foreign language documents. Though the alignment of intra-language content is new, it is closely related to cross-language alignment. There has been considerable work in this area including work with domain knowledge (lexical information) and without [15, 24, 28, 79]. The system described in this book utilizes WordNet, a large existing linguistic knowledge base, for scoring word similarity. Rigau and Agirre use WordNet in conjunction with a cross-lingual dictionary to build a cross-language lexicon for information retrieval and alignment [108]. Other researchers have focused on discovering this knowledge directly from the text data.

Given feature vectors of varying granularities (characters, words, sentences, etc.), computation of a best alignment path varies from the simple shortest line approach described above to image-based approaches advocated by Church [24]. The image-based approaches construct a *dot plot*, a square image of size $(n_1+n_2)^2$. Feature correspondences are plotted in this image, and line detection is used to find a path. Church plots coincidental characters in an attempt to discover a lexicon with no examination of the actual words. Fung and Church apply the same technique to matching word pairs with more general results, particularly when one of the languages is non-Roman [42]. These approaches suffer from quadratic scaling problems in that they are based on image sizes that are $\Omega(n_1 n_2)$.

2.4   TEXT-TO-SPEECH ALIGNMENT

Another correlation application presented in detail is text-to-speech alignment, the location in speech audio of the presentation of the transcript words. Most previous work on text-to-speech alignment has been concerned with automatic corpora labeling, the accurate location of sound elements such as phones in speech audio [3, 125, 130]. The process is applied to very short audio segments and is used to generate standard training and testing data. These systems are designed for precise alignment of very short segments of audio, not for entire texts. They are not designed to effectively recover from alignment failures or to scale to hours of content.

The importance of alignment of text to speech audio has been recognized in the Informedia [53] and News-on-demand [52, 80] projects at Carnegie Mellon University. The Informedia project seeks to index speech-based audio using automatic transcription. Whenever possible, they have taken advantage of the availability of transcript data. However, their approach to synchronization is to perform automatic transcription on the audio without knowledge of the transcription and then align the text transcripts based on word matching, hoping for some minimum recognition performance. The News-on-demand project utilizes closed-captioned digital video, but has observed that the caption content can lead or lag the video by up to 20 seconds.

Most approaches to searching speech content assume no available transcription data. Of particular interest is work at Cambridge University [16] and the

Swiss Federal Institute of Technology [113]. A good introduction to speech recognition technologies can be found in [102]. Cole, et al. describe recent developments in the field [25].

2.5   CONTRASTING AREAS

A core of this work is media synchronization. This should not be confused with the conventional multimedia topic of synchronization [1, 6, 19, 69, 84]. Typically, synchronization in multimedia is concerned with the synchronized presentation of content. Synchronized presentation assumes synchronization data either already exists (as in video-audio streams) or is explicitly supplied as an element of the authoring process (as in spatio-temporal composition).

2.6   PUBLICATIONS RELATED TO THE WORK

There have been several publications related to this work. This work is being performed in the Dartmouth Experimental Visualization Laboratory (DE-VLAB) and is closely related to the Speak Alexandria, Hear Homer [73], and Fuseum projects [32, 70]. The IMAGETCL multimedia algorithm development environment is described in [90]. The IMAGETCL infrastructure for multiple media stream analysis is presented in [72, 93, 94]. Information on multiple media correlation has been described in [95]. An application of multiple media correlation to medical imagery is described in [89]. Cross-modal retrieval of scripted speech audio is described in [97]. A general description of cross-modal information retrieval is in [91]. The use of synchronization in electronic and multimedia publishing systems is discussed in [74, 33].

2.7   MEDIA MODELS

Some of the most mature work in the field of multimedia today is in formal models for media data. Gibbs, Breiteneder, and Tsichritzis have presented widely accepted models [45, 46]. However, this previous work has focused on storage, presentation, and authoring of multimedia data. Computed synchronization is primarily concerned with multimedia data *analysis*. The existing models are not well adapted to analysis. This book introduces new models and operations for analysis of multimedia. In particular, the formally diverse media classes of static media and temporal media are combined into a new class of *causal media*, providing a common framework for simultaneous analysis.

New terminology and operations are introduced in this book for the transformation of media objects from one type to another. This is a prerequisite for domain translation, the conversion of media data into forms more suitable for analysis. This work generalizes the work of Gibbs et al. and provides tools for describing operations necessary during the media data analysis process.

One of the most important of the new media models is the *media representation graph* (MRG). MRGs are a new graphically-based model for media data that is unique in its ability to represent many media types, including temporal media such as audio and video, static media such as text and images, and hypermedia such as World Wide Web presentations. This model provides a single media representation for all of the computational approaches presented in this book and allows many problems to be solved using a single, simple tool.

2.8 MULTIPLE MEDIA CORRELATION

The primary theoretical contributions of this work are models for multiple media correlation. Many existing models exist for signal correlation and for aligning two media objects temporally. This work derives the multiple media correlation model, a more general model for computed synchronization that accounts for both causal (temporal) and spatial synchronization. The concept of normalization, the synchronization of media objects to an arbitrary normalization coordinate system, is presented as a more general computational alternative to synchronization.

Multiple media correlation is presented in three forms in this book: a continuous formulation, a discrete formulation, and a ranked-results formulation. Most of the applications presented herein are based on the use of the discrete formulation. The continuous formulation provides a fertile ground for future applications which are more analytical in nature.

Multiple media correlation solutions must obey certain constraints for a solution to exist. Conditions under which a solution will not exist are described and new constraints are defined which can guarantee solution existence.

2.9 ALGORITHMIC SOLUTIONS

This work was motivated by real-world problems which required (automatic) computed synchronization. As experimental work on these problems progressed, several new algorithms were developed for solving these problems. Gradually, a general pattern of similarity evolved into a multiple media correlation model and a single algorithm appropriate for a large class of problems. This algorithm, presented in Chapter 4, is the first general solution for N-way computed synchronization. The algorithm is very general and appropriate for a large class of problems.

The performance analysis of the new algorithm assumes unconstrained algorithm input. However, for many specific problem instances the performance is shown in this book to be significantly improved. One of these instances, synchronization to continuous media such as audio and video, is actually quite common. Two special cases of algorithm input constraints are described which are both common, and naturally result in improved performance.

Several approaches are presented which further improve algorithm performance. A characteristic of multimedia data analysis is that media objects are often very large, so algorithm performance improvements are very important. The performance improvements developed include comparison caching, MRG optimization, and the general practice of pruning, a method for paring a problem solution down to just the important or most likely candidate alignments.

An important new concept introduced in this book is *edit tolerance*, the ability to synchronize media objects in the presence of errors. Real content often has errors between components. A speech presentation may skip over textual content, a document may not include some words, etc. Practical computed synchronization systems must take these errors (edits) into account. This book presents new formal constructs for edits and demonstrably practical edit tolerance approaches.

In real-world applications, the synchronization of two or more media objects will sometimes fail. For example, real media objects often have periods of high noise or completely obscured content. In such cases, the media alignment does not discriminate content very well, so the system should interpolate an alignment over the region that does not match well. This book introduces the concept of *enforced interpolation* and provides algorithmic approaches to its implementation.

2.10   PARALLEL TEXT ALIGNMENT

Two major applications of multiple media correlation are described in this book. These applications were chosen both for their general utility and as representations of many of the major features of multiple media correlation.

Parallel text alignment is the computed synchronization of two texts which enjoy a written language translation relationship with each other. The most common example of parallel text alignment is the alignment of alternative language presentations. This book represents the first known work on alignment of common language presentations (intra-language), specifically multiple English language translations based on a foreign language root-document. This application has been shown to be very useful in the study of Classic literature and in the critical analysis of alternative translations. The techniques presented can also apply to cross-language text alignment.

The multiple media correlation parallel text alignment solution is also the first approach to parallel text alignment to apply global synchronization technologies. Previous approaches have used greedy local techniques and statistical character, word, sentence, and paragraph associations. The new approach presented in this book formulates the problem as a multiple media correlation problem.

2.11   TEXT-TO-SPEECH ALIGNMENT

The multiple media correlation solution to text-to-speech alignment presented in this book is the first known attempt to directly align textual transcripts to speech-based audio on a large scale. Previous alignment work has focused on short segment alignment for speech corpus development. The text-to-speech alignment solution presented in this book allows for practical and accurate retrieval of speech-based content in multimedia databases. It is the first such application to use the transcript as the entire vocabulary and language model in a speech recognition-like tool.

Text-to-speech alignment provides a good demonstration of many of the algorithmic enhancements described in this book. Transcriptions, though widely available, are often quite error laden, either through erroneous presentation or though deliberate editing out of content to save presentation time. Audio quality varies widely. Consequently, text-to-speech alignment is a significant test of edit tolerance mechanisms and enforced interpolation.

Also described are methods and tools for the evaluation of text-to-speech alignment results. As a new application area, no known-correct test corpus exists. This book demonstrates building test data-sets using hand-marking and converting an existing speech recognition corpus into a document useful for text-to-speech alignment testing.

2.12   THE XTRIEVE CROSS-MODAL INFORMATION RETRIEVAL SYSTEM

The major system component of this book is the Xtrieve cross-modal information retrieval system. Xtrieve is the first IR system to exploit cross-modal information retrieval. Consequently, it is one of the few query-based IR systems in existence that can accurately and quickly retrieve audio and video content as well as text.

Xtrieve exploits two modalities for retrieval of multimedia content, indexing and browsing. Indexing allows for the query-based retrieval of content, but indexing solutions beyond text-based technologies are rare and very limited at this time. Cross-modal information retrieval allows text-based query processing results to be extended to complicated media such as audio and video. Media browsing is the manual traversal of a media object using VCR-like controls, mouse selections, etc. Xtrieve introduces cross-modal browsing, where results discovered in one media object are simultaneously presented in an alternative media object. Xtrieve is the only known system to support cross-modal browsing.

The difficulty of searching video and audio content has limited the development of multimedia databases. Xtrieve is one of the first multimedia database systems to allow practical query-based retrieval of multimedia data. As a result,

Xtrieve development led to many new ideas in the selection and presentation of multimedia data in a database system. Xtrieve supports *granularity control*, the control of retrieval sizes so as to limit the temporal duration of a result presentation. Granularity control, in conjunction with media browsing, makes it much easier for a user to find specific content in time-based media.

Text data in Xtrieve is indexed in levels to support granularity and is subjected to analysis for computed synchronization. Consequently, text data is subject to three types of processing: display, multi-level indexing, and synchronization. Xtrieve illustrates the importance of structured document formats such as SGML in a cross-modal information retrieval system [116]. As in many SGML-based systems, style sheets are used to associate format with the SGML document structure so that documents can be nicely displayed on the screen. However, Xtrieve extends this idea by using style sheets to associate analysis, in this case multiple media correlation, with selected parts of a document and to associate indexing granularity with different selected parts of the document.

2.13   FUTURE APPLICATIONS

Two applications are presented in considerable detail in this book. In addition, Chapter 8 describes many more potential applications for the technologies developed in this book, including the analysis of medical imagery and the alignment of slide-based lecture presentations, two projects currently active in the DEVLAB. Possible uses for multiple media correlation are described in varying detail, illustrating the great potential for future work in multiple media correlation.

3.   ORGANIZATION OF BOOK

This book is structured top down, first describing the theoretical framework, then demonstrating the technology in implementation. The early chapters focus on models and algorithms for general computed synchronization applications. Two specific applications for this technology are then presented. These applications demonstrate the generality and utility of the algorithm and models. The applications form the indexing core of the Xtrieve cross-modal information retrieval system described in Chapter 7. Finally, a closing chapter lists many future applications for this technology.

Chapter 2 describes the terminology for succinctly describing media types and media objects. This chapter also introduces the *media representation graph*, a powerful tool for media object representation and a foundation for the algorithms in this book. Chapter 3 presents the basic models for multiple media correlation. The new models presented in Chapter 3 expand on previous correlation and pattern recognition models to provide a simple and general, yet highly usable description for the correlation of two or more media objects.

Chapter 4 presents a general algorithmic solution for this model. This solution can be applied to a wide variety of problems in multiple media correlation.

Chapter 5 is the first of two major application chapters. This chapter presents the specific application of intra-language text-to-text alignment. Results are demonstrated on ancient texts and Bible translations. Chapter 6 is the premier application of multiple media correlation, text-to-speech alignment. Text-to-speech alignment makes possible simple and accurate queries into speech-based multimedia data. It also provides tools for automating the labor-intensive captioning process.

Chapter 7 describes the Xtrieve cross-modal information retrieval system. Xtrieve utilizes the technology presented in this book to support query-based retrieval of multimedia data. As a full system implementation, the Xtrieve development project allowed exploration of the concept of cross-modal information retrieval and experimentation with a full function multimedia retrieval system.

Multiple media analysis is a new and general field. As such, there is considerable room for future work. Chapter 8 describes additional applications for multiple media correlation and discusses future directions for this research. Some of these applications and future directions are already in development at the DEVLAB and the Dartmouth Medical School.

Chapter 2

MEDIA, MULTIMEDIA, AND SYNCHRONIZATION MODELS

Deducing and utilizing relationships, (specifically synchronization relationships) among audio, video, text, and other media objects must necessarily build upon the foundation of a strong understanding of the underlying media. The focus of this chapter is the description of models for media objects and media synchronization data. These models are used in Chapter 3 to describe multiple media correlation and in the remaining chapters to describe the solution and implementation of that model in general and specific applications. This work differs from the existing base of literature on media models by providing for media analysis.

Media types are typically divided into three classes: static media such as text, time synchronous media such as audio and video, and complex multimedia presentations requiring object composition models for description. The existing literature is primarily concerned with three issues when media data models are formally presented: synchronized delivery, synchronized presentation, and the construction of composite media presentations. This chapter extends the work of Gibbs et al. with the goal of accommodating a fourth usage: multimedia data analysis [46]. Multiple media correlation often occurs on media types that are not necessarily both static or time synchronous. Also, the analysis techniques presented in this book often require the transformation of a media type to another, more appropriate type. This chapter describes mechanisms and operations for such transformations. The bulk of the chapter is devoted to media models and terminology, constructing a concrete model on which to base synchronization technologies.

An important new contribution of this chapter is the *media representation graph* (MRG), a graphical model for media objects. Media representation graphs provide a single media model that unifies and can represent most media types including text, audio, video, and hypermedia. Indeed, the presented algorithmic solutions for computed synchronization in this book will utilize MRGs for all input representation.

Section 1. describes the related work in media models that forms the foundation for the models in this chapter. Section 2. defines the concepts of media, multimedia, and media streams. The operations which convert media objects to new types are defined in Section 3.. The definition and use of media elements is discussed in Section 4.. The media representation graph is introduced in Section 5.. Section 6. introduces models for synchronization data, the computed result of multiple media correlation.

1.   RELATED WORK

Multimedia is an emerging field and many of the earlier or existing results are models for media data. Much of this work is closely related to models developed for textual data by Salton and others [111]. In particular, structured text, as evidenced by SGML and related standards [5, 116], constitutes the foundation for most existing hierarchical media models. These standards have led to similarly structured multimedia data standards such as HyTime [84].

The literature is replete with models for time-based media types and media ordering. Gibbs, Breiteneder, and Tsichritzis [45, 46] describe *timed streams*, a generalization of temporal media types. In the Gibbs et al. model, timed streams assume media objects consist of media data (frames, samples, etc.) combined with a discrete time system, a mapping from media object indices to moments in time, a specific temporal requirement. Thus, a major goal of the Gibbs, et al. temporal media representations is synchronized presentation, not analysis or correlation.

Synchronized presentation assumes the existence of implicit or explicit synchronization information between multiple media stream objects that is utilized to present composite media objects in a timed presentation with bounded timing errors between elements [69, 51]. This differs from the requirements of *computed media synchronization*, as defined in this book, in that media synchronization data is not assumed to exist a priori and the computed data may need to be of a higher density than require for presentation. Text is typically presented without regard to time, whereas a computed synchronization between text and speech may exist at the sub-word level.

Multimedia composition models have been developed to model combination of component media objects into presentations. Common composition models include spatio-temporal composition [65], Object Composition Petri nets [69], and time-line models [51]. Synchronization models have focused on the synchronized delivery and presentation of multimedia content and are presented by many authors [10, 99, 69].

2. MEDIA, MULTIMEDIA, AND MEDIA STREAMS

The word "media" is a general term meant to represent both the "how" and "what" in communication and information exchange. Gibbs, et al., refer to media as both "how information is conveyed" and "the materials and forms of artistic expression" and distinguish *digital media* from *natural media*, natural media implying reliance on physical elements and digital media implying reliance on discrete representations [46].

Virtually all content routinely referred to today as *multimedia* can also be considered *media*. Gibbs, et al., in fact, use the terms interchangeably. However, the distinction in the term *multimedia* is the co-existence of two or more media. A video clip with an associated sound track is a multimedia object composed of sound and video media objects. An audio clip or a document is not considered multimedia under this strict interpretation. The author of this book has been known to use the term "monomedia" on occasion for this class of data.

DEFINITION 2.1 (MEDIA) *Media are any means of transmitting, storing, and presenting information. This definition does not limit media to conventional computer media technologies such as video, audio, and text, but also includes binary data, medical imagery, and analog media technologies such as broadcasting and sound.*

DEFINITION 2.2 (MEDIA TYPE) *A media type is a data type describing the format and representation of media data. Often the term media is applied to both the generic data types (as in audio, video, and images), and to specific instantiations of those data types (a video clip or a document). To avoid possible confusion, this book utilizes the term media type to refer to a specific data type and media object to refer to an instantiation of that type.*

DEFINITION 2.3 (MEDIA OBJECT) *A media object is a specific instance of a media type.*

At the most basic level, a media object is a function of time, space, input, and state. Access by time and space is obvious, but it is also common that a multimedia presentation will be highly dependent upon a user access pattern or external input. Access to a World Wide Web page may depend upon the authored content, user profile information that has been stored, the user access pattern that led to the page, and news or stock price input that modified the page contents. Hence, an entirely general mathematical model of media (and multimedia) would have to be of the form $f : T \times I \times S \rightarrow D \times S$. T is a vector of dimensions (a multidimensional space) and represents access to the media data. Locations in an image, the address of a web page, or even the specific time a web page is accessed are examples of spatial parameters for a media object. I is any input to the media object that will modify the object state and presentation. In the case of a web application, user input to data forms or real-time stock quotation feeds are examples of input. D is the domain of the data (images, audio samples, composites of many components, etc.). S is the sets of possible object states. The media object state can be modified as a function of the input.

Modeling media data as a general function of state, spatial parameters, and input results in a very general model that is complex and difficult to characterize, requiring component models such as Object Composition Petri Nets (OCPN) [69], multi-structured models [67], hypermedia models [10], or other spatio-temporal composition technologies. However, this generality is nearly always related to composite multimedia presentation and can often be described using combinations of less complex component media.

2.1   CONTINUOUS AND DISCRETE MEDIA

Information spans two worlds, the analog and digital worlds. Nature is inherently analog and continuous; computers are digital and discrete. Hence, it is common to refer to *continuous media* and *discrete media*. Continuous media are analog media types and cannot be represented in finite storage without sampling. Discrete media are media types that can be represented by a mapping of integers to elements of the media.

In this book, media in the analog world is referred to as "continuous media". However, this is not meant to imply underlying continuity of the waveforms of the media type. Indeed, discontinuity is common in models of analog media (though less common in actuality). An "edit" in an analog signal may induce discontinuity through an instantaneous signal transition. Conventional television broadcasting uses continuous analog waveforms to represent the contents of a scan line, but the lines and the video fields are discrete.

2.2   MEDIA STREAMS

Many media types can be expressed as a function of one or more real variables. The implication is that the media presentation is consistent and static (reproducible in only one form) and has no state. For example, audio is a one dimensional function of time and video is a three dimensional function $\mu(t, x, y)$, where t represents time and x, y are positions within an image. Text is a one dimensional discrete function of sequential character or word presentation $\mu(s)$. Media which can be expressed in such an ordered form are referred to in this book as *media stream types*.

DEFINITION 2.4 (MEDIA STREAM TYPE) *A media stream type is any media type that can be expressed as a multidimensional function of real variables. More precisely, a media stream can be expressed in the form* $\mu : \Re_1 \times \ldots \times \Re_N \rightarrow$

D. D is the media domain, the presentation format (or natural format) of the media. D can (and usually does) include the empty set for points in the range which do not map to other members of the domain of the media stream. $\Re_i, i = 1, ..., N$ are the ordering variables for the media object.

The definition assumes, for simplicity, that a media stream type is a function of real variables, even when the media type is discrete. Discrete media are modeled in this framework by mapping non-integral points to the empty set or a null domain value (such as zero for a real-valued domain). This is similar to the assumption that the sampling operation is considered to be the multiplication of a real-valued signal by an impulse function, as described by Bellanger [12].

The word "stream" is due to the ordered nature of the media. A media stream type can be accessed sequentially by each of the ordering variables. Examples of ordering variables include time and space. A video object can be presented as a continuum of image data, ordered by a variable t or as a sequence of horizontal cross-sections for different values of y.

DEFINITION 2.5 (ORDERING VARIABLE) *An ordering variable is any one of the real variables which form the range of a media stream type. Mapping real variables to elements of the media domain necessarily implies distinct orders of presentation or access. Ordering variables can present media in orders that are different from the natural order of appearance or an alternative mapping.*

An instantiation of a media stream type is a *media stream object*. Streaming media is often utilized in "live" settings. An example is the capture of audio and video for transmission and remote presentation. In this case, the term "object" may seem inappropriate in that the entire media object never exists in storage. However, this example does fit the above definition and the presentation could, in fact, be stored and accessed as an object.

Not all media types can be described as media stream types, in particular those that require state, so media stream types are a proper subset of the general set of media. However, media stream types are appropriate for describing many common media formats such as audio, video, text, and images. They are also appropriate for describing many components upon which more complicated compositional models are built.

2.3   CAUSAL MEDIA STREAM

Some media stream types have an underlying primary ordering, represented by a dominant ordering variable. This ordering may be time, as in the case of an audio signal, or a sequential nature to the content, as in the case of text. A primary ordering is often exploited as an indexing means for storage of media; the media objects are stored sequentially based on the ordering, so that retrieval for presentation is more efficient. Many media types have more than one such ordering. Video can be described as a three dimensional function of t, x, and y. However, in the case of video, the temporal ordering is usually considered dominant. Media types with more than one ordering dimension can still be described as having an ordering on a single dimension and are referred to as *causal media streams*[1].

DEFINITION 2.6 (CAUSAL MEDIA STREAM TYPE) *A causal media stream type is a media stream type that has a dominant ordering. This ordering is typically related to storage, presentation, and transmission of media objects. Any causal media type can be expressed as a function of one variable:* $\mu : \Re \rightarrow D$, *where D is the domain of the causal media function, the possible values of the media type for a given value of the ordering variable.*

Obviously, any media stream type can be considered a causal media stream type by simply declaring one variable to be the dominant variable. Similarly, the choice of a dominant variable may be completely arbitrary, so a media object might be changed from one causal media stream type to another by simply changing the choice of ordering variable. The distinction is entirely an enforced distinction for an application. Video is considered a causal media stream type ordered on time because time is a natural ordering users are accustomed to and a sensible ordering for storage and transmission.

The functional representation of a causal media stream can be continuous or discrete. Continuous functions represent analog media data. Streaming media that can be represented using continuous functions are referred to as *continuous streaming media*. If the ordering function is discrete, as is often the case in computational applications, the media type is referred to as *discrete streaming media*. The terms "streaming" and "continuous" are not synonymous. A "streaming media type" implies sequential presentation or access, be it of discrete or continuous elements. A "continuous media type" implies that the underlying functions that model the media are locally continuous.

For some media types, such as video and audio, the dominant ordering variable is time. Media types ordered on time are traditionally called *time-based media*. Other media types, such as text, are not considered to be fundamentally time-based at all, though they are considered to be ordered on a dominant ordering variable such as a character index into a document. An image is a single discrete event, and has no fundamental ordering in time. Although the term *time-based media* has enjoyed widespread acceptance in the literature, the class of media it describes, a subset of causal media streams, is easily extended to include any content that is also ordered on a single variable, but is not necessarily considered to be ordered on time.

2.4   FUNCTIONAL MODELS AND BLOBS

The models presented thus far have been functional models, i.e., models of media types best expressed using mathematical functions. Functional models are useful because they allow for simple mathematical manipulation of causal media types and because they are a general representation that can be applied to all of the other models in this chapter. The Binary Large Object (BLOB) model of discrete media is similar in that it also describes a media object with the minimum amount of information, i.e., as a sequential list of bytes. Both functional and BLOB models represent "black boxes". Positional information goes in, media data comes out. This is, in fact, the function of interpretation, a media transformation operation described in Section 3.1 — to convert black boxes into a more readily understood form.

3.   MEDIA TRANSFORMATIONS

Media objects can exist in many similar or equivalent forms. Video can exist as a continuous function of time and space, as in nature. Broadcast video exists as a discrete sequence of raster images, each composed of continuous line data. In computer applications, video might be represented as a set of discrete matrices or as an MPEG encoded compressed data file. Each of these media objects is presenting the exact same underlying information, but in different forms so as to be compatible with the presentation environment or take advantage of temporal and spatial redundancy to decrease storage space or transmission bandwidth. The differing storage and presentation formats each imply some loss of information. This section is concerned with transformations among various representations of the same media, both with and without loss.

3.1   INTERPRETATION, DERIVATION, AND TRANSFORMATION

Interpretation and *derivation* are common existing terms for relations among media objects [46]. Interpretation refers to the conversion of a *binary large object* (BLOB) to a media type suitable for display or manipulation. A BLOB is basically a sequence of bytes, a representation of a media object with all detail hidden. An interpretation is a mapping of a BLOB to a media object. An example is the mapping of compressed video frames in a BLOB to image data in memory for display. A derivation is a computation of a new media object from an existing object and is typically used to describe processes in the manipulation and authoring process. An example is the processing of a video frame to increase brightness. The following are formal definitions of interpretation and derivation, as quoted from Gibbs et al.

DEFINITION 2.7 (INTERPRETATION [46]) *An interpretation, I, of a BLOB B, is a mapping from B to a media object. For each object, I specifies the object's descriptor and its placement in B. If the object is a media sequence, then for each media element, I specifies the element's order within the sequence, its start time, duration, and element descriptor.*

DEFINITION 2.8 (DERIVATION [46]) *The derivation (D) of a media object o_1 from a set of media objects O is a mapping of the form $D(O, P_D) \rightarrow o_1$, where P_D is the set of parameters specific to D. o_1 is called the derived object. The information needed to compute a derived object, including references to the media objects and parameter values used, is called a derivation descriptor.*

The above terms describe similar operations. For example, the act of decompression is specifically defined as an interpretation, but is compression a derivation? Is segmentation a derivation? Derivation is assumed to be *parameterized*, incorporating a set of parameters which describe the derivation operations, while interpretation is not; however, it is common for decompression, a BLOB interpretation, to be parameterized with different display resolutions, quality factors, etc.

The operation described by both of these terms is the parameterized transformation of one media object to another. This book uses the more general term *transformation* to denote this operation.

DEFINITION 2.9 (TRANSFORMATION) *A transformation T from one media object $\mu \in M$ to another media object $\mu' \in M'$ is a function $T : M \times \Pi \rightarrow M'$, where Π represents a set of parameters specific to T. Transformation is denoted $\Rightarrow_{T,\pi}$, where $\pi \in \Pi$ is a specific parameterization of the transformation. In many cases the parameterization is assumed and can be omitted.*

Using this model, the decompression of a BLOB $\beta(s)$ representing a compressed data file is denoted $\beta \Rightarrow_{T,\pi} \mu$, where T is the decompression transformation and π is any parameterization of the decompression operation (image size, quality, processor time available, etc.).

3.2   EQUIVALENCE TRANSFORMATIONS

An *equivalence transformation* is an invertible transformation. Lossless compression is an example of a invertible transformation. *Lossless compression* is the transformation of a media object to a representation that exploits temporal and spatial redundancy so as to decrease storage requirements and transmission bandwidth while allowing for identical reconstruction of the original content. If lossless compression of a media type M is denoted C, then there exists an operation C^{-1} such that $\mu \Rightarrow_C \Rightarrow_{C^{-1}} \mu'$ implies $\mu = \mu'$. (Transformations are naturally transitive operations.) If a transformation is invertible, the transformation is considered to be an *equivalence transformation*.

DEFINITION 2.10 (EQUIVALENCE TRANSFORMATION) *A transformation T is an equivalence transformation if there exists an inverse transformation T^{-1}*

such that the composition of the transformation and the inverse transformation forms an identity transformation. Notationally, $\mu \Rightarrow_{T,\pi} \Rightarrow_{T^{-1},\pi} \mu$, where $\pi \in \Pi$ is a parameterization of the transformation operation. Equivalence transformations are denoted $\mu \equiv_{T,\pi} \mu'$. An equivalence transformation is an invertible transformation.

Obviously, not all transformations are equivalence transformations. Selection of a specific cut from a video cannot be reversed so as to restore the entire video. However, under certain conditions the transformation may appear to perform an equivalence operation, even though exactly reconstructing the original content is impossible. An example of such a transformation is lossy compression. *Lossy compression* is similar to lossless compression, except that the compression/decompression process reconstructs a representation of the original with some induced distortion. This distortion, an error between the original media object and the compressed/decompressed version, is assumed to be perceptually insignificant. The degree of imperceptibility can often be varied, typically in an inverse relationship to compression ratio (the effectiveness of the compression process at decreasing space or bandwidth requirements).

One method for assessing of the quality of reproduction following a lossy operation is the application of a *fidelity* factor. A fidelity factor F is a predicate that compares two media objects. The predicate is true-valued if the media objects are similar enough to meet the fidelity criteria.

The media analysis techniques presented in this book often require the transformation of a media object to a form easier to compare. This transformation requires some invertibility in order to maintain a relation to the original media object. However, the quality of the object may be severely degraded. A transformation that maintains a limited amount of invertibility up to a fidelity factor is a *semi-equivalence transformation*.

DEFINITION 2.11 (SEMI-EQUIVALENCE TRANSFORMATION) *A transformation T is a semiequivalence transformation under fidelity criterion F if there exists an inverse transformation T^{-1} such that for $\mu \Rightarrow_{T,\pi} \Rightarrow_{T^{-1},\pi} \mu'$, the predicate $F(\mu, \mu')$ is satisfied. Semi-equivalence transformations are denoted $\mu \tilde{\equiv}_{T,\pi} /mu'$.*

Chapter 5 describes a system for the alignment of translations of foreign language texts. The documents to be aligned are transformed into another form, the media representation graph described later in this chapter. That transformation discards much of the structure of the original document including content markup, inter-word spacing, and most punctuation. However, the operation is invertible in that the original document content can be reproduced with sufficient accuracy that locations in the original document can still be deduced after the analysis. Specifically, the byte offset of every word in the original file can be reproduced from the media representation graph. A fidelity measure that ensures the content of the original and reproduced documents are the same up to loss of punctuation and inter-word spacing could easily be devised for this example. Hence, the transformation from the document to the media representation graph is a semi-equivalence transformation.

4.   MEDIA ELEMENTS

Section 2. described the most basic of media models: media, media streams, and causal media streams. This section extends these definitions by examining the media function domain, specifically the elements of a media object at points in the ordering space (values of the ordering variables). This work extends the Gibbs terminology for segmental and hierarchical descriptions of media. The description of the domain of media objects as *media elements* is used to simplify the comparison of media objects. *Elemental* structure is important in analysis. Individual bits convey very little information; larger structural units are far more useful. Computed synchronization solutions align not the bits or bytes, but larger units of analysis.

The use of the term *media element* in this book is more general than in Gibbs et al. wherein a media element exists only in the context of a timed stream [45]. This distinction clears up some ambiguity about the validity of groupings in non-temporal media, as well as non-causal media. Hypermedia presentations, for example, a media type that is not at all temporal, can be subdivided into smaller units, the hypermedia *nodes*, each of which is a media element.

DEFINITION 2.12 (MEDIA ELEMENT) *A media element is a logical unit of analysis or presentation.*

Media types usually have many possible logical units of analysis or presentation. Digital media has a smallest unit in the form of a bit, but larger units also exist. Aggregates of bits are bytes. Bytes may, in turn, be grouped into integers, floating point values, or characters. Beyond these strictly mechanical aggregates exist groupings which represent structural elements of the media type. Examples for digital video include the contents of one video frame, a sequence of frames which represent a complete camera cut, or all of the frames that have red balls in them. Selection or identification of logical units applies equally well to discrete and continuous media. Broadcast radio signals can be subdivided temporally into news programs, commercials, or music.

4.1   CAUSAL MEDIA ELEMENTS

Causal media stream types can be expressed in the form $\mu : \Re \to D$, where D is the domain of the media function. The domain can be as simple as a single real value or as complex as a function space describing images. If the media type is only defined for integral values of the range, the media type is discrete.

The function values at points in the discrete ordering space are referred to as *causal media elements.*

DEFINITION 2.13 (CAUSAL MEDIA ELEMENT) *A causal media element for a discrete causal media stream object $\mu : \Re \to D$ is any $d \in D$ such that $\mu(s) = d$ for some $s \in \Re$.*

Recall that a media element is defined as a logical unit of analysis or presentation. Clearly text can be described as a sequence of characters. However, it is often more desirable that text be treated as a sequence of words. In such a case, an analysis application can transform the character-based media object into one with words as the media element. Let $\mu(s)$ be a discrete media object mapping points in a causal ordering space to characters. A transformation T can be devised such that $\mu(s) \Rightarrow_T \mu'(s)$ transforms $\mu(s)$ to a new media object that is a mapping of points in a causal ordering space to words.

In this book, computed synchronization is always based on the alignment of media elements. As an example, text-to-speech alignment, as described in Chapter 6, converts audio, a discrete function of the form $\mu : I \to I$, where I is the set of integers, to media elements consisting of estimates of the probability that each of a set of speech sounds are present in a 10 millisecond range of the audio. The audio, at various sample rates, is converted to a new causal media object such that the causal ordering space is integers representing 10 millisecond intervals of the audio. The domain of this new function, the media element, is a vector of real values representing the probability estimates. This transformation is a semi-equivalence transformation because the original audio stream can be reconstructed from these probabilities, but only with a great deal of loss.

The common description in the literature of time-based media objects as a function $\mu(t)$ of time can also be applied to causal media elements. The only change in notation is the use of the ordering variable s instead of t so that it will not be confused with "time".

4.2   HIERARCHICAL MEDIA ELEMENTS

Media elements often exhibit an inherent hierarchical structure. New media elements can be constructed as aggregates of underlying media elements. Table 2.1 lists hierarchical media elements for several common media types. The hierarchical nature of many media types provides a flexible tool for better description of the media type. Gibbs et al. describe media as being constructed in a hierarchical structure from simple to more complex objects [45]. Their description assumed temporal media. This book uses similar terminology, but extends the model to allow a more general meaning.

A common example of hierarchical media elements is the inherent tree structure in *standard generalized markup language* (SGML) documents [5,

Table 2.1.   Examples of hierarchical media elements.

Media type	Media elements
Text	Characters, words, sentences, paragraphs, sections, chapters, books
Text	Characters, words, lines, scenes, acts, plays
Video	Pixels, frames, cuts, scenes
Audio	Samples, waveform cycles, notes, utterances
Graphics	Points, lines, polygons, polyhedra

116]. SGML provides a mechanism for describing a hierarchical segmentation of a text document into logical units. Examples of subdivisions include lines, speeches, scenes, and acts of a play. Examples in other media types include the division of video into logical browsing units [7], and grammar based models of media such as Flavor [31].

Hierarchical media elements are useful, but should not be considered to be a complete and unique mechanism for the description of content. Even the widely accepted technique of hierarchical markup of textual content has been criticized as too restrictive [105]. In particular, such models do not allow for overlapping media elements. As an example, all of the lines of a play spoken by one particular actor is a selection from the document lines rather than a segmented element of the content. Consequently, hierarchical models are a tool, but not an exclusive model.

4.3   MEDIA ELEMENT TRANSFORMATIONS

A common transformation in computed synchronization applications is the selection of a more appropriate media element. As the last section illustrated, multiple media element structures can be defined for most media types. SGML documents can be described as sequences of bytes, words, or document sections. Each of these representations is a different causal media stream type. The types are related to each other through equivalence transformations (or semi-equivalence transformations when the alternative representations sacrifice some content). Implementation of these transformations may only require computation of an index that translates the causal ordering systems.

In computed synchronization applications the input to a solution algorithm is typically an alternative representation of a media object that is based on media elements more appropriate for comparison and alignment. Consequently, transformations that modify the choice of media elements or compute alternative media elements are very common and are referred to as *media element transformations*.

DEFINITION 2.14 (MEDIA ELEMENT TRANSFORMATION) *A transformation operation that converts a media type to an new type based on an alternative media element is a media element transformation. The transformation may be a grouping of media elements into aggregates, a break-down of an aggregate media element into components, or the computation of a totally new media element representation.*

Media element transformations can be equivalence or semi-equivalence transformations. Examples of media element transformations include translation of a character representation to a word representation, translation of a sequence of audio samples to a sequence of fixed duration audio frames (sets of samples), translation of words into sets of pronunciation units which represent how the word can be spoken, and translation of a hypermedia node into a set of media objects that were composed to form the node.

Media elements are elements of the domain of a functional representation of a media object. The domain does not in any way indicate the presentation order of the object. Causal media objects present media elements sequentially, but causal media objects can be transformed into media objects which do not present the media elements sequentially. As an example, pronunciation of a word can have alternatives. Words are presented sequentially, but the presentation sequence for an equivalent media object based on the pronunciation of the word will have alternative paths through the media object coordinate system depending upon the chosen word pronunciation. Media elements define the "what", not the "when", of media objects.

5.   MEDIA REPRESENTATION GRAPHS (MRG)

The purpose of a media model is to adequately describe the behavior of a media object. For many media types, simple causal (sequential) models are insufficient for describing media object behavior. It may also be the case that a media object has many possible alternative presentations in another modality. Aligning to media elements in a computed synchronization application may require the discovery of the selected presentation in that modality. This section introduces the *media representation graph* (MRG), a powerful new tool for describing media objects, modeling complex behavior, and structuring alternative presentation.

Section 4. introduced media elements as a unit of analysis or presentation. A media object that can be transformed to a finite set of media elements can be described graphically by assigning the media elements to vertices of the graph and using edges to represent possible orders of presentation of the media elements. As an example, causal media elements can be described graphically using vertices for media elements and edges to indicate the sequential, causal presentation of the elements, as shown in Figure 2.1, a simple example based on words from a text. The media elements in this example are the words of the text. Edges represent possible transitions from element to element, in this

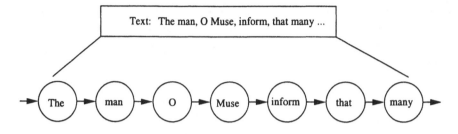

Figure 2.1.   Causal media elements represented as a graph.

case permitting only sequential presentation. A graphical model of the media element presentations for a media object is a media representation graph model of the object.

DEFINITION 2.15 (MEDIA REPRESENTATION GRAPH) *A media representation graph is a set of vertices representing media elements and a set of edges representing possible transitions from element to element. One vertex is identified as a start vertex. A presentation of a media object represented by a media representation graph is a path through the MRG.*

The construction of an MRG is dependent upon the ability to represent a media object as a finite set of media elements and a set of media element transitions. This transformation may or may not be an equivalence transformation. In Figure 2.1 the transformation is not an equivalence transformation, since the punctuation has been omitted.

MRG models are not, strictly speaking, equivalent to Finite Automata [61]. A finite automaton consists of a set of states and a set of labeled transitions between states. In an MRG, it is the state that is labeled rather than the transition. Obviously, an MRG can be translated to an equivalent finite automaton. However, the MRG is more indicative of the structure of media element presentations and models a large number of media types in a clear, distinct way.

5.1   HYPERMEDIA MRGS

Graphical models are the optimum tool for modeling hypermedia objects [84]. Hypermedia is a prevalent data structure representing multimedia presentations. Hypermedia combines composite media elements including documents, images, etc. (hyperdocuments) with *links* (hyperlinks), which are references to other media elements which can be traversed during presentation. If the content is entirely textual, hypermedia is referred to as "hypertext". The links in hypermedia correspond directly to the transition edges in a graphical model. Figure 2.2 illustrates an MRG model of a simple hypermedia document. The World Wide Web is a common example of hypermedia documents.

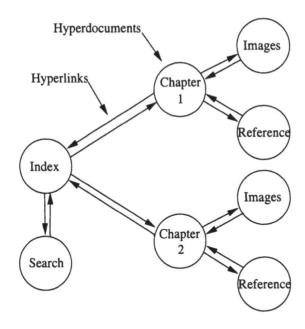

Figure 2.2. A hypermedia document represented as a media representation graph.

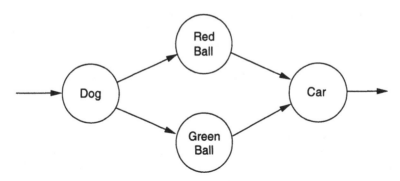

Figure 2.3. An MRG representation of the sequence dog, ball, car.

Assume an MRG μ' as a transformation of a causal media element object μ. Each media element in μ is represented by a vertex in μ'. However, what if more than one presentation of the same media element is possible? In the context of analysis, this may often be the case. Suppose the object consists of graphical images presented sequentially: dog, ball, car. What color ball will be presented? If red and green balls are equally possible, then the transitions could be dog, red ball, car or dog, green ball, car. A graphical model provides a simple means of indicating this uncertainty, as illustrated in Figure 2.3.

This is a powerful feature of media representation graphs. An MRG can model another media type *with more detail*. The models are equivalent, since

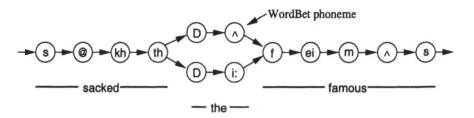

Figure 2.4.   An example media representation graph accommodating two alternative pronunciations of the word "the".

both the causal media object and the MRG present dog, ball, car. The causal model captures the distinction of ball color in the domain of the media function μ. It is implied by the description "ball" that a ball can be red or green. The selection of a particular ball color requires spatial selection, selection of one of the alternatives for the media element. The MRG model *moves the spatial selection into the same framework as the causal selection: paths in the MRG.*

A more concrete example is the text-to-speech alignment application presented in Chapter 6. In that application, a textual document representing the script of an audio segment is aligned with the audio of a vocalization of that script. The script is modeled as a sequence of media elements, in this case, words. However, many words have alternative pronunciations. Alternative pronunciations mean nothing in a textual (SGML) representation since all pronunciations map to a single spelling of the word. However, the word instance implies the alternative pronunciations. For analysis, an alignment between the text and audio requires the discovery of the pronunciation actually used. The first step in the alignment process is the conversion of the simple causal media stream model (words) into an MRG wherein vertices represent sequences of pronunciation units, in this case WorldBet phonemes. Alternate pronunciations are indicated by parallel paths in the MRG. An example of such a model is presented in Figure 2.4. This MRG fragment represents pronunciation of the words "sacked the famous". The word "the" has two alternative pronunciations: "D ^" and "D i:", where "D" is the "th" sound, "^" is the "ah" sound as in "above", and "i:" is the "iy" sound as in "beet."

MRGs can model complex phenomena. Continuing with the Chapter 6 example, it is not known when users will pause between words. Linguistic research can predict these pauses, but not with any certainty. Also, various sources of noise may exist between words. Speech systems use various models for noise and pauses. Figure 2.5 illustrates how an MRG is used to model the possible noise and pauses between words. The two vertices between the words "run" and "the" model ".gar" (garbage or noise) and ".pau" (pause). The media element transition edges allow for all possible combinations of noise and silence between words, or the case of no inter-word content at all.

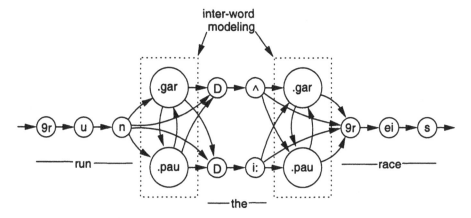

Figure 2.5. Graphical modeling of pauses and noise between words for text-to-speech synchronization.

5.2   DURATION MODELING IN MEDIA REPRESENTATION GRAPHS

In a discrete media model, media elements are assumed to have some duration, or period of presentation. Even non-temporal media such as discrete images have a period of at least one causal index. Two types of media element durations are possible: fixed and variable. A fixed duration implies that every media element is presented for the exact same period; variable durations imply differing presentation periods. As an example, audio can be modeled as a sequence of audio samples, with each sample having a fixed duration (due to a uniform sample rate). The presentation of a textual document will typically be of variable duration, since different words require different amounts of time to read or speak. "Duration" in this section is assumed to be causal duration, duration modeled as a range of the causal ordering variable (which includes temporal duration).

Variable duration media elements complicate the analysis process. If media objects are subject to simultaneous analysis, it is difficult to compare media elements if one or more of the elements have variable durations. Consequently, this book will always transform variable duration models into fixed duration models. In an MRG, a variable duration media element is equivalent to repetition of a fixed duration media element. The fixed duration of media elements is assumed to be implicit in the structure of the media element. There are three possible approaches to the modeling of duration in a media representation graph: explicit loop-back edges, implicit loop-back edges, or bounded duration.

The simplest of these is the *loop-back edge*. A loop-back edge is an edge from a vertex to itself. This is the common approach to modeling duration in

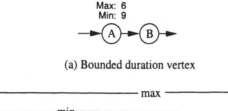

(a) Bounded duration vertex

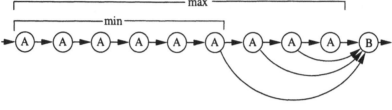

(b) Equivalent conventional MRG vertices

Figure 2.6.   Illustration of the equivalence of a bounded duration MRG with a conventional MRG.

graphical models and assumes duration is modeled by the repetition of a state. *Explicit loop-back edges* are defined when used. *Implicit loop-back edges* are an assumption of loop-back edges on every non-end vertex in the MRG. The use of loop-back edges assumes a base duration for a vertex in the graph. Commonly, this is the minimum step size for durations. In the text-to-speech synchronization example, the minimum vertex duration is the fixed audio frame sampling size.

Bounded duration, the definition of a fixed upper and lower limit for vertex duration, is modeled as an annotation on a vertex. A minimum and maximum duration and a duration step size are specified as an annotation on the vertex[2]. Either the minimum or maximum duration can be omitted. Omitting the minimum duration implies a minimum duration of one. Omitting the maximum duration implies no bound on the element duration at all. Bounded durations are equivalent to conventional MRG models as illustrated in Figure 2.6. The single bounded duration vertex labeled "A" in 2.6(a) is equivalent to multiple vertices as presented in 2.6(b), where each of the multiple vertices other than the one labeled "B" represent that same media element. The sequential group of vertices labeled "min" ensures the minimum duration, while the edges from the remaining vertices to the vertex labeled "B" represent possible intermediate terminations of the duration of media element "A" up to duration *max*. Section 2.1 describes additional duration modeling approaches which allow for interrelations among element durations.

An obvious modification of this construct is to add a loop-back edge to the last *min* vertex if no maximum duration is specified. A minimum duration of zero is problematic, since it implies an option is to bypass the vertex completely.

Sequential presentation of n vertices with $min = 0$ would imply $O(n^2)$ edges. It is assumed that $min \geq 1$ and that any bypass of vertices is modeled explicitly.

5.3   WEIGHTED AND MARKOVIAN MEDIA REPRESENTATION GRAPHS

The modeling of multimedia data for analysis purposes often requires data structures that represent the varying possibilities of alternate transitions among media elements. One path may be more likely than another, or a path may be penalized to indicate that it represents a rare occurrence. The media representation graph model achieves this with the addition of weights to the edges. Such a model is referred to as a *weighted media representation graph*. Weights on edges have several uses in the model, the most common being the explicit specification of probabilities of different vertex transitions. In addition, weights are used to *penalize* certain transitions or elements of a model. As an example, additional edges may be added between vertices to accommodate deletion or insertion within the media model. These edges model either skipping over content or a temporary transition to inserted content. However, these edits are considered to be lower probability events, so a weight is associated with the edge that penalizes the edge transition.

A weight may or may not be related to the probability of a particular presentation format. When weights are introduced into graphical models, the *path cost accumulation function* must be explicitly indicated. If the weights are indicative of probability, the total weight for a path should be the product of the edge weights. However, if the weights are arbitrary, or if they have been translated to some alternative coordinate system, the accumulation function may be any arbitrary function. Additive accumulation is common in this book and more closely related to conventional graph theory.

If the edge weights are assumed to be probabilities and obey all of the criteria required of probability distributions, the weighted MRG model describes a Markov process [47]. Let s_i represent the state of a stochastic process at causal index i, where the range of i is assumed, without loss of generality, to be the set of integers. A process is said to have the *Markov property* if for any $j \geq 2$ the conditional probability of state s_j is

$$P(s_j | s_{j-1}, ..., s_1) = P(s_j | s_{j-1}) \qquad (2.1)$$

This property is often called the "past-forgetting" property and simply states that only the most recent state matters in the determination of the probability of a new state. This property is easily modeled using weights in a graphical model as shown in Figure 2.7. Such a model is referred to as a *Markovian media representation graph model*.

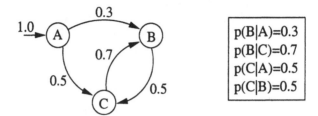

Figure 2.7.   Illustration of the Markov property of a graphical model with weights.

5.4   SEMI-ACYCLIC MODELS

The use of loop-back edges in graphical representations of media objects implies cycles in the MRG. Indeed, many representations are cyclic. Figure 2.8 illustrates two media models, an MRG model for a slide-based lecture presentation and an MRG model for spoken representation of text. The slide presentation is clearly cyclic, since slides can be presented in any order, with the only criteria that a period of no slide presentation exist between slides. Though the phonemic MRG in Figure 2.8(b) is cyclic due to both loop-back edges and the cyclic modeling of noise and silence between vertices, it does have a characteristic that, if the noise and silence vertices are oriented vertically in relation to each other, the process must proceed left-to-right, though it can cycle at any vertex column.

A graph is referred to as *semi-acyclic* if it possesses this property. Formally, a graph is *semi-acyclic* if it can be partitioned into two or more subgraphs by grouping vertices into sets wherein edges between the sets do not form any cycles. Figure 2.8(b) includes a partitioning of the graph that illustrates the semi-acyclic nature of the graph.

The semi-acyclic property is useful in media models in that it implies "progress". In other words, it implies that the media type is presented sequentially rather than arbitrarily.

5.5   CAUSALLY VARYING MEDIA REPRESENTATION GRAPHS

Assume a semi-acyclic MRG media object that represents the alternative presentations of a sequential time-based media object. Elements of the MRG closer to the start vertex are more likely at the beginning of the time-based media than at the end. The opposite holds true for vertices at the end of the model. Assume the existence of a function $\gamma(i, v)$, where i is a vertex number and v is a relative causal ordering variable for the sequential presentation of the media. v is typically normalized to the range $[0, 1]$. This function represents a weighting of each of the vertices for different values of s. This weighting can be additive or multiplicative and is treated as a *vertex visitation penalty*.

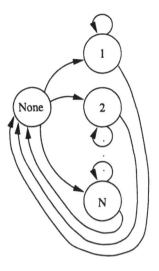

(a) Slides MRG

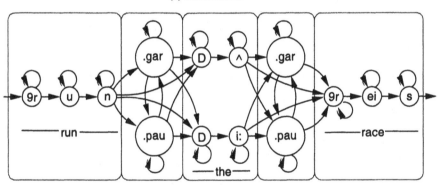

(b) Phonemic MRG

Figure 2.8.   Cyclic and semi-acyclic media models.

A multiplicative penalty is multiplied by the path weight at each vertex. An additive penalty is added to the path weight.

Multiplicative examples often indicate probability distributions on localities within a Markovian media representation graph. The value of $\gamma(i, v)$ cannot simply be multiplied by the value of the incident edge probabilities in a Markovian MRG, however. If $\gamma(i, v)$ is any value other than 1, the Markovian property of the graph would be violated. Hence, this value is, instead, associated with the vertex itself. $\gamma(i, v)$ provides an additional probability distribution for the vertices of the graph at points in time. For this distribution to be valid, the following property must hold:

$$\sum_i \gamma(i, v) = 1, \forall v \qquad (2.2)$$

Additive examples are more common when the edge weight is also considered additive and are used exclusively in this book. MRGs with an associated vertex visitation penalty are referred to as *causally varying MRGs*. This property can apply to both MRG and Markovian MRG models of media.

6.   SYNCHRONIZATION MODELS

Media models are concerned with describing the presentation or analysis of media elements or functional representations of media. Synchronization models are concerned with describing inter-media relationships such as the relation of the words in a textual document to times in an audio file when the words are spoken. This section describes different classes of media synchronization models.

DEFINITION 2.16 (SYNCHRONIZATION DATA) *Synchronization data is a mapping from the coordinate systems of one media object to those of another. This mapping does not have to be among the causal ordering variables, but can include mappings within media elements.*

DEFINITION 2.17 (SYNCHRONIZATION TYPE) *A synchronization type is a specific data type for synchronization data and describes the format of the synchronization data.*

DEFINITION 2.18 (SYNCHRONIZATION OBJECT) *A synchronization object is an instantiation of a synchronization type.*

This terminology is similar to that for media types and objects. There may be some confusion between the conventional multimedia field of *synchronization enforcement*, the use of existing synchronization data to ensure that the components of a multimedia presentation are presented in proper relationship to each other, and the focus of this work, the automatic computation of synchronization data. Although the approaches to synchronization determination are very different among these diverse research topics, the results are the same: causal and spatial relationships among media objects. Hence, the terminology "synchronization" has been retained. This book commonly uses the term *alignment* as an alternative to synchronization. This terminology choice is typically made in relation to specific applications due to the existing use of the term in relation to parallel text alignment (see Chapter 5).

6.1   CAUSAL AND SPATIAL SYNCHRONIZATION

There are two distinct classes of synchronization types: *causal synchronization* and *spatial synchronization*. It is common for the literature to refer to *temporal synchronization* as well. However, the term "causal synchronization" includes temporal synchronization and is more general and is, therefore, used in this work. Causal synchronization is the relationship among the causal ordering variables of two or more causal streams. Spatial synchronization defines relationships between individual media elements. As an example, the synchronization of an audio track to a video track is a causal synchronization. At any point in time a location in the ordering space of the audio (time) is associated with a location in the ordering space of the video. A synchronization between a fixed duration audio frame and moving lips in a video frame is a spatial synchronization. The audio media element (the audio frame) is associated with a location in the video frame (pixels centered on a moving lip, for example.)

What these classes of synchronization are describing is the relationship among the media objects specified by the synchronization type. Hence, these are referred to as classes, not types. A specific synchronization type may include both classes. Indeed, many synchronization models used for media composition do include both types in that they specify both spatial and temporal relationships, though it is also common for spatial and temporal relationships in a presentation to be specified independently using differing models, as in Little and Ghafoor [69]. In that work temporal synchronization is specified using Petri nets while spatial synchronization is specified using spatial hierarchies.

6.2   IMPLICIT, EXPLICIT, AND COMPUTED SYNCHRONIZATION

There are two types of synchronization objects: implicit and explicit. *Implicit synchronization* is synchronization data that is inherent to the media type and not explicitly specified. The most common implicit synchronization is if two or more media objects are based on an identical causal ordering variable, such as time. Uniform frame rate digital video and an associated sound-track are implicitly synchronized because they are both captured using sampling based on aligned clocks. *Explicit synchronization* is synchronization data that has been designed into the media object. Specifically, it is the explicit definition of relationships among media elements. If digital video is captured at varying frame rates or frame dropping is allowed, the alignment between the frame data and the audio sound-track must be specified for each frame. This is an example of explicit synchronization. Common video data formats such as *audio/video interleaved* (AVI) and *QuickTime* include structures for the explicit specification of synchronization data.

Computed synchronization is synchronization data discovered by analysis of the media data. Computed synchronization data is not a type, but rather a source of synchronization data.

6.3   FUNCTIONAL MODELS OF SYNCHRONIZATION

The most general model of synchronization is the functional model, in which two media types are related to each other via a mathematical function. Such a function can be as simple as $\tau(s)$, wherein one media ordering variable is mapped to the domain of another. This simple mathematical model is used often in this book.

However, it is not always sufficient for a functional model to be of the form $\tau : S_\alpha \to S_\beta$, where S_α is the functional range of media type α and S_β is the range of media type β. A general model must necessarily allow for arbitrary range and domain with each media type. It cannot be stated for all cases what the structure of the elements under synchronization will be. Examples can include the relation of arbitrary subsets of the range of the causal ordering coordinate system of one media object to that of another. A synchronization object could explicitly relate all of the speeches by Hamlet in a script to all of the spoken lines in audio, for example. A completely general functional model for synchronization is $\tau : \mathcal{P}(S_\alpha) \to \mathcal{P}(S_\beta)$, where $\mathcal{P}(A)$ is the power set of A, and S_α and S_β are the ranges of two functional representations of media objects.

6.4   POINT-WISE SYNCHRONIZATION

A simple synchronization type is *point-wise synchronization*, the specification of alignment at specific points. This mechanism is very similar to the concept of *barrier synchronization* in parallel computing [4], which enforces alignment of independent processing threads at specific points in the executable code. Common uses of point-wise synchronization are the presentation of multiple elements at the same time or the spatial alignment of the elements on a display.

Point-wise synchronization need not be coarse-grained. If many such points are selected, point-wise synchronization approaches functional models in accuracy, with a corresponding increase in storage and computational requirements.

6.5   RANGE MODELS AND SYNCHRONIZATION COMPRESSION

Point-wise synchronization assumes synchronization of unique media elements. Often this is not the case. In particular, it is often more beneficial to describe synchronization as the relationship among intervals of media elements. An example is the description of a computed synchronization between two textual documents. The point-wise alignment of every word actually means very little; it is the relationship among larger linguistic units such as sentences and paragraphs that carries the true meaning.

A *range synchronization type* is a model for synchronization data wherein the data maps an interval (range) in one media object to another. This model is assumed to be equivalent to the additional models of point-to-range and range-to-point by simply specifying a range that is a single point. Range synchronization is modeled mathematically as $\tau : S_\alpha \times S_\alpha \rightarrow S_\beta \times S_\beta$.

Range synchronization is very useful in that it allows for the more efficient storage of point-wise or discrete functional synchronization data, particularly when a dense media type is correlated to a sparse media type. When text is aligned to speech, the number of media elements in the text is very small relative to that of the audio (which may have tens of thousands of audio samples for each word). A point-wise synchronization based on even the common speech recognition frame size of 10 milliseconds has 100 entries per second of speech audio. These can readily be compressed into ranges representing the duration of the words in the audio media object.

6.6　SYNCHRONIZATION MODEL INVERTIBILITY

A synchronization type provides a means for converting points or intervals in one media object to related points or intervals in a second media object. In many cases an inversion exists such that an object that allows synchronization of media object μ_β with media object μ_α can be inverted to allow for inverse synchronization. This is not guaranteed in general.

It might be assumed that a computed synchronization between media objects μ_α and μ_β would be symmetrical. However, this is not always the case. Often, the process is considered to be the synchronization of one media object to another. As an example, two intervals in one media object may map to the same interval in a second media object, perhaps due to repetition of content. Mapping each interval to the common interval is not a problem, but mapping the common interval back to two simultaneous intervals in the inverse cannot be done in the range model.

Although invertibility is not guaranteed, it can often be approximated. Of the presented media synchronization types, point-wise synchronization and range synchronization are the most common in practice. Range synchronization allows the relation of a range of content in one media object to a related range in another. It is useful for aligning words to audio or text paragraphs to text paragraphs, and in many other applications. If one of the ranges is a single point, this method models the relation of musical notes to audio presentation, presentation slides to video, and other applications. A useful approximation for inversion of a range synchronization type is described in Chapter 7.

7.   SUMMARY

This chapter has developed a foundation of media and synchronization data types. Media and multimedia are shown to be similar concepts and to be very broad terms. The generalization of causal media is presented as an alternative to the more common temporal media model because many ordered media types such as audio and text can present virtually identical information and need a structure that allows them to be related to each other without regard to differing coordinate systems.

The more complex models presented in this chapter, such as the media representation graph model, not only provide a tool for modeling some existing media, in particular hypermedia presentations, but also provide a tool for modeling intermediate representations for analysis. Given the powerful tools of transformation and equivalence, two media objects which would be difficult to compare can be converted to equivalent, yet more logically comparable, domains or transformed into non-equivalent, yet salient (representative), domains.

The following chapters introduce methods for computing synchronization information between media objects and illustrate how the media models presented in this chapter relate to computed synchronization. In particular, the media representation graph is shown to be a powerful tool for describing media objects for analysis. Two additional special cases of media representation graphs are presented in Chapter 4. These cases, the causal MRG and the synchronous MRG have certain advantages in the algorithm presented in that chapter.

Notes

1 The term "causal" has been chosen in this work due to its close relation to the more common term "temporal". The term implies an ordering, without the unnecessary connotation that the ordering is specifically time. This choice was made due to the wide-spread use of the term "temporal" in the multimedia community.

2 More complex models of duration are obviously possible wherein the possible durations are other than just a minimum to a maximum with a fixed step size. However, these are difficult to model in a general way.

Chapter 3

MULTIPLE MEDIA CORRELATION

This chapter develops general models that form the framework for computed synchronization solutions. The goal of computed synchronization is the automatic determination of causal and spatial synchronization among media objects. The models that are developed provide a basis for the construction of solutions to real-world problems in media synchronization, as well as a basis for proving solution validity. Techniques based on these models are collectively referred to as *multiple media correlation* (MMC). Chapter 4 presents algorithmic approaches to solving these models.

The derivation of a general model for multiple media correlation begins in Section 1. with a model applicable to continuous media. This derivation is then used as an example in Section 2. to derive a similar discrete model of multiple media correlation more useful in sampled and discrete media element applications. A ranked results model is presented in Section 3.. The ranked results model is designed to select not just the single optimal result, but also the M highest ranked results and is, therefore, useful in applications requiring selection of multiple alternative solutions.

In addition to presenting the multiple media correlation model, Section 4. places these models in the context of other approaches to media and signal comparison and representation. Specifically, the relationship between the new models presented in this book and dynamic time warping, cross-correlation, and least squares approaches is discussed.

1. THE CONTINUOUS MODEL

Let $\mu_1(s_1), ..., \mu_N(s_N)$ represent N continuous media objects with $s_i \in \Re, \forall i = 1, .., N$. It is not required that the domain of the media be real valued in this model. It is assumed that there exists some relationship among these media objects such that causal and/or spatial synchronization is meaningful.

The problem of synchronization of *unrelated* media objects is difficult to quantify. Examples of unrelated media objects include text transcripts and speech audio where the transcript does not represent the presented text or alignment of two text documents with no common theme or content. What does it mean to align two unrelated media objects, spatially or causally? If the media components under alignment are unrelated, the alignment information will be meaningless. Since the solution approaches described in Chapter 4 are guaranteed to terminate, a result is always computed. However, correlation of unrelated media objects cannot be assumed to produce meaningful information.

1.1   CAUSAL NORMALIZATION

The first issue to be addressed in development of a model is causal synchronization, the alignment of the causal coordinate systems of the constituent media elements so as to maximize a correlation measure between the media objects. A synchronization function is a mapping from the coordinate system (time, character offsets, etc.) of one media object to that of another. To explicitly define such a mapping as an element of a mathematical model would require that one media object be declared a "master" object against which all of the other media objects are aligned. This is not only an asymmetrical concept, it is also less general than *causal normalization*.

DEFINITION 3.1 (CAUSAL NORMALIZATION) *Causal normalization is the alignment of a set of media objects to a single normalization coordinate system. The alignment consists of a set of mappings from the normalization coordinate system to each of the media object coordinate systems. The normalization coordinate system is arbitrary and need not coincide with any of the media object coordinate systems.*

DEFINITION 3.2 (CAUSAL NORMALIZATION FUNCTION) *A causal normalization function is a function that maps a causal normalization coordinate system to the coordinate system of a media object.*

Causal normalization functions can be converted to synchronization functions in most cases using function inversion. The relation between normalization and synchronization is discussed in Section 1.3. Causal normalization functions are sometimes referred to as *causal warping functions* because they change the rate of presentation of a media object. For example, a causal normalization function might change the rate of playback of an audio object so as to maximize the alignment with moving lips in a video object. The video of the moving lips is also a media object, so a causal normalization function exists that maps a normalization coordinate system to the video coordinate system (time). A good choice for this second causal normalization function is $\tau(s) = s$ because it is easily inverted.

For correlation to be quantified, some a priori measure of the similarity among media elements is necessary. This measure is expressed as a function of N media elements. Functions that measure the similarity (or dissimilarity) of media elements and indicate closer relationships with decreasing values are often referred to as *distortion* or *dissimilarity* functions [50, 102]. Let $\rho(\mu_1(s_1), ..., \mu_N(s_N))$ be a real-valued point-wise dissimilarity function, where $\mu_i, i = 1, ..., N$ represent functional models of media objects. The function is defined on the media elements. This function is referred to in this work as the *correlation function* and serves as a measure of the dissimilarity of the media objects.

It is assumed for now that the measure of dissimilarity can be performed locally on individual media elements. This is obviously not always the case. Measuring the dissimilarity of function spectra (frequency domain representations of signals for example) cannot be done using point-wise comparison of two real-valued functions, since media elements or single points in a function space do not convey spectral information. Windowed comparison, the comparison of a (potentially infinite) range of values in each of the constituent media objects, is required for spectral similarity measures and other distortion measures. Windowed comparison is supported as the model is further developed.

Decreasing values of the correlation function indicate increasing local similarity. Example distance functions include inner product operations (as in cross-correlation), Euclidean distance, or Manhattan distance. This problem is constructed as a minimization problem, effectively the minimization of dissimilarity. It could equally well be formulated as a maximization problem, maximizing the similarity, by simply negating the distance function[1].

Let $\tau_1(s), ..., \tau_N(s)$ be a set of causal normalization functions. A goal of multiple media correlation is to choose a causal normalization function for each media object that minimizes the total dissimilarity (the result of the correlation function) among the media objects over the range of the objects. The distance between the media elements at a point s in the normalization space is:

$$\delta_s = \rho(\mu_1(\tau_1(s)), ..., \mu_N(\tau_N(s))) \tag{3.1}$$

An estimate of the similarity of an interval of the domain of ρ of width Δs, and centered on s is $\rho(\mu_1(\tau_1(s)), ..., \mu_N(\tau_N(s))\Delta s$. Applying simple calculus, the similarity of the media under causal normalization is expressed in Equation 3.2, assuming the limit as the size of the interval tends to zero.

$$D(\mu_1, ..., \mu_N) = \lim_{\Delta s \to 0} \sum_{s=-\infty}^{\infty} \rho(\mu_1(\tau_1(s\Delta s)), ..., \mu_N(\tau_N(s\Delta s)))\Delta s$$

$$= \int_{-\infty}^{\infty} \rho(\mu_1(\tau_1(s)), ..., \mu_N(\tau_N(s)))ds \qquad (3.2)$$

For this measure to exist, the integral must exist and be real valued. It is not required that the distance measure be positive. Since the problem is stated as a minimization problem, the accommodation of inner product formulations or other inherently maximizing formulations necessarily requires use of negative (or scaled) distance measures.

Linear causal normalization is the use of linear equations as causal normalization functions. An example linear causal normalization function, assuming s is a coordinate in the causal normalization coordinate system, would be:

$$\tau(s) = \alpha s, \alpha \in \Re \qquad (3.3)$$

Linear causal normalization has limited utility, but does provide an illustration of how general normalization function spaces are modeled in practice using *parameterization*, the selection of a function from a function space based on selected parameters, in this case α. Linear causal normalization also provides a tool for demonstrating some potential problems with causal normalization solutions, as discussed later in this chapter.

Linear causal normalization lends itself well to simple solution strategies because of the limited search space (one degree of freedom per media object). However, most applications require more complicated normalization functions. Causal normalization functions can be subject to all of the potential constraints that time-normalization functions are subject to. For a detailed description of some possible time-normalization constraints, see Rabiner and Juang [102]. The following constraints are adapted from that text to this more general framework. Note that some constraints are optional and must be specified for a problem instance.

DEFINITION 3.3 (ENDPOINT CONSTRAINTS) *The endpoint constraint specifies that if each media object $\mu_i(s_i), i = 1, ..., N$ has a distinct starting point s_{i_0} and ending point s_{i_1} in the media object coordinate system, then there exist values s_0 and s_1 such that for all causal normalization functions $\tau_i(s_0) = s_{i_0}$ and $\tau_i(s_1) = s_{i_1}$, for $i = 1, ..., N$. The media objects are assumed to start and end together, regardless of the coordinate system on which they are mapped. Causal normalization functions meeting this criterion are said to be endpoint constrained.*

The endpoint constraint is a common constraint when matching presentations of words with each other, where it is assumed that the presentations begin and end with the same content. This is an optional constraint that must be specified for all causal normalization functions in a problem instance. It is also possible to constrain only the start or end of the causal normalization functions to coincide, rather than both ends, as indicated in the endpoint constraint.

DEFINITION 3.4 (MONOTONICITY CONSTRAINT) *The monotonicity con-straint states that* $s_\alpha \geq s_\beta$ *implies* $\tau_i(s_\alpha) \geq \tau_i(s_\beta)$. *This is an optional constraint that can be specified for any of the causal normalization functions in a problem instance. This constraint is an indication that the causal normal-ization functions must be monotonically non-decreasing.*

Causal normalization functions are selected from a candidate function set T_i, where $\tau_i \in T_i, i = 1, ..., N$, so as to minimize the dissimilarity of media objects under causal normalization, i.e. to minimize the function $D(\mu_1, ..., \mu_N)$, as defined in Equation 3.2. An issue in the determination of candidate function sets is the possibility of *solution scaling*, the existence of congruent normaliza-tions with differing scaling factors (multiplicative relationships) on the causal normalization coordinate system.

Solution scaling is easy to demonstrate. Let ρ be a correlation function constrained to two media objects. Let $T_i : i = 1, 2$ be candidate causal normalization function sets of the form $\tau_i \in T_i$ implies $\exists \alpha \in \Re$ such that $\tau_i(s) = \alpha s$ (the set of linear causal normalization functions). Then either no possible solutions or an infinite number of identical solutions for Equation 3.2 are possible. To show this, assume a minimized solution is possible with the choice of constants $< \alpha_1, \alpha_2 >$, such that $D(\mu_1, \mu_2) > 0$. Then:

$$D(\mu_1, \mu_2) = \int_{-\infty}^{\infty} \rho(\mu_1(\alpha_1 s), \mu_2(\alpha_2 s)) ds \qquad (3.4)$$

The choice of α_1 and α_2 minimize the value of $D(\mu_1, \mu_2)$, so:

$$D(\mu_1, \mu_2) \leq \int_{-\infty}^{\infty} \rho(\mu_1(2\alpha_1 s), \mu_2(2\alpha_2 s)) ds \qquad (3.5)$$

Then:

$$\int_{-\infty}^{\infty} \rho(\mu_1(2\alpha_1 s), \mu_2(2\alpha_2 s)) ds =$$
$$\frac{1}{2} \int_{-\infty}^{\infty} \rho(\mu_1(\alpha_1 s), \mu_2(\alpha_2 s)) ds =$$
$$\frac{1}{2} D(\mu_1, \mu_2) \qquad (3.6)$$

This implies that $D(\mu_1, \mu_2) \leq \frac{1}{2} D(\mu_1, \mu_2)$. However, $D(\mu_1, \mu_2)$, a contra-diction. For the alternative case of $D(\mu_1, \mu_2) < 0$, simply replace the value of 2 in the example with $\frac{1}{2}$. The only remaining case is if $D(\mu_1, \mu_2) = 0$. In such a case, an infinite set of solutions exist of the form $\alpha_1'/\alpha_2' = \alpha_1/\alpha_2$.

DEFINITION 3.5 (SOLUTION SCALING) *A problem instance P of Equation 3.2 exhibits solution scaling if for every choice of causal normalization functions* $< \tau_1, ..., \tau_N >$ *yielding solution* $D(\mu_1, ..., \mu_N)$ *and for every real valued constant* $\epsilon > 0$, *there exists an alternative choice of causal normalization functions* $< \tau'_1, ..., \tau'_N >$ *yielding solution* $D'(\mu_1, ..., \mu_N)$ *and a real valued constant* α *such that the conditions* $\alpha > 1 + \epsilon$ *or* $\alpha < 1 - 1/\epsilon$ *and* $\tau_i(s) = \tau'_i(\alpha s), \forall i = 1, ..., N$ *are true and* $D'(\mu_1, ..., \mu_N) < D(\mu_1, ..., \mu_N)$.

What solution scaling implies is that causal normalization function sets are not guaranteed to yield a solution. As an example, when correlating two audio steams, the streams could be played twice as fast by doubling each of the causal normalization functions. The total stream duration is then cut in half, dividing the value of the integral by two. This process can be repeated, producing a result approaching zero in the limit. The inclusion of the constant ϵ ensures that an asymptotic solution (α approaching 1 in the limit) is not an instance of solution scaling.

One solution to the scaling problem is to introduce scaling constraints that ensure solution scaling can not occur. Several such constraints are possible:

DEFINITION 3.6 (LOWER-BOUND SCALING CONSTRAINT) *Let T be a set of candidate causal normalization functions. The lower-bound scaling constraint applies to set T if for each* $\tau \in T$, *there exists some* $\beta \leq 1$ *such that* $\forall \tau' \in T$ *and* $\alpha, s \in \Re$, $\tau(s) = \tau'(\alpha s)$ *implies* $\alpha \geq \beta$. *The lower-bound scaling constraint applies to the set* $\mathcal{T} = \{T_i : i = 1, ..., N\}$ *of sets of candidate causal normalization functions if the constraint applies to any member of* $\mathcal{T}$. *The lower-bound scaling constraint limits the expansion of a causal normalization function domain implied by multiplying the coordinate system by a value less than one.*

DEFINITION 3.7 (UPPER-BOUND SCALING CONSTRAINT) *Let T be a set of candidate causal normalization functions. The upper-bound scaling constraint applies to set T if for each* $\tau \in T$, *there exists some* $\beta \geq 1$ *such that* $\forall \tau' \in T$ *and* $\alpha, s \in \Re$, $\tau(s) = \tau'(\alpha s)$ *implies* $\alpha \leq \beta$. *The upper-bound scaling constraint applies to the set* $\mathcal{T} = \{T_i : i = 1, ..., N\}$ *of sets of candidate causal normalization functions if the constraint applies to any member of* $\mathcal{T}$. *The upper-bound scaling constraint limits the shrinking of a causal normalization function domain implied by multiplying the coordinate system by a value greater than one.*

DEFINITION 3.8 (RANGE-BOUND SCALING CONSTRAINT) *A set T of candidate causal normalization functions is range-bound scaling constrained if both the lower- and upper-bound scaling constraints apply to set T. Likewise, the range-bound scaling constraint applies to set* $\mathcal{T}$ *of sets of candidate causal* *normalization functions if both the lower- and upper-bound scaling constraints apply to set $\mathcal{T}$.*

These constraints are important elements of the multiple media correlation model. Most solution strategies specify one of these constraints to ensure solution scaling can not occur.

Clearly, none of these constraints is met by the set of linear causal normalization functions. A set of causal normalization functions which does not exhibit solution scaling in a particular problem instance is said to be *scaling-invariant*. It is important to note that it is not the set of functions alone that induces solution scaling, but rather the combination of candidate function sets and choice of correlation function ρ.

THEOREM 3.1 *Let $\mathcal{T}$ be set of sets of candidate causal normalization functions for an instance of Equation 3.2 such that $\mathcal{T}$ is upper-bound scaling constrained and let ρ be chosen such that $D(\mu_1, ..., \mu_N) > 0$ for all non-trivial media instances[2]. Then the instance is scaling-invariant.*

Proof. The proof is by contradiction. Let the problem instance P not be scaling-invariant. Let $< \tau_1, ..., \tau_N >$ be a choice of causal normalization functions yielding solution $D(\mu_1, ..., \mu_N)$. Since $\mathcal{T}$ is upper-bound scaling constrained, there exists some i such that $T_i \in \mathcal{T}$ is upper-bound scaling constrained. Then for τ_i in the initial solution there exists some $\beta \geq 1$ such that $\forall \tau' \in T$ and $\alpha, s \in \Re$, $\tau(s) = \tau'(\alpha s)$ implies $\alpha \leq \beta$. Let ϵ in the definition of solution scaling be β. Then there exists an alternative choice of causal normalization functions $< \tau_1', ..., \tau_N' >$ yielding solution $D'(\mu_1, ..., \mu_N)$ and a real valued constant α such that $\alpha > 1 + \epsilon$ or $\alpha < 1 - 1/\epsilon$, $\tau_i(s) = \tau_i'(\alpha s), \forall i = 1, ..., N$ and $D'(\mu_1, ..., \mu_N) < D(\mu_1, ..., \mu_N)$. Since $D(\mu_1, ..., \mu_N) > 0$, the value of α must be greater than 1, which implies that $\alpha > 1 + \epsilon$, implying that $\alpha > 1 + \beta$. However, for the chosen τ_i, $\alpha \leq \beta$, a contradiction.

LEMMA 3.1 *Let $\mathcal{T}$ be an lower-bound scaling constrained set of sets of candidate causal normalization functions for an instance of Equation 3.2 and let ρ be chosen such that $D(\mu_1, ..., \mu_N) < 0$ for all non-trivial media instances. Then this instance is scaling-invariant.*

Proof. The proof of Lemma 3.1 is similar to that of Theorem 3.1 and is omitted here.

The range-bound scaling constraint is a "harder" constraint than either the upper- or lower-bound scaling constraints, so Theorem 3.1 and Lemma 3.1 both apply.

The scaling constraint may seem restrictive in that it limits the space of available scaling functions. The alternative, of course, is to apply a scaling factor, a constant multiplicative factor related to the selected causal normalization function (see Section 4.2 for an example of this approach in dynamic time warping). However, scaling factors complicate the model considerably, since the factor must be closely related to and dependent upon the choices of causal normalization functions. Chapter 4 presents algorithmic approaches that satisfy the scaling constraint. Of these approaches, two worth noting are to limit one media causal normalization function to the identity function or to enforce a global alignment constraint limiting scaling of all media objects. The use of an identity function for one of the media types is actually quite intuitive, in that it implies that the other media are to be aligned to one media object already in a reference coordinate system such as real time. The identity function clearly meets the range-bound scaling constraint. Global constraints limit the matching solution process so as to allow only specific ranges of causal normalization, thereby also enforcing the range-bound constraint.

Given Equation 3.2, a modified equation based on selection of optimal causal normalization functions is:

$$\eta = \arg \min_{\tau_i \in T_i, i=1...N} \int_{-\infty}^{\infty} \rho(\mu_1(\tau_1(s)), ..., \mu_N(\tau_N(s))) ds \qquad (3.7)$$

Equation 3.7 is similar to *dynamic time warping*. Some of the differences are pointed out in Section 4.2. The major difference is the generalization of the model to continuous systems and the explicit specification of the scaling constraint.

1.2   SPATIAL NORMALIZATION

Equation 3.7 provides a mechanism for causal (and temporal) normalization, but only for functions than can be aligned on a point-wise basis. This model will now be extended to include a mechanism for spatial normalization and the alignment of media elements larger than a single point in the causal space.

Spatial normalization is a difficult concept to model because the spatial characteristics of functional media models are not clearly defined. Nothing is implicitly known about the domain of the media functions. Hence, it is assumed that normalization requires functional spatial selection or spatial warping. Let the sets of functions $\Psi_i, i = 1, ..., N$ be sets of *spatial normalization functions*. The objective of maximizing the correlation both spatially and causally, is stated as in Equation 3.8.

$$\eta = \arg \min_{\tau_i \in T_i, \psi_i \in \Psi_i, i=1...N} \int_{-\infty}^{\infty} \rho(\psi_1(\mu_1(\tau_1(s))), ..., \psi_N(\mu_N(\tau_N(s)))) ds$$
$$(3.8)$$

The spatial normalization function as presented in Equation 3.8 still assumes that all spatial normalization can be done on a single point in the media function space. However, the question arises: is point-wise alignment sufficient? As discussed in Section 4., the media element, as indicated by a single point in the causal ordering space, often conveys little information. As an example, the text-to-speech alignment system presented in Chapter 6 seeks to align units of sound large enough to convey information about the phonetic content of the unit. A single point does not convey that level of information. Hence, it is typically necessary that the spatial normalization functions and correlation functions be able to process, for a point in the normalized causal ordering space, a *window* of the media coordinate space. A simple modification of Equation 3.8 accommodates windowed analysis:

$$\eta = \arg \min_{\tau_i \in T_i, \psi_i \in \Psi_i, i=1...N} \int_{-\infty}^{\infty} \rho(\psi_1(\mu_1 \circ \tau_1, s), ..., \psi_N(\mu_N \circ \tau_N, s))ds \quad (3.9)$$

Equation 3.9 is referred to as the *continuous formulation of multiple media correlation*. It provides a model for spatial and causal normalization and synchronization of multiple media objects.

The function space Ψ_i does more than just provide for spatial synchronization in this model. It also provides for domain translation to a *correlation domain*, an important element of most solutions of the model. It is difficult to construct appropriate correlation functions with disparate media parameters; as an example, what does it mean to compare text, a discrete set of language representations, to audio, a one-dimensional function representing sound pressure? However, comparison of standard sound units such as phonemes to an estimate of the probability that a given sound represents a phoneme is much less complicated. Even when two or more media are of the same type, they may be too complicated to correlate directly. For this reason, it is implicit in this model that all media objects under correlation can be translated to a common domain for comparison by a correlation function ρ.

Domain translation can be thought of as the translation of a media object to another media object with different media elements that exist in the normalization coordinate system and are more appropriate for comparison. This is a media element transformation. Computed synchronization as presented in this book nearly always subjects the component media elements to many levels of transformation. A text document is translated to a media representation graph (MRG) (see Section 5.) consisting of sequential words. Domain translation then translates the elements of the MRG to windows of several words that are used for word comparison. This is the process used for parallel text alignment in Chapter 5. The model presented in this chapter assumes domain translation is performed entirely in the mathematical model. However, Chapter 4 illustrates that domain translation can be equivalently performed or partially performed prior to solution of the model as problem input preprocessing.

In the text-to-speech synchronization application described in Chapter 6, ρ combines log-likelihood values through simple addition. This is equivalent to multiplication of the probability of a sound unit at a particular time by the probability that the sound unit is emitted at that time. The logarithm operation is necessary to convert a product space to a summation space and to avoid numeric underflow.

Example domain translation functions for text-to-speech synchronization are: ψ_1: translation from words to a representation of units of sound and ψ_2: translation from sounds to an estimation of the probability that a sound matches a given sound element. The possible translations for ψ_1 are indicated by the possible pronunciations for a given word and the possible durations of each sound element. ψ_2 is computed using speech feature recognition tools.

It should be emphasized that the result of this equation, η, is not the minimized result of the integral, but, rather, the functions that achieve this minimization. This model specifies a structure for defining and selecting functions that maximize the correlation. The resulting functions indicate necessary causal and spatial normalizations. The set of selected causal normalization functions indicate the causal synchronization to a normalized causal coordinate system that maximized correlation. The set of selected spatial normalization functions indicate the appropriate spatial synchronization for maximum correlation.

1.3   RELATION BETWEEN NORMALIZATION AND SYNCHRONIZATION

Synchronization data is a mapping from the coordinate system of one media object to that of another. The preceding sections have emphasized *normalization*, the mapping of an arbitrary normalized coordinate system to each of the media object coordinate systems. Normalization is a general model for solution strategies. However, pair-wise synchronization among media objects is usually the desired result.

Let μ_α and μ_β be two media objects and $\tau_\alpha(s)$ and $\tau_\beta(s)$ be the causal normalization functions which normalize the causal ordering of these objects to a common coordinate system denoted by s. The synchronization function $\tau(s_\alpha)$ mapping μ_α to μ_β is:

$$\tau(s_\alpha) = \tau_\beta(\tau_\alpha^{-1}(s_\alpha)) \tag{3.10}$$

The ability to convert normalization to synchronization is dependent upon the ability to invert the computed causal normalization function of at least one media object.

2. DISCRETE MODEL

The model in Equation 3.9 is designed for continuous (analog) applications. This model is inappropriate for two other important application areas: discrete (sampled) applications and discrete media elements in continuous media. These applications require a discrete causal normalization space, so a discrete version of Equation 3.9 is presented in this section. This formulation is referred to as the *discrete formulation of multiple media correlation*.

$$\eta = \arg \min_{\tau_i \in T_i, \psi_i \in \Psi_i, i=1...N} \sum_{s=-\infty}^{\infty} \rho(\psi_1(\mu_1 \circ \tau_1, s), ..., \psi_N(\mu_N \circ \tau_N, s)) \quad (3.11)$$

Equation 3.11 is developed using a process analogous to that used for Equation 3.9 and that process is not repeated here. Equation 3.11 is more commonly applied in computer applications. The use of the discrete formulation does not imply discrete media types, however. For analytical purposes, the media may be assumed to be an underlying continuous function, or continuous media applications may use hardware to sample media elements from continuous media input. In such an application, it is assumed that the result of ψ_i is only valid at the summation sample points, but that ψ_i may utilize the continuous nature of the underlying signal.

In Section 1. it was shown the the spatial normalization function required, as its parameters, both the warped media function and the normalized causal ordering variable. In the continuous case, this requirement accommodates windowed domain translation and spatial normalization, wherein the value of ψ_i for any value of s is dependent on more than one point in the causally warped media, typically a (potentially infinite) neighborhood of s. In discrete applications, the result of ψ_i is assumed to be a discrete media element. As with windowed analysis, it is rare that a media element can or would be computed based on a single point in the causal ordering space. In speech applications, media elements often represent 10 millisecond fixed audio frames based on windowed observations of the underlying sampled speech waveform.

Solution scaling is also an issue in the discrete formulation, though the definition of solution scaling must be modified:

DEFINITION 3.9 (SOLUTION SCALING (DISCRETE)) *A problem instance P of Equation 3.11 is said to exhibit solution scaling if for every choice of causal normalization functions $< \tau_1, ..., \tau_N >$ yielding solution $D(\mu_1, ..., \mu_N)$ and for every integer constant $\epsilon > 1$, there exists an alternative choice of causal normalization functions $< \tau_1', ..., \tau_N' >$ yielding solution $D'(\mu_1, ..., \mu_N)$ and an integer constant α such that $\alpha \geq \epsilon$ and the conditions $\tau_i(s) = \tau_i'(\alpha s), \forall i = 1, ..., N$ or $\tau_i'(s) = \tau_i(\alpha s), \forall i = 1, ..., N$ are true and $D'(\mu_1, ..., \mu_N) < D(\mu_1, ..., \mu_N)$.*

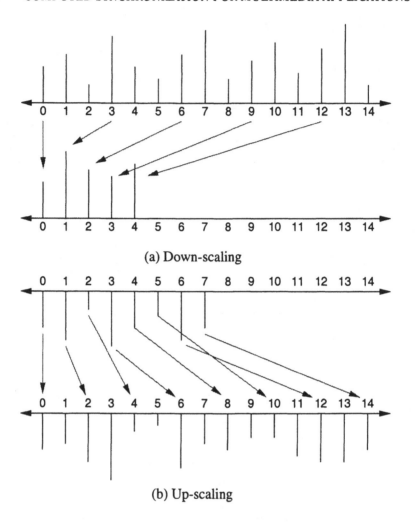

Figure 3.1.   Solution scaling in discrete applications.

The primary difference between this definition and Definition 3.5 is the discrete relationship among causal normalization functions during scaling. Figure 3.1 illustrates scaling in a discrete environment. In Figure 3.1(a), the choice of α is 3. The upper graph illustrates media object points under correlation for values of s following application of a causal normalization function $\tau(s)$. Immediately below this graph is the same media object following application of a causal normalization function $\tau'(s)$. In this case, $\tau'(s) = \tau(3s)$. In Figure 3.1(b), the alternative relation exists: $\tau(s) = \tau'(2s)$.

Although the definition of scaling must be modified to accommodate a discrete causal normalization space, the scaling-invariants, Theorem 3.1 and

Lemma 3.1, still apply. The proof is similar in discrete applications and is omitted here.

3.   EXTENDED MODELS

Both Equation 3.9 and Equation 3.11 select optimal solutions. In many cases the optimal solution is only one of a set of desired solutions. An example is the localization of lip motion within a video sequence through correlation with the sequence audio. One model for this solution would be to correlate motion estimates from an audio analysis with motion vectors for pixels on the screen. For this approach, the result should be more than just a single optimal pixel, but rather the set of pixels that represent the moving lips. Other examples include information retrieval applications wherein a set of maximally ranking solutions provides a mechanism for plotting precision versus recall, a common measure of performance in information retrieval [111].

Equation 3.11 can be extended to compute a ranked set of solutions. This model, a logical computational extension of Equation 3.11 is called the *ranked results discrete formulation of multiple media correlation*. Such an extension is similar in structure to the *K-best paths* extension used in dynamic time warping. In speech systems the best selected word at any point in time may not fit well with the best match for the next word because the new match may require the first word match be shorter or longer than the computed optimal. Consequently, it is useful to compute a set of best matches so that a locally suboptimal path that has a more appropriate length can be chosen for the first word match. Local optimality is sacrificed in favor of global optimality in this approach. This is a consequence of applying synchronization models in layers, searching for phonetic sounds, then combining those sounds into words, and finally combining the words so as to effectively match a context model or two or three word combinations. The techniques for speech content analysis presented in this book are single-layer, and do not suffer from the problems associated with matching multiple layers of smaller unit alignments.

Extension of ranked results modifications to the continuous formulation is not obvious, in that an infinite set of results may exist within any range of integral results, so that model is not further discussed.

4.   RELATION TO OTHER MODELS

Many models for comparing or aligning media exist. Multiple media correlation is meant to be a general model in that it includes both spatial and temporal normalization by design. Examining other models illustrates the generality of this new model and shows the roots of this generality.

None of the models presented here model spatial normalization. Instead, it is assumed that spatial normalization is accomplished by testing the model against multiple alternative input combinations. As an example, dynamic time warping is a common approach to speech recognition. A spatial element of a dynamic time warping-based general speech recognition system is the choice of words at a particular time. The temporal element is the matching of a word template to the utterance. In such a system, the matching to multiple candidate words simply occurs in parallel, using multiple solution instances [22, 102].

4.1   CROSS-CORRELATION, INTER-CORRELATION, AND LEAST SQUARES

The most basic task of media correlation is an assessment of similarity. One approach to the measurement of similarity is the computation of a *correlation coefficient*, a value ranging from $+1$ for identical signals to -1 for signals that are exact opposite (inverted phase signals for example). A real-valued time-bounded function $s_i(t), 0 \leq t \leq T$ (usually referred to as a signal in this application) can be characterized by its energy, defined as:

$$\mathcal{E}_i = \int_0^T s_i(t)^2 dt \tag{3.12}$$

This chapter assumes media objects that are either undefined or zero-valued beyond the bounds of the ordering variable. This section assumes time-bounded functions are zero-valued beyond the function bounds. Under that assumption, Equation 3.12 can be stated as:

$$\mathcal{E}_i = \int_{-\infty}^{\infty} s_i(t)^2 dt \tag{3.13}$$

The real-valued correlation function for the signals s_i and s_j is defined as [101]:

$$\rho_{i,j} = \frac{1}{\sqrt{\mathcal{E}_i \mathcal{E}_j}} \int_{-\infty}^{\infty} s_i(t) s_j(t) dt \tag{3.14}$$

For time-based (causal) real-valued signals, comparison can also be defined as a function of the offset between the two signals. This function is called the *inter-correlation function* or the *cross-correlation* function [12, 128]:

$$h_{i,j}(s) = \frac{1}{\sqrt{\mathcal{E}_i \mathcal{E}_j}} \int_{-\infty}^{\infty} s_i(t) s_j(t + s) dt \tag{3.15}$$

The analogous discrete versions of these functions are:

$$\mathcal{E}_i = \sum_{t=-\infty}^{\infty} s_i(t)^2 \tag{3.16}$$

$$\rho_{i,j} = \frac{1}{\sqrt{\mathcal{E}_i \mathcal{E}_j}} \sum_{t=-\infty}^{\infty} s_i(t)s_j(t) \tag{3.17}$$

$$h_{i,j}(s) = \frac{1}{\sqrt{\mathcal{E}_i \mathcal{E}_j}} \sum_{t=-\infty}^{\infty} s_i(t)s_j(t+s) \tag{3.18}$$

Equations 3.14 and 3.17 do not accommodate causal normalization and Equations 3.15 and 3.18 accommodate causal normalization only as a pure offset. The value s that maximizes $h_{i,j}(s)$ is the offset that maximizes correlation of the two signals. The general models for multiple media correlation are designed to optimize a set of parameters that will maximize correlation, not provide an invariant measure of correlation. Consequently, Equations 3.14 and 3.17 are useful tools for assessing the quality of correlation after causal and spatial normalization. Configuring Equations 3.9 or 3.11 in a pair-wise application to maximize correlation with only pure offsets requires a correlation function of the form: $\rho(x_1, x_2) = -x_1 x_2$ and causal normalization functions of the form $T_1 = \{\tau(t) = t\}$ and $T_2 = \{\tau(t) = t + \alpha : \alpha \in \Re\}$. Clearly, multiplication by a constant positive value has no effect on the choice of α that maximizes correlation, so the the constant energy scaling multiple utilized in the above equations need not be included in this formulation.

An interesting difference between multiple media correlation and inter- and cross-correlation techniques is the application of *energy scaling* (the inverse energy product in each of the above equations). Energy scaling is used to normalize the function results so as to compute comparable values for signals with differing durations and relative amplitudes. A similar scaling could have been applied in multiple media correlation. The disadvantage of energy scaling in causal normalization minimization equations such as Equation 3.9 is that an infinite set of proportional solutions (identical up to a constant causal scaling factor) are always possible.

Closely related to inter-correlation techniques are techniques that seek to minimize the squared error [48]. A least squared error can be determined by minimizing the quantity:

$$E = \frac{1}{s_2 - s_1} \int_{s_1}^{s_2} |\mu(s) - \mu_a(s)|^2 ds \tag{3.19}$$

Equation 3.19 has been adapted from Giordano and Hsu to use notation similar to that used in the rest of this chapter [48]. In this equation, E represents the average squared error. The goal of least squares approaches is to best approximate the arbitrary function $\mu(s)$ with an approximation function $\mu_a(s)$ over the interval $s_1 \leq s \leq s_2$. Least squares estimation is a powerful tool useful for signal prediction, filter estimation, and many other functions. Multiple media correlation can be formulated as a least squares problem by choosing $\rho(x, y) = (x - y)^2$ as a correlation function. A large class of least squares solution strategies can then be applied to problems that fit this formulation.

4.2   DYNAMIC TIME WARPING

Dynamic time warping is a model for the temporal alignment of two signals [102]. Dynamic time warping is used in speech recognition systems and for the alignment of parallel translations [22, 43]. The dynamic time warping equation is:

$$d(\mathcal{X}, \mathcal{Y}) \triangleq \min_{\phi} \sum_{k=1}^{T} d(\phi_x(k), \phi_y(k)) m(k) / M_\phi \qquad (3.20)$$

In this equation, d represents a dissimilarity function such that larger values indicate increasing lack of similarity. It is assumed in this model that the comparison is among media elements. $m(k)$ is a path weighting coefficient. Often omitted, the path weighting coefficient allows for variation in the relative value of matches over time. It is possible to weight the system so as to require better matches for lesser values of k and less strict matching for greater values of k. M_ϕ is a path weighting coefficient dependent upon the choice of temporal warping functions ϕ. The model requires M_ϕ as a consequence of not requiring a scaling constraint.

Clearly, dynamic time warping and the discrete formulation of multiple media correlation are closely related. The use of a scaling constraint simplifies the model. Appropriate choices of ψ_i can provide a function identical to that of the path weighting coefficient.

5.   SUMMARY

Multiple media correlation provides a tool for formulating solutions to spatial and causal normalization problems. Synchronization data can then be readily derived from computed normalization data. The models presented in this chapter are very general and, in fact, overlap some existing techniques such as inter-correlation and dynamic time warping. However, the models presented in this chapter provide a framework for a larger class of problems than previous solution approaches. Chapter 4 shows that a large class of problems can be formulated in this form and solved efficiently.

The model presented in this chapter is a new contribution of this work and is more general than is necessarily required for the applications presented in this book. However, the reason for this generality is to provide a framework for not only the applications and algorithms presented hereing, but for a wide class of media computed synchronization problems. In particular, greater exploration of the potential of spatial normalization is a subject of considerable interest for future work.

Notes

1 Prior publications of this work have, indeed, presented a maximization formulation. This has been changed due to the "shortest path" approaches which have been commonly employed in the solution algorithms [95, 89, 96].
2 A trivial media instance is a set of media objects with one or more members having zero duration.

Chapter 4

ALGORITHMS FOR
MULTIPLE MEDIA CORRELATION

Chapter 3 presented a general model for multiple media correlation. This chapter presents a specific algorithmic solution strategy for that model. As presented, multiple media correlation is a very general model and a single solution approach encompassing all possible applications is not practical. However, the solution approach presented in this chapter is appropriate for large classes of problems, namely those which can be expressed using media representation graphs (MRGs). Media representation graphs are discussed in Section 5..

Two variations of the algorithm presented in this chapter have been implemented as components of the Xtrieve cross-modal information retrieval system described in Chapter 7. The implementations are completely general and oblivious to the underlying media types. All that is required to apply the solutions is a method for building the necessary media representation graphs and a media element comparison strategy. Chapters 5 and 6 describe how solutions are constructed for two distinct problems and Chapter 8 describes briefly many other possible applications.

The general algorithm presented gives an N-way solution for causal and spatial normalization of N weighted, additive media representation graphs. This is a general solution and can be applied to a large variety of problems. Causal media stream models and Markovian media representation graph (presented in Chapter 2) can be converted through equivalence relationships to media representation graphs compatible with this algorithm. Enhancements of the algorithm demonstrate that causal variation, Markovian representations, and error modeling are easily accommodated.

1. GENERAL SYNCHRONIZATION APPROACHES

Section 6.2 described two synchronization data types: implicit and explicit. This chapter describes sources of synchronization data, and so it is useful to define synchronization data sources in the context of these different synchronization data types.

1.1   INHERENT SYNCHRONIZATION

Some media object sets are *inherently synchronized* because they exist and are captured in a synchronized state. A simple example is simultaneous audio and video recording. In most cases the audio and video data are captured simultaneously and the synchronization source is the inherent temporal simultaneity of the capture process. Inherent synchronization does not imply *implicit synchronization*, synchronization inherent to the *media type*, as opposed to the media data source. If audio and video are captured simultaneously with video frame and audio sample timing from identical clocks, the synchronization is implicit. However, if frame drops (loss of frames during capture), analog frame rate imperfections, or other potential sources of timing errors are possible, explicit alignment between the audio and video data is required. audio/video interleaved (AVI) and QuickTime files include explicit synchronization data identifying relationships between audio and video data for these very reasons [29].

Closed-caption digitized video is considered inherently synchronized from an application point of view, since the synchronization exists in the off-air monitoring acquisition mechanism [109]. However, this synchronization did not always exist and had to be created at some point in time.

1.2   MANUAL SYNCHRONIZATION

Synchronization among media streams is a surprisingly useful tool and has been an element of some applications for many years. Up to now, automatic solutions have been lacking and manual solutions have been used. The most common example is closed-captioning of video broadcasts. Program captioning is typically based on known script material. However, the alignment between the broadcast and the script is not known, so the captions are aligned manually by an operator. Live broadcasting often requires the generation of a transcript "on-the-fly" by a *steno-captioner* [109]. Live transcription alignment quality suffers in relation to script alignments due to the increased complexity of the task and the latency of the steno-captioner.

1.3   COMPUTED SYNCHRONIZATION

A *computed synchronization data* is synchronization data produced as a result of the automatic analysis of media objects. The result of a synchronization computation is one or more explicit synchronization objects, because the synchronization relationships are explicitly defined by the synchronization objects. Computed synchronization is the main subject of this book.

2. MEDIA REPRESENTATION GRAPHS AS SYNCHRONIZATION OBJECTS

Section 5. presented media representation graphs as a powerful and general model for media objects. Causal media element models can be converted directly into MRGs by simply converting the elements into a sequential list of vertices, each vertex representing a media element. Variations in causal progress (effectively causal warping) are modeled using loop-back edges and duration modeling. Spatial alternatives are modeled with parallel paths. The media representation graph is a very natural media type for synchronization algorithms.

Some examples of media representation graph models for media types that may undergo synchronization are presented in Figure 4.1. This figure illustrates the power of the MRG data structure, and graphical representations of media types in general, in computed synchronization applications.

This work presents the notion of synchronization of *media representation graph,weighted* with explicit loop-back edges and additive edge weights. Causal variation of the MRG model is presented as an algorithmic extension. Increasing the MRG edge weights is considered inhibitive, and best weights are minima. Hence, edges which induce no path penalty have a zero weight.

2.1 MARKOVIAN MEDIA REPRESENTATION GRAPHS

In a Markovian media representation graph, all MRG edge weights are assumed to be probabilities; decreasing weights are considered inhibitive and best weight values are close to one. This is in contrast to the inhibitive increasing weights of general MRGs. Markovian media representation graphs can be converted to weighted media representation graphs by applying the formula $w_e = -ln(p_e)$ to edges e weights with probability p_e. w_e is the new edge log-likelihood weight and is compatible with the multiple media correlation model. The logarithm operation converts the multiplication to addition, while the sign change makes all values positive with increasing weights considered inhibitive. Probability values of one, indicating a path that imposes no penalty, translate to weights of zero.

Converting probabilities to weights has several other practical advantages. If an implementation utilizes only probabilities, the long path lengths (typically many thousands of vertices) are equivalent to very large products of values in the range $0 \leq x \leq 1$ and induce numeric underflow problems. Also, conversion from products to sums allows a Bayesian probabilistic problem to fit in the summation-based discrete model of multiple media correlation.

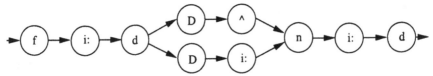

Phonemic MRG - Sounds representing text

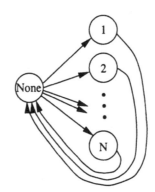

Slide presentation MRG

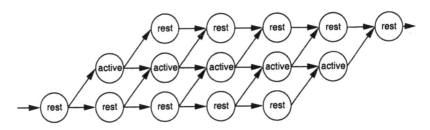

Delayed activation MRG segment

Brain hemodynamic response simulation

Figure 4.1.   Media representation graphs for various media synchronization alternatives.

2.2   NOTATION

A media representation graph instance is denoted μ_i, $i = 1, ..., N$ for the N MRGs input to a problem instance. The vertex set for the graph is denoted $\mu_i.V$. Vertices in the graph are considered to be indexed in an arbitrary order such that $\mu_i(s) \in \mu_i.V$ represents a single vertex in the MRG μ_i and $1 \leq s \leq |\mu_i.V|$. Directed edges in the graph are represented as $(\mu_i(s_1), \mu_i(s_2)) \in \mu_i.E$. All of the vertices reachable from vertex $\mu_i(s)$ are denoted $reachable(\mu_i(s))$. The weight of an edge is denoted $w(\mu_i(s_1), \mu_i(s_2))$. A path in a media representation graph is represented using the function $\tau_i(s), 0 \leq s \leq S$, where s and S are integers and the function τ_i is a mapping from an integer causal index to a vertex index.

τ_i is also referred to as a list of *visited vertices* $< \mu_i(\tau_i(0)), ..., \mu_i(\tau_i(S)) >$. The usage is equivalent and is clear in context. A path τ_i in MRG μ_i is valid if $(\mu_i(\tau_i(s-1)), \mu_i(\tau_i(s))) \in \mu_i.E, \forall s = 1, ..., S$.

Index $s = 1$ is the unique start vertex for an MRG. End vertices in MRGs are optional. The index for an end vertex is specified as $\mu_i.end$. If no end vertex is specified, $\mu_i.end = \infty$. Comparison of N MRG elements (from N media representation graphs, of course) is denoted as $\phi(\mu_i(\tau_i(s)), ..., \mu_N(\tau_N(s)),)$ and is assumed to produce a real-valued result. It is assumed that the result of a media element comparison and all edge weights in all MRGs are non-negative, though this requirement is relaxed in some applications.

A *supervertex* n refers to an ordered list of vertex indices such that one index for each media representation graph is included. The set of supervertices is the cross product of all constituent MRG vertex sets. A path that normalizes all of the media representation graphs visits a vertex in each graph for each value of s. The list of vertices visited simultaneously in this way for one value of s is a supervertex. The comparison of all of the elements of a supervertex is denoted $\phi(n)$. A *supergraph* M is a directed graph where each vertex is a supervertex. An edge (n_1, n_2) exists in M if and only if $(\mu_i(n_1[i]), \mu_i(n_2[i])) \in \mu_i.E, \forall i = 1, ..., N$. This states that a path exists from one supervertex to another if and only if paths exist between all vertices which are elements of the supervertex. A *synchronized transition* from coincident vertices, those vertices associated with a single supervertex, to coincident vertices associated with another supervertex assumes the path exists in all media representation graphs under normalization. The weight of an edge in the supergraph is the sum of all of the weights of the constituent edges: $w(n_1, n_2) = \sum_{i=1}^{N} w(\mu_i(n_1[i]), \mu_i(n_2[i]))$.

A supergraph is closely related to the *Cartesian product graph* of a set of graphs [13]. The definitions of a supergraph and a Cartesian product graph utilize the same construction rules, though supergraphs are directed and include a rule for defining edge weights.

A vertex n is an *end vertex* of the supergraph if $\mu_i.end = \infty$ or $n.v[i] = \mu_i.end, \forall i = 1, ..., N$. By the definition of an end vertex in a media representation graph, every vertex in the supergraph is an end vertex if no explicit end vertex is specified in the constituent MRGs. However, it is a requirement in the algorithm presented that a reachable explicit end vertex exist for at least one constituent MRG and that all end vertices have out-degree 0. This is a termination condition for the algorithm. Without this constraint, a minimum weight solution to the correlation problem is an empty path. Media representation graphs are allowed one explicit end vertex. Supergraphs can have multiple end vertices.

3.   GENERAL MRG OBJECT CORRELATION

Given N media representation graphs, this section presents general approaches for computing an *optimal correlation* among these graphs. This solution assumes positive weighted media representation graphs and $\phi(n) \geq 0, \forall n \in M$, where M is the supergraph constructed from the N MRGs.

A valid and complete path in an MRG is a path that exists in the MRG and reaches the end vertex if an end vertex is defined (recall that end vertices are optional for MRGs). An optimal correlation is defined to be the set of valid and complete paths $\tau_i, i = 1, ..., N$, and a path length S such that:

$$\eta = \arg \min_{S \geq 0, \tau_i \in T_i, i=1...N} \left(\sum_{s=1}^{S} \sum_{j=1}^{N} w(\mu_j(\tau_j(s-1), \tau_j(s))) + \right.$$

$$\left. \sum_{s=0}^{S} \phi(\mu_1(\tau_1, s), ..., \mu_N(\tau_N, s)) \right) \qquad (4.1)$$

Each of the computed causal normalization functions represents a path in its associated media representation graph. Each value of s is a point of correspondence among the vertices of the graphs and subject to computation of the correlation function. The weights of the edges traversed for each media type are added to the correlation function.

Equation 4.1 very closely resembles equation 3.11, repeated here:

$$\eta = \arg \min_{\tau_i \in T_i, \psi_i \in \Psi_i, i=1...N} \sum_{s=-\infty}^{\infty} \rho(\psi_1(\mu_1 \circ \tau_1, s), ..., \psi_N(\mu_N \circ \tau_N, s)) \quad (4.2)$$

The predominant differences between Equations 4.2 and 4.1 are the summation bounds, the addition of edge weights to the equation, and the elimination of the ψ spatial selection terms. The summation bounds in Equation 4.1 are considered to extend to infinity. It is assumed that correlation beyond bounds produces a zero value. The edge weights are considered an element of the match weight in this model. Edge weights are considered a cost of a vertex visit and, therefore, a component of the media element comparison.

The value of the correlation for a vertex is the sum of the result of function ρ and the weights of the edges that were traversed to reach the vertices in all of the media objects. If viewed as a probabilistic model, as in the Markovian media representation graph, the *probability of a vertex correlation* is the product of the probabilities of the match itself and the probabilities of visiting the vertex. These probabilities are converted to sums when the model is translated to an additive weighted media representation graph, but the same principles apply.

Equation 4.1 can be exactly reformulated as Equation 4.2 based on the following choices for ψ_i and ρ:

$$\psi_i(f, s) = \begin{cases} (f(s), w(f(s-1), f(s))) & 0 < s \leq S \\ (f(s), 0) & s = 0 \\ (\emptyset, 0) & \text{otherwise} \end{cases} \qquad (4.3)$$

$$\rho((v_1, w_1), ..., (v_N, w_N)) = \begin{cases} 0 & s < 0 \text{ or } s > S \\ \phi(v_1, ..., v_N) + \sum_{j=1}^{N} w_j & \text{otherwise} \end{cases}$$
$$(4.4)$$

The elimination of ψ in Equation 4.1 as a solution model is due to the increased ability of the media representation graph to translate many applications of spatial normalization to causal normalization. However, the need for spatial normalization and domain translation is not eliminated, so an alternative model incorporating these features is presented as Equation 4.5:

$$\eta = \arg \min_{\tau_i \in T_i, \psi_i \in \Psi_i, i=1...N} \left(\sum_{s=1}^{S} \sum_{j=1}^{N} w(\mu_j(\tau_j(s-1), \tau_j(s)))) + \right.$$
$$\left. \sum_{s=0}^{S} \rho(\psi_1(\mu_1 \circ \tau_1, s), ..., \psi_N(\mu_N \circ \tau_N, s)) \right) \qquad (4.5)$$

This equation is more general. Domain translation may require windowed analysis of more than one media object vertex. Indeed, this is the case for the specific application of text-to-text alignment presented in Chapter 6. Again, Equation 4.5 could be converted to the exact form of Equation 4.2 using techniques similar to those of Equations 4.3 and 4.4.

A requirement for solution existence is the existence of a path in the super-graph from the start vertex to an end vertex. The existence of such a path is not guaranteed by the existence of paths in the constituent media representation graphs, as illustrated inFigure 4.2. Any valid path from start to end in graph μ_1 will have an even number of vertices. A valid path in graph μ_2 will have an odd number of vertices. As a consequence, the supergraph, shown in Figure 4.2(b), has no reachable end vertex. Unreachable supervertices, including the end supervertex C,4 are omitted from Figure 4.2(b).

The path existence constraint is specified as a precondition to the algorithms in this chapter rather than being explicitly tested since most applications have solvable problem instances by design. Testing for the existence of a path in the supergraph can be done in time and space linear in the number of vertices and

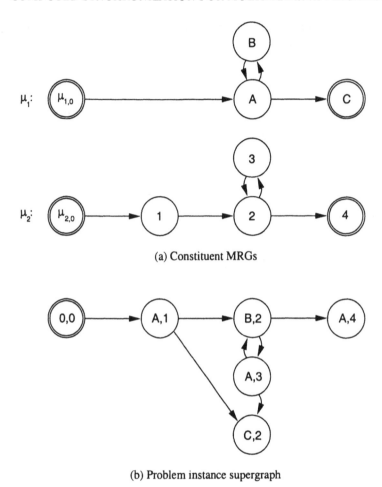

(a) Constituent MRGs

(b) Problem instance supergraph

Figure 4.2.   Media representation graph problem instance that exhibits no possible solution.

edges in the supergraph. The algorithm solution iterations can also be bounded to the size of the supergraph. If no solution is found by that time, no solution exists.

The requirement of non-negative weights on edges and as vertex scores is common for graph algorithms. Should negative weights be allowed, cycles in the graph could induce monotonically decreasing path weights, yielding infinite solutions.

3.1   SCALING INVARIANCE

For a multiple media correlation solution to exist at all, the problem instance must be scaling-invariant as defined in Section 1.1. Without the explicit inclusion of end vertices on at least one media object, the problem is not scaling invariant, since the solution could be scaled to length zero for a trivial optimal solution. However, the inclusion of an explicit end vertex on one of the media objects prevents that problem.

THEOREM 4.1 *If multiple media correlation is to be performed on a set of media objects represented by media representation graphs such that one of these graphs has a specific end vertex specified, the problem instance is scaling invariant.*

Proof: By assumption, at least one of the media representation graphs has a specific end vertex. For a specific media object μ of the constituent problem MRGs that has an end vertex, let τ be any path from the start vertex to the end vertex. Then, τ is a candidate causal normalization function and a member of T, the set of causal normalization functions, for this media object. Since the length of τ is finite, there must exist some $\beta \leq 1$ such that $\forall \tau' \in T$ and $\alpha, s \in \Re, \tau(s) = \tau'(\alpha s)$ implies $\alpha \geq \beta$, because there is a shortest path length X such that for any path length S, $S \geq X$. Then $\beta \geq X/S$. Hence, by Theorem 3.1, the problem instance is scaling invariant.

3.2   ALGORITHMS

The computation of an optimal solution for multiple media correlation is closely related to the shortest path in the supergraph. This leads to the following trivial solution algorithm:

Algorithm 4.1 (Trivial solution to general N-way weighted media representation graph normalization problem.):

1: Construct a supergraph G from all constituent MRGs
2: **for all** $(v_1, v_2) \in G.E$ **do**
3:     // *Add incident vertex correlation score to edge weight*
4:     $w(v_1, v_2) \leftarrow w(v_1, v_2) + \phi(v_2)$
5: **end for**
6: Compute single-source shortest paths from start vertex of G
7: Select the end vertex in G with the shortest path

A natural choice for single-source shortest paths for this algorithm is Dijkstra's algorithm, since the supergraph is constrained to meet its requirements [26]. Once a supergraph shortest path is found, all that remains is to map the path to the constituent MRG vertices.

Algorithm 4.1 is rarely practical in media applications. The reason is that media applications involve large media representation graphs and vertex counts in the tens and hundreds of thousands are typical. Since the supergraph size is a product of the constituent MRG sizes, supergraph sizes in the billions and trillions of vertices are common. Also, in many applications an entire media representation graph may not exist at any one time. Therefore, a more practical algorithm is needed.

Algorithm 4.2 presents an alternative solution to the general N-way weighted media representation graph normalization problem.

Algorithm 4.2 (N-way weighted media representation graph normalization.):

1: // **Initialization phase**
2: // *Create an empty search tree*
3: $root.v[i] \leftarrow 1, \forall i = 1, ..., N$
4: $root.parent \leftarrow \emptyset$
5: $root.children \leftarrow \emptyset$
6: $root.weight \leftarrow 0.$
7: $root.s \leftarrow 0$ // *The tree depth of the root.*
8: $tree \leftarrow \{root\}$
9: // *The set of active vertices for a given value of s:*
10: $active \leftarrow tree$
11: // *The current best completed path:*
12: $done.v \leftarrow \emptyset$ // *No vertex is done, yet*
13: $done.w \leftarrow \infty$ // *The weight of the best done path*
14: $s \leftarrow 0$
15: // **Forward search phase**
16: **while** $active \neq \emptyset$ **do**
17:    $s \leftarrow s + 1$
18:    // *The new active level is initially empty*
19:    $newactive \leftarrow \emptyset$
20:    // *For all of the active vertices:*
21:    **for all** $a \in active$ **do**
22:       // *For every supervertex reachable from an active vertex:*
23:       **for all** $r \in reachable(a.v[1]) \times ... \times reachable(a.v[N])$ **do**
24:          // *Compute a weight for this supervertex*
25:          $w \leftarrow \phi(r) + w(a.v, r)$
26:          **if** $\exists n \in tree$ such that $n.v = r$ **then**
27:             // *This supervertex has been visited before*
28:             // *Move to leaf here if it is a better weight on this path*
29:             Let $n \in tree$ such that $n.v = r$
30:             **if** $w < n.weight$ **then**
31:                // *Remove from parent's subtree and make a's child*
32:                $n.parent.children \leftarrow n.parent.children - n$
33:                $n.parent \leftarrow a$
34:                $n.weight \leftarrow w$
35:                $n.s \leftarrow s$
36:                $a.children \leftarrow a.children \cup \{n\}$
37:                $newactive \leftarrow newactive \cup \{n\}$
38:                // *Remove any children of n from search tree*

39:                       **while** $n.children \neq \emptyset$ **do**

40:                         Let $n_1 \in n.children$

41:                         $n.children \leftarrow (n.children \cup \{n_1.children\}) - n_1$

42:                         $tree \leftarrow tree - n_1$

43:                   **end while**

44:               **end if**

45:         **else**

46:             *// This supervertex has not been visited before*

47:             *// Add a new vertex n to the search tree*

48:             $n.v \leftarrow r$

49:             $n.parent \leftarrow a$

50:             $n.children \leftarrow \emptyset$

51:             $n.weight \leftarrow w$

52:             $n.s \leftarrow s$

53:             $a.children \leftarrow a.children \cup \{n\}$

54:             $newactive \leftarrow newactive \cup \{n\}$

55:             $tree \leftarrow tree \cup \{n\}$

56:         **end if**

57:       **end for** *// All vertices reachable from a*

58:     **end for** *// All active vertices*

59:     *// Determine vertices which are done*

60:     **for all** $a \in newactive$ **do**

61:       **if** $\mu_i.end = \infty$ or $a.v[i] = \mu_i.end, \forall i = 1, ..., N$ **then**

62:         $newactive \leftarrow newactive - a$

63:         **if** $a.weight < done.weight$ **then**

64:           $done.v \leftarrow a$

65:           $done.weight \leftarrow a.weight$

66:         **end if**

67:       **end if**

68:     **end for** *// All new active vertices*

69:     *// Early path termination condition (optional)*

70:     **for all** $a \in newactive$ **do**

71:       **if** $a.weight \geq done.weight$ **then**

72:         $newactive \leftarrow newactive - a$

73:       **end if**

74:     **end for** *// All new active vertices*

75: **end while** *// Forward search phase*

76: *// **Backtracking phase***

77: **if** $done.v = \emptyset$ **then**

78:     *// No solution exists*

79: **else**

80:     $m \leftarrow done.v$

```
81:    for j = m.s, ..., 0 do
82:      for i = 1, ..., N do
83:        τᵢ(j) = m.v[i]
84:      end for
85:      m ← m.parent
86:    end for
87: end if
```

Upon examination, Algorithm 4.2 is an alternative approach to single-source shortest paths that has been modified to match the multiple media correlation problem specification. The following analysis illustrates this fact in more detail. The important difference in this application is that the algorithm proceeds *synchronously*, computing candidate paths which are all the same length at any point in time. Also, the active vertex list provides a tool that is used for controlling the search space actually accessed.

3.3   OPTIMAL SUBSTRUCTURE

This algorithm takes advantage of the optimal substructure of the problem and is, in fact, a dynamic programming solution [115]. Each child vertex at any step in the algorithm represents the end of a least weight candidate path $\tau =< n_0, ..., n_s >$ in the supergraph from n_0 to n_s of length s. The optimal substructure of the problem is that any sub-path $\tau' =< n_0, ..., n_{s-j} >$ of τ is also a least weight path from n_0 to n_{s-j} of length $s - j$. This is easy to show, since should any lesser weight path $\tau'' =< n_0, ..., n_{s-j} >$ exist, it could be substituted for the path τ' to produce a lesser weight path.

All algorithm candidate paths in the supergraph are simple, having no cycles. This is clear because any attempt to add a new vertex to a path (lines 26 to 56) checks to see if the vertex already exists in the search tree. If a path to the vertex already exists, it is either replaced with a lesser weight path or left as the only path. Likewise, it is not possible that the removal of a heavier subtree (lines 32 to 43) removes a path to a, because that would leave a heavier version of vertex n along the path to the new, lighter version, a contradiction of the monotonically increasing path weight implied by non-negative edge and correlation weights.

3.4   TERMINATION

The only question relative to termination is whether the *while* loop (Line 16) terminates. Termination of this loop is dependent upon one of two events: (a) all paths have reached end vertices in the supergraph or (b) all current candidate path weights have exceeded a candidate best path weight. Option (a) is guaranteed to occur when the maximum path length in the supergraph is reached, since all paths are simple. However, it is far more common in practice that option (b) occurs due to the early path termination condition tests in lines 70 to 74.

3.5   PERFORMANCE

Let (V_S, E_S) be the vertices and edges of the supergraph. The number of executions of the *while* body is clearly bounded by $|V_S|$, since all paths are simple. Each algorithm step iterates over the set of active vertices, also bounded by $|V_S|$, and tests all reachable vertices, a maximum of $|E_S|$ total tests. The tree existence test in line 26 can be implemented in $O(\log V_S)$ time[1]. This test can also be done in constant time assuming the entire supergraph exists (each supergraph vertex has an associated pointer to its location in the search tree). However, as discussed, this is rarely the case. Implementations of this algorithm have used red-black trees as a mechanism for this determination [26]. Combining these elements, the worst case time bound for Algorithm 4.2 is $O((V_S + E_S)V_S \log V_S)$. This time bound is sub-optimal relative to Dijkstra's algorithm. However, several special problem instances are discussed that yield much better performance. Also, this large bound assumes the entire search space is examined. In practical applications the search space is significantly decreased.

Since a media representation graph is a relatively unconstrained general graph, the supergraph vertex count $|V_S|$ can, and often is, the product of the vertex counts for the constituent media representation graphs: $|V_S| = O(\prod_{i=1}^{N} |\mu_i|)$. Figure 4.3 illustrates a worst case for a supergraph. In this example, all vertices are reachable from all other vertices in the constituent graphs (excepting the start and end vertices, of course). All combinations therefore, are possible for supergraph vertices and all vertices in the supergraph are reachable from all other vertices. Hence, edges can be quadratic in the number of vertices.

The performance computations do not include the time to construct the supergraph, which no longer needs to be constructed, since the only need for the graph is determining reachable supervertices. Reachable supervertices can be determined by finding all vertices reachable for all constituent MRGs from a current supervertex and applying a cross product operation.

Space performance of the algorithm is based on the size of the search tree. (The active list is the leaves of the search tree.)

4.   SPECIAL CASE MRGS

While algorithm 4.2 is very general, its performance is highly dependent upon the specific MRG formats and the comparison methodology used. Several special cases of MRGs exist that allow for more detailed performance bounding

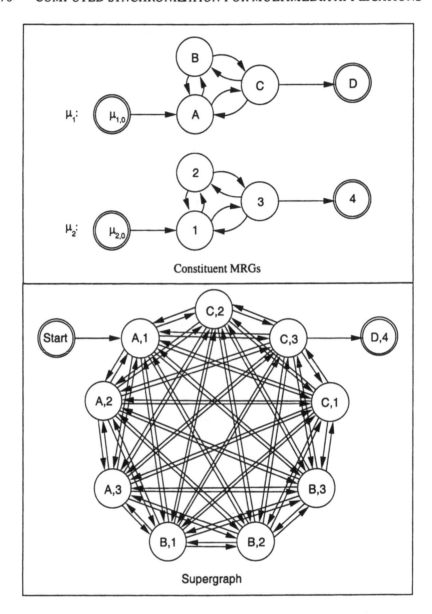

Figure 4.3.   Example of worst case supergraph.

in many practical applications. This section describes a few of these special cases.

4.1   SYNCHRONOUS COMPONENTS

A *synchronous media representation graph* is an MRG that is a list of vertices with no loop-back edges and one end vertex. Each causal step advances one vertex in the graph. Synchronous MRGs model time-step processes such as audio or video media elements, so they are quite common in practice. The inclusion of one or more synchronous MRGs as input to Algorithm 4.2 has a significant effect on the running time. The number of *while* body iterations is exactly the number of vertices in the synchronous MRGs. If more than one synchronous MRG is constituent to a problem instance, all synchronous MRGs must be of the same length, or no solution is possible.

An additional bound is based on the fact that the active supergraph vertices for any step of the algorithm can only include those that have a single vertex from each synchronous MRG included. At step $s = 5$, for example, only supergraph vertices which include the fifth vertex from each of the constituent synchronous MRGs can be active. The reachable vertices also includes only those which include the sixth vertex from each of the synchronous MRGs, because the only edge that exists from vertex five is to vertex six in these graphs. Hence, the number of active vertices is bounded by $O(\prod\{|\mu_i| : i \neg synchronous\})$.

This usage presents a significant performance improvement, in that it bounds the algorithm steps to a fixed number and it limits the number of active vertices. For pairwise normalization, wherein one media object is represented by a weighted MRG μ_1, and the other a synchronous MRG μ_2, the total number of algorithm steps is exactly the number of vertices in the synchronous MRG, $O(V_2)$. The total operations per step (relax operations) is bounded by the number of vertices in μ_1 (which may all be active) plus the number of edges in μ_1 (which may all be relaxed). For this simple pair-wise application, the determination of whether a supervertex is in the search tree can be reduced to a reference to the tree node attached as an annotation to the vertices in μ_1. Consequently, the running time is bounded by $O((V_1 + E_1)V_2)$.

4.2   RELATION TO VITERBI'S ALGORITHM

The specific case of alignment of one synchronous MRG to one unconstrained MRG reduces to a case very similar to that of Viterbi's algorithm, a popular approach to *maximum a posteriori* decoding [37, 110]. Viterbi's algorithm decodes a code as a sequence of symbol probabilities in combination with a Markov model for the symbol conditional probabilities. The Markov model assigns a probability for each state given any other state, with paths that cannot be traversed given a zero probability. In practical applications, all of the symbol probabilities and the model probabilities are converted to log-likelihood values by simply applying a logarithm. Zero probability edges are assumed to have infinite negative weight. Viterbi's algorithm, formulated in notation similar to that of Algorithm 4.2 is presented as Algorithm 4.3.

Algorithm 4.3 (Viterbi's algorithm):

1: // **Initialization phase**
2:   // *$\omega(s, i)$ is the weight of vertex i at time s*
3:   $\omega(0, 1) = 0$
4:   // *$\pi(s, i)$ is the predecessor of vertex i at time s*
5:   $\pi(0, 1) = nul$
6:   **for** $i = 2, ..., |\mu_1.V|$ **do**
7:     $\omega(0, i) = -\infty$
8:     $\pi(0, i) = nul$
9:   **end for**
10: // **Forward phase**
11: **for** $s = 1, ..., |\mu_2.V|$ **do**
12:     // *Get the log of the symbol probability*
13:     $\rho \leftarrow \mu_2(s)$
14:     **for** $i = 1, ..., |\mu_1.V|$ **do**
15:       // *No path to state initially, so $-\infty$ weight*
16:       $\omega(s, i) = -\infty$
17:       $\pi(s, i) = nul$
18:       **for** $j = 1, ..., |\mu_1.V|$ **do**
19:         $\omega' \leftarrow \rho + w(\mu_1(j) + \mu_1(i)) + \omega(s - 1, j)$
20:         **if** $\omega' > \omega(s, i)$ **then**
21:           $\omega(s, i) = \omega'$
22:           $\pi(s, i) = j$
23:         **end if**
24:       **end for**
25:     **end for**
26: **end for**
27: // **Backtracking phase**
28: max $\leftarrow$ arg$_i$ max $\omega(|\mu_2.V|, i)$
29: path $\leftarrow < max >$
30: **while** $\pi(max) \neq nul$ **do**
31:     // *Build list from the path*
32:     path $\leftarrow < \pi(max) > \| < path >$
33:     max $\leftarrow \pi(max)$
34: **end while**

In practice, enhancements are incorporated into the algorithm to increase efficiency, the most obvious being the computation of a path weight only for edges with non-zero probability.

Viterbi's algorithm is an instance of *trellis decoding*. A trellis is a time-indexed directed graph representing the transitions of a code over time. Definitions for a trellis vary in the literature. The following definition by Trachtenberg, based on two earlier definitions by Massey and McEliece, is indicative of common descriptions.

DEFINITION 4.1 (TRELLIS [75, 76, 123]) *A trellis T=(V,E) of rank n is a finite, directed, edge-labeled graph with the following properties:*
1. *Each vertex $v \in V$ has an associated depth $d \in 1, ..., n$.*
2. *Each edge $e \in E$ connects vertices at depth i to depth $i + 1$, for some i.*
3. *There is one vertex A at depth 0 and one vertex B at depth n.*

Figure 4.4 presents an example of trellis decoding. In this example a simple communications model expects three possible symbols as input: A, B, and C. At each point in time the probability of each symbol is estimated. This estimate can be based on direct observation combined with an estimate of the channel noise, for example. The table in Figure 4.4 includes some example symbol probabilities for the optimal sequence: A, B, A, C, A, B, C. The highlighted edges of the trellis correspond to this sequence. As an example, the weight of the edge to the first B vertex of the trellis, assuming a multiplicative model (not log-likelihoods), is 0.5, the edge weight, multiplied by 0.6, the symbol probability.

The single vertex at depth n is the maximum a posteriori path at time n; it represents the max argument in the Viterbi backtracking phase. The trellis searches to the full width at time n, but only paths that reach the maximum path are considered valid. Of these paths, only one path is optimum, and followed in the backtracking phase.

Viterbi's algorithm computes a modified breadth-first search of the trellis, effectively searching for the maximum weight path. Algorithm 4.2 is searching for a least-weight path on the supergraph. Supergraphs are not at all guaranteed to be a trellis. Differences between Algorithm 4.2 and Viterbi's algorithm are listed in Table 4.1.

4.3   CAUSAL COMPONENTS

A *causal media representation graph* is an MRG that is a list of vertices with loop-back edges and an explicit end vertex. If Algorithm 4.2 is applied to a set of causal MRGs, the analysis is a special case. To illustrate, assume two causal MRGs, μ_1 and μ_2. Any path in the supergraph built from these two graphs has edges that advance in one graph, advance in both, or repeat elements of both, since this is the only edge transition support in the constituent MRGs. Figure 4.5 illustrates the options. From supervertex A1, the options are A1, B1, A2, B2. However, the case of repeating vertices in both media objects never occurs in an optimum path, because shortest paths in the supergraph are simple paths. Hence, the number of steps in the algorithm is bounded by $O(V_1 + V_2)$. For this special case, the algorithm running time is bounded by

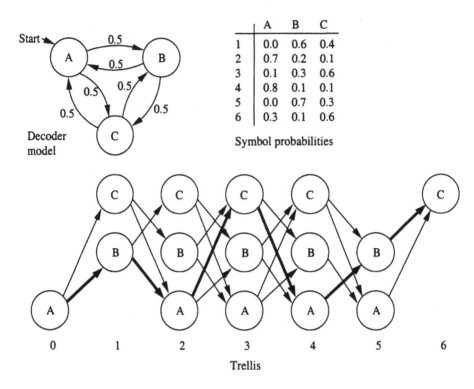

	A	B	C
1	0.0	0.6	0.4
2	0.7	0.2	0.1
3	0.1	0.3	0.6
4	0.8	0.1	0.1
5	0.0	0.7	0.3
6	0.3	0.1	0.6

Symbol probabilities

Figure 4.4.   Example trellis and trellis decoding.

Table 4.1.   Comparison of Algorithm 4.2 to Viterbi's algorithm.

Algorithm 4.2 *Multiple Media Correlation*	Algorithm 4.3 *Viterbi's Algorithm*
Trellis decoding only in synchronous applications	Trellis decoding
Builds search tree that is a subset of the supergraph	Builds a trellis
Search is based on supergraph that need not be computed	Trellis is based on Markov model
General media element comparison model	Symbol probability model
General weights model	Log-likelihood or Bayesian model

$O(V_s(V_1 + V_2) \log V_s)$, where V_s is the number of vertices in the supergraph. Again, the log factor is due to the determination of vertex existence in the search tree. Edges are omitted from this asymptotic running time since they are linear in the number of vertices.

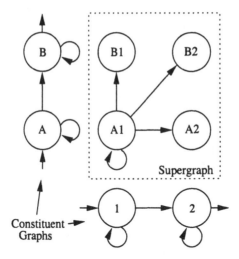

Figure 4.5. Possible transitions for the case of application of Algorithm 4.2 to two causal MRGs.

The example is easily extended to an N-way normalization of N causal MRGs. The analysis is an obvious extension of the above example. The running time is $O(V_s(\sum_{i=1}^{N} V_i) \log V_s)$.

5.   STRATEGIES FOR PERFORMANCE

The algorithmic solution presented in this chapter computes an optimal solution. However, for most applications the polynomial space and time performance is not tractable, so performance improvements are necessary. Three classes of performance improvements are presented in this section: constant improvements, efficient input construction, and solution approximations. *Constant improvements* do not affect the asymptotic running time, but do decrease the running time by improving the performance at each algorithm step. *Efficient input construction* seeks to increase performance by decreasing MRG sizes. *Approximations* trade solution optimality for performance. This section describes performance improvement approaches which can be applied to Algorithm 4.2 in each of these areas. The specific application examples describe the consequences or trade-offs made by approximation algorithms.

The performance of Algorithm 4.2 is dependent upon several factors: the number of algorithm steps, the size of the active search space at each step, the number of graph edges traversed at each step, and the comparison function performance. The options for performance improvement presented in this section are related to these three areas.

Performance is a significant issue in this work due to the large size of media representations. Audio in Chapter 6 is modeled as a synchronous media representation graph with 100 vertices per second of audio. Thirty minutes of audio is equivalent to 180,000 MRG vertices. Text is modeled using sound approximations called *biphones*, which average close to 100 vertices per second of presented text. An example synchronization problem normalized a 188,990 vertex biphonemic MRG and a 248,413 vertex synchronous audio MRG.

5.1   COMPARISON CACHING

The complexity of the media element comparison function varies considerably for differing applications. The parallel text alignment system presented in Chapter 5 performs a windowed textual comparison based on word searches in the WordNet lexical database of the English language [11], a computationally complex operation. The text-to-speech alignment system presented in Chapter 6, on the other hand, reduces the media element comparison to a simple table lookup.

The number of media element comparison operations per algorithm step is dependent upon the number of active supergraph vertices and the average MRG out-degree. Obviously, each of these can be very large. However, the number of combinations is specifically limited to the number of supergraph vertices. If the number of supergraph vertices that can be active at any one algorithm step is limited, as discussed in Section 4., the number of possible comparisons is even less. The same comparison is repeated in each algorithm step for each active edge traversed that ends in the same supergraph vertex. A significant performance improvement can be gained by caching, or saving temporarily, comparison function results, either per algorithm step or for the duration of the algorithm. Such a strategy was found to lead to 100X performance improvements in the text-to-text alignment program, mostly due to poor performance of the WordNet lookup process.

5.2   MRG LIMITATION STRATEGIES

The performance of Algorithm 4.2 is asymptotically dependent upon the size of the media representation graphs. Any decrease in the size of these data structures significantly improves performance. Indeed, the graphical representations of vocabulary in speech recognition systems are carefully tuned to decrease the symbol space for this very reason. The most common reduction in size is the merging of parallel, identical paths. Figure 4.6 illustrates the reduction of both leading and trailing paths to single vertices. This is a common reduction when speech is involved, since many words have common prefix and suffix elements. Of course, the edge weights must be compatible with this reduction. Other likely possibilities for decreasing MRG size include decreasing the media element space to a smaller number of items (using a more compact or less redundant representation), increasing the causal duration of media elements,

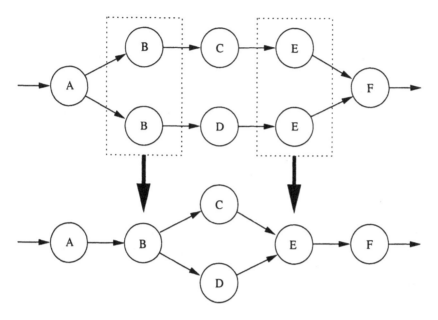

Figure 4.6.   Merging of identical MRG paths.

or limiting the spatial resolution of selection (spatial resolution translates into parallel paths in the MRG).

5.3   PRUNING STRATEGIES

In Algorithm 4.2, the search space quickly expands to include a significant percentage of the active space in the supergraph. No amount of MRG reduction or functional acceleration will help when the size of the tree is expected to grow to 4×10^{10} vertices, as in one text-to-speech alignment example. Some significant limit on this search space is not only required for performance, but logical. It is not necessary that all of the search space be examined. In the text-to-speech application, for example, the algorithm is proceeding synchronously with the audio media elements. Each audio media element can logically be expected to align with text media elements within a reasonable range, not anywhere in the transcript.

A common approach to decreasing search space is to apply a pruning,heuristic [104], eliminating paths from consideration after each step of the algorithm based on the path weight. The idea is to eliminate unlikely paths from consideration. There are several approaches to determining the paths to prune.

The first approach, common in speech recognition systems, is based on definition of a *pruning,parameter* $\beta > 1$. After each algorithm step, the minimum weight in *active* is determined, say ω_{min}. All vertices $a \in active$ such that $a.weight > \beta\omega_{min}$ are removed from *active*. This is the approach used in the CMU Sphinx-II speech recognition system [104]. Use of a multiplicative pruning parameter is referred to as *pruning,proportional*.

The second approach is a slight variation on the first approach and was recognized in this research as more useful in computed synchronization applications than proportional pruning. This technique is again based on a pruning parameter $\beta > 0$. All vertices $a \in active$ such that $a.weight > \omega_{min} + \beta$ are removed from *active*. This method is called *additive pruning*. Path weights increase monotonically for each algorithm step. As the algorithm proceeds, the best paths will typically have an initial common path followed by a branching into different paths. This is due to the fact that the paths are paths within a tree. The common path results in an additive value common to all paths, effectively offsetting the path weights by the additive bias. Consequently, the ratio of the best path weights tends to decrease over time. Empirical evidence suggests that the difference between among the highest ranking paths is a more indicative measure of path difference than the ratio. Hence, an additive pruning factor is more sensible than a multiplicative factor. The use of additive pruning is also suggested by the log-likelihood model where a proportional pruning of probabilities is equivalent to additive pruning of log-likelihood values.

A difference between this application and the Sphinx-II system is the length of the paths. Speech recognition systems are searching shallow, but wide, sets of possible matches in the form of many parallel word matches. Hence, the monotonic increase in the path weight is not a significant factor in those systems.

The third approach simply prunes all but the α least weight paths. As an example, if only the 2000 least ranking members of *active* are retained after each algorithm step, the running time is bounded to $O(\alpha \lambda S)$, where λ is the maximum out-degree for any supergraph vertex and S is the number of iterations of the *while* body, the duration for synchronous media elements or the length of the optimal path. The search tree is bounded to $O(\alpha S)$ memory usage as well. This technique is referred to as *ranked pruning*.

Of these approaches, ranked pruning has been found to be more applicable to media normalization problems than proportional or additive pruning. Media normalization problems have a unique characteristic that the pruning parameter determines the coverage of the search space that can be active at any time, effectively lower-bounding the search range for the application. This search range often translates to a distance range representing causal coverage of synchronization content (the range of text that may be subject to alignment to one point in a vocal presentation of that text, for example).

Given the application of pruning (and all applications demonstrated in this work employ pruning), a logical enhancement is to also prune the search tree recursively, pruning not only leaf nodes, but also any redundant paths leading only to pruned leaf nodes. Algorithm 4.4 performs this function. The algorithm is applied to each vertex removed from the active set. The operation is called *recursive tree pruning*.

Algorithm 4.4 (Recursive tree pruning):

```
1:  // Prune the vertex p from the actives set
2:  function prune(p)
3:  p.parent.children ← p.parent.children − p
4:  if p.parent.children = ∅ then
5:      // The parent is now childless, so
6:      // recursively prune the parent
7:      prune(p.parent)
8:  end if
```

Given a pruning parameter α, the memory requirement for the search tree is bounded by $O(\alpha S)$. Recursive tree pruning operations can remove no more than this number of tree vertices, so the operations per step have an amortized performance of $O(\alpha)$.

The worst case tree space usage remains αS vertices, even if pruning is employed. However, the only way to achieve such a tree is if all paths in the tree are parallel. Each branch in the tree decreases the tree width at that step by at least one. In practice, the tree tends to collapse to a single path relatively quickly, yielding a tree that consists of a long list followed by a small tree at the end.

5.4   PATH COMPRESSION

The depth of the search tree is S, which can be rather large when media objects are subjected to multiple media correlation. The tendency of the search tree to collapse to a long list with a small tree at the end can be exploited to significantly decrease memory usage through the application of *path compression*. Two path compression approaches have been developed: the list can be flushed to disk as it becomes available, or compression/redundancy reduction techniques can be applied to reduce the memory usage for the list. Both techniques are used in the Xtrieve system described in Chapter 7.

6.   EDIT STRATEGIES

A major goal of this work has been the development of tools which can be applied to consumer and commercial media applications. In real-world applications, two or more media objects under correlation may not match as precisely as expected due to errors. Errors are changes in content relative to the expected result and are referred to as *edits*. Human transcription operators make mistakes, performers misread scripts, and people routinely insert additional content. Indeed, none of the test data utilized in the evaluation of the text-to-speech application described in Chapter 6 has been error-free. Hence, effective methods for detecting and managing errors are required.

This section describes tools for handling edits in media objects under correlation. Three edit types exist: insertions, deletions, and substitutions. The terminology used in this section assumes synchronization of a media object μ_2 that may have errors to an assumed correct media object μ_1.

Insertions are content added to μ_2 which do not exist in μ_1. Insertions include alliteration and "ad-libs" in speech, extra slides or hand-draw figures in presentations, and additional front-matter in a translation. *Deletions* are content which exist in μ_1, but not in μ_2. Common deletions include skipped content in presentation, skipped slides, or accidental omissions. In the Chapter 6 test data, deletions have been found to be far more common and extensive than insertions, assuming the textual transcription represents the correct content. *Substitutions* are local changes in content. A substitution can be modeled as simply the combination of an insertion and a deletion.

Obviously, some symmetry exists in this problem. If the assumption of correctness is reversed, the notions of insertion and deletion are reversed. Indeed, the question arises, why model both? One reason is that the methods for modeling insertions and deletions as presented herein require modifications of the media representation graph that convert content such as speech audio from strictly synchronous. This induces a performance penalty, since the advantages of the application of Algorithm 4.2 to a synchronous MRG are lost.

Application of deletion modeling techniques to all input to Algorithm 4.2 can violate the scaling constraint by allowing deletion of content from all MRGs. As a simple example, modeling insertion and deletion simultaneously by allowing deletion from both media under correlation results in a trivial solution wherein both media are completely deleted, leaving only matching start vertices. Finally, if only one media object in an N-way problem may have insertions, it is more sensible to model the insertions for the single object rather than modeling deletions for the other $N - 1$ media objects.

6.1   ERROR TOLERANCE

Most applications of Algorithm 4.2 are timing tolerant in that they include variable-duration modeling in at least one of the constituent MRGs. The most common variable-duration modeling technique is the use of loop-back edges. In the presence of variable-duration modeling, a media object can "stretch" or "shrink" in the presence of edits. This results in some range of the normalization space, $[s_\alpha, s_\beta]$ in which the correlation function scores are poor, either due to a substitution over the range, insertion errors during the range, or due to the alignment playing "catch-up" over a range in the presence of a deletion. The ability of the normalization to tolerate such an error is dependent upon the overall quality of the remaining match. An estimate of the expected error penalty per causal normalization step for the bad match is:

$$\varepsilon = \frac{\sum_{s=s_\alpha}^{s_\beta} \phi(\mu_1(\tau_1(s)), ..., \mu_N(\tau_N(s)))}{s_\beta - s_\alpha + 1} -$$

$$\frac{\sum_{s=0}^{s_\alpha - 1} \phi(\mu_1(\tau_1(s)), ..., \mu_N(\tau_N(s)))}{S - s_\beta + s_\alpha - 1}$$

$$\frac{\sum_{s=s_\beta + 1}^{S} \phi(\mu_1(\tau_1(s)), ..., \mu_N(\tau_N(s)))}{S - s_\beta + s_\alpha - 1} \tag{4.6}$$

Equation 4.6 computes the difference between the average bad match range correlation weight and the average good match range correlation weight. Edge weights are omitted in this example because they remain the same over an equivalent range of the MRG. Bad matches may induce different paths, though, that would affect the path edge weights. However, the difference is rarely significant in practice. The total error weight for the error range is $(s_\beta - s_\alpha + 1)\varepsilon$. For an error to be ignored due to the weight of good matches, the total error weight must be small relative to the range of the good matches over which the error weight is spread. The range is determined by the average frequency of errors and by path pruning. A good rule of thumb determined in experimental usage has been a $10 : 1$ range of errors to good match spread. A single word error in a speech document is considered to require about ten words of good match to overcome the error. Hence, small errors are tolerated very well. However, larger errors can break the system out of synchronization for a considerable range. Chapter 6 describes error tolerance experience.

6.2 DELETION MODELING

An obvious solution for deletion tolerance is the inclusion of edges in the MRG that model all possible deletions by simply bypassing or jumping over content. However, this approach is not practical for two reasons. Jumping all possible deletion combinations requires a quadratic number of deletion edges. Since media object models are often very large, on the order of hundreds of thousands of vertices, quadratic edge counts are often not feasible and would slow performance considerably. Also, allowing for every possible deletion possibility expands the forward search space to a parallel application of all future content, effectively reducing the local media alignment problem to open vocabulary automatic transcription. Three solutions for this problem have been devised which are much more practical.

The first solution is *heuristic deletion edges*, edges added to the MRG which bypass a logical and common deletion unit. In text-to-speech alignment, it has been discovered that the vast majority of large deletions correspond to

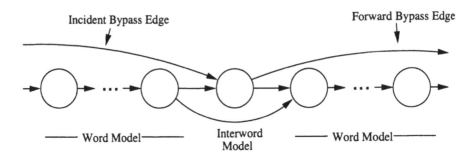

Figure 4.7.   Bypass edges relative to word subgraph.

paragraphs or sentences (or lines in a play). Hence, bypass edges are placed around those units. This technique is based on knowledge of the structure of the content and the types of deletions common in that content. Heuristic bypass edges have been found to be a highly effective bypass alternative due to the common structure of many deletions.

The next two solutions are based on hierarchical sets of bypass edges. These techniques are blind to the content, requiring only that the content be semi-acyclic. Since it is not practical to bypass every possible deletion combination, it is obvious that any deletion requires the traversal of more than one bypass edge if some alternative bypass path exists. Assuming $b > 1$ bypass edges are traversed, there must exist some aligned content between each sequential pair of bypass edges. If the bypass edges are among elements of a semi-acyclic MRG (as described in section 5.4), each bypass edge connects one subgraph to another subgraph. In practice, this connection is usually to vertices within the subgraph. Examples include connections incident on a word, exiting after the word, or incident on a model for space between words.

Figure 4.7 illustrates application of bypass edges to an MRG modeling a transcription that will be aligned to a spoken utterance. In this example, a model for inter-word spacing has been used as the vertex (actually a vertex group) between bypass edges. The inter-word spacing vertex is bypassed by design of the language model, not as a deletion accommodation. Inter-word spacing is not predictable. Should the second word modeled in the figure be deleted, the forward edge would be taken. This implies that the inter-word spacing model is also in the path, even if there is no inter-word spacing to the next word. However, this in-line accumulation of extra vertices is a necessary tradeoff if a quadratic bypass edge load is to be avoided.

It seems logical that bypass edges should be added in a hierarchical set such that for each level, $2^L - 1$ vertices are bypassed. Figure 4.8 illustrates the naive approach to such a structure. Construction of the bypass edges is trivial, and the number of added edges is linear in the number of MRG vertices. Deletion

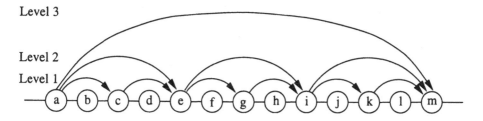

Figure 4.8.　　Basic hierarchical bypass edges.

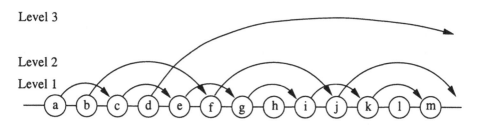

Figure 4.9.　　Bounded out-degree hierarchical bypass edges.

of the range $d - f$ would require that e remain in the path. Deletion of $c - l$ would require that c, e, and i remain in the path. The number of intermediate vertices that must be traversed for a deletion of length D is $O(\log D)$. Extra traversal vertices in the path are kept to a minimum.

The approach in Figure 4.8, while effective, does have a major drawback in practice, particularly when combined with pruning. As Algorithm 4.2 proceeds, it maintains a list of candidate paths in the search tree. When pruning is employed, the width of the deepest level of the tree is bounded by the pruning parameter. Note, however, that the number of vertices reachable in Figure 4.8 from vertex a within a limited number of steps is very large. Also, this construct causes an unbalanced out-degree for vertices in the graph. A factor in the algorithm performance is the average out-degree for active vertices. This structure causes rapid branching in the tree on the high out-degree vertices such as vertex a and more rapid branching later in the tree as other high out-degree vertices are reached. The search space becomes dominated by high out-degree vertices, impacting performance. In experimentation, this structure was found to rapidly expand the search tree such that a large number of paths had similar scores and pruning width had to be increased for effective matching. The simple solution to this problem is to bound the out-degree of vertices in the presence of bypass edges.

Figure 4.9 illustrates the *bounded out-degree bypass edge system*. Only bypass levels 1 to 3 are presented in this figure for symmetry with Figure 4.8. An identical number of bypass edges (up to boundary conditions) are included.

The only modification to the placement algorithm is that each level is offset by $2^{L-1} - 1$. The intermediate steps remain logarithmic. However, the search tree branch factor for each vertex is increased by only one. In practice, this structure has been found to be far more effective than that of Figure 4.8.

6.3   INSERTION MODELING

An insertion is an inclusion in μ_2 not modeled by the media representation graph μ_1. Insertions can be thought of as the inverse of the deletion problem. However, as discussed earlier, simple addition of deletion edges to μ_2 is not a practical solution.

Small insertions resemble small deletions or substitutions in that the alignment process is tolerant due to the weight of the larger surrounding match. However, larger insertions can and do cause problems. Again, a semi-acyclic MRG is assumed. Let $[s_\alpha, s_\beta]$ be the range of the causal normalization variable such that $\mu_2 \circ \tau_2$ over that range for all candidate match paths covers the insertion. For this period, it is assumed that all candidate paths for τ_1 have advanced beyond the point following the insertion (for example, if the string "abcd" is to be matched to "abxcd" and all paths have moved beyond "c" in string one when "c" is reached in string two). Should this not be the case, the insertion is not a problem and can be recovered from directly. A simple way of viewing this problem is that all matchings in μ_1 have advanced too far. This is typically the case in the presence of insertions, since, assuming no insertion modeling and a semi-acyclic MRG, all paths in the semi-acyclic MRG can either stall due to loop-back edges or advance. Long term loop-back edges tend to accumulate larger scores than other alternatives in the search space and get pruned. If the search paths can jump backwards when such a condition occurs, the resynchronization point can be found.

Figure 4.10 illustrates the problem. Assume two semi-acyclic MRGs μ_1 and μ_2 with an insertion in μ_2. Since the MRGs are semi-acyclic, a 2-D graph can be used to plot the alignment of the vertex groups. Advancement in μ_1 is indicated by vertical motion in the graph, advancement in μ_2 by horizontal motion. Since both media types are semi-acyclic, the slope of the normalization line is bounded between 0 and ∞. The dark line is the ideal path, assuming the insertion is ignored. When an insertion occurs, an ideal match would proceed over the insertion without advancing the match in μ_1, as evidenced by the horizontal line during the insertion period. In practice, a large insertion typically induces such a large error weight that an alternative path becomes the leader, especially in the presence of pruning, which may have completely eliminated all paths that would intersect with the ideal path in the future. Such a bad match path is illustrated by the dotted lines.

If the search range after the insertion includes the possibility of stepping back in the media representation graph, this back traversal can allow the system to

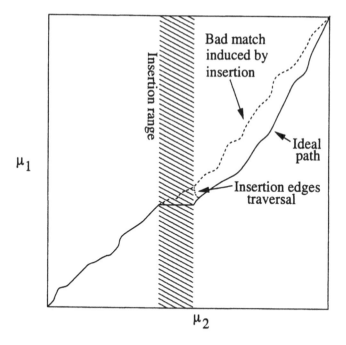

Figure 4.10.   Insertion effect on synchronization.

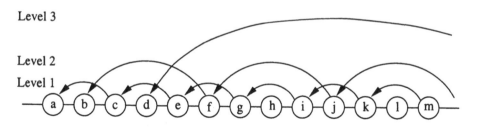

Figure 4.11.   Insertion bypass edges.

resynchronize, albeit with some intervening vertices. This is also illustrated in Figure 4.10. A hierarchical structure similar to the deletion model can be used to model insertions, with the modification of edge direction reversal. Figure 4.11 illustrate bounded out-degree hierarchical insertion modeling. As in Figure 4.9, hierarchical levels beyond 3 are not shown, so edges incident on *h* and *l* are not included.

6.4   COMBINED INSERTION AND DELETION MODELING

Clearly, simultaneous insertions and deletions are possible in many media normalization applications. However, simple inclusion of both insertion and

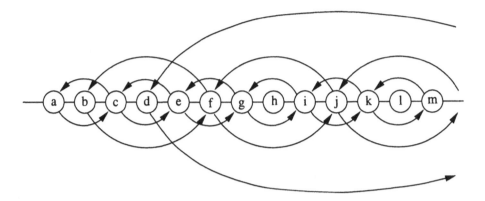

Figure 4.12.   Insertion and deletion bypass edges.

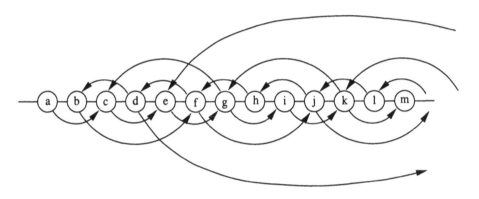

Figure 4.13.   Insertion and deletion bypass edges.

deletion edges, as in Figure 4.12 creates many simple cycles in the media representation graph. These redundant paths clutter the search space. A simple means of avoiding simple cycles is to offset the insertion edges relative to the deletion edges as in Figure 4.13. All of the simple cycles are then broken. Cycles are still possible, as in "bcdbcd...", but the minimum cycle length is increased, requiring more context for a cycle to match.

6.5   ISSUES OF EDIT MODELING AND CONTEXT

The inclusion of edit modeling edges expands the search space considerably during algorithm execution. Figure 4.14 is a visualization of the search space during an execution of Algorithm 4.2. In this figure, a transcript from Act 1, Scene 2 of *Hamlet* is aligned to an audio presentation of that act. This figure was created by an instrumentation of Algorithm 4.2 that outputs image rows as the algorithm progresses. The image rows indicate the vertices in the text MRG that are active by shadings other than black. No bypass edges are included in

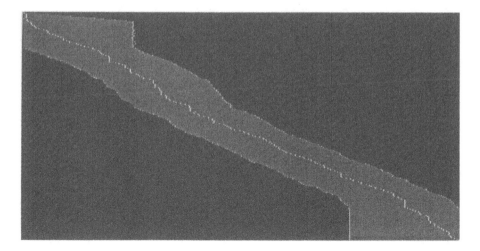

Figure 4.14.   Algorithm 4.2 search space with no edit modeling.

the algorithm input MRGs and the transcript is predominantly correct, up to local word errors. Time in the audio proceeds from top to bottom, the transcript words are presented sequentially left to right. The width of the gray area for an image row indicates the active search range. The range maintains a fixed width band in the vicinity of the current best path, the bright white line. The current best candidate path ends do not imply the best overall paths, so this line does not represent the final alignment.

Figure 4.15 illustrates the same problem instance, with the exception that insertion and deletion modeling have been included. The search space remains dense near the best current match, but extends much farther in either direction. A relatively large search range is available. This has the advantage of allowing for insertions and deletions, but does decrease the near-in search space. Hence, the pruning parameter must be increased when edit modeling is in use.

Care must be taken when using edit modeling so as to not obliterate the advantage of *context*. Edit modeling edges allow paths within the media representation graph that do not correspond to normal media object presentations. The order of media object presentation represents context, a limitation of matching possibilities. Matching of noisy or occluded content is more effective in the presence of a larger context. However, edit modeling edges can allow arbitrary traversal of the model, potentially penalizing context.

The issue is that use of bypass edges should be rare. Traversal of these edges should be only in the case of edits. The simplest means of ensuring that bypass edge traversal is rare is to penalize that traversal. This penalty is modeled by adding a weight to the bypass edge. This weight should be large enough that it

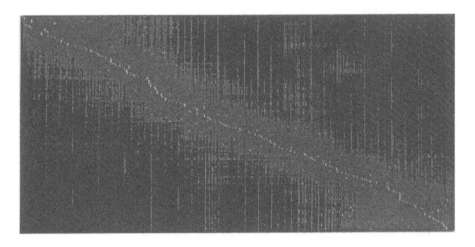

Figure 4.15.   Algorithm 4.2 search space with insertion and deletion modeling.

must be distributed over a relatively large number of vertices. The application chapters describe statistical approaches used for selecting bypass edge weights.

7.   ENHANCEMENTS

As presented, Algorithm 4.2 is a general solution to a wide class of problems. However, several of the enhancements of media representation graphs presented in Chapter 2 are not accommodated by this algorithm, specifically causally varying MRGs and duration modeling. This section describes enhancements to Algorithm 4.2 that accommodate these additional features.

7.1   CAUSALLY VARYING MRGS

Section 5.5 described causally varying media representation graphs as having an associated weighting function $\gamma(i, v)$, where i is a vertex number and v is a relative causal ordering variable for the sequential presentation of the media. It is assumed that the weighting function result is additive. It is trivial to extend Algorithm 4.2 by adding the weighting function to each alignment step in the algorithm, provided v, a relative measure of the distance into the MRG, can be determined. The length of a match is not known *a priori* in Algorithm 4.2 except in the case where one of the media objects is synchronous (as in Section 4.1), so causal variation can only be applied for that special case, though the most likely use of causal variation is in the presence of synchronous time-based media such as audio or video.

A common application of causally varying MRGs is the interpolation of an estimated normal weighting curve over the MRG. When synchronization becomes impossible due to noise or other uncertainties in the data analysis process, this curve helps the system to advance an alignment. This process is referred to as *enforced interpolation*. As an example, the text-to-speech application described in Chapter 6 has limited utility when the content is a singing voice with rich musical backgrounds. The music overwhelms the speech feature recognition system, and the singing voice does not present speech in its normal form. Since the alignment is no longer based on reliable information it is logical that it interpolate the alignment over the song. Normal distributions are very natural in this application. The modified formula used is [58]:

$$\gamma(i, v) = -\ln \left(\frac{1}{\sigma\sqrt{2\pi}} e^{\frac{-(\delta(i)-v)^2}{2\sigma^2}} \right) \tag{4.7}$$

The function $\delta(i)$ translates a vertex index into an average relative position for the vertex in a causal ordering of the media object. σ is the standard deviation specified for the causal variation. This formula is a point-wise approximation of a normal distribution obtained by selecting a point in the middle of the range in the curve rather than integrating over a range in the curve. However, it is an efficient approach and has been found effective in practice. The peak of the curve moves from the beginning of the media object at time $v = 0$ to the end of the media object at time $v = 1$. The application of the $-ln$ function converts the probability-like function to a weight such that decreasing probability is increasing weight.

Equation 4.7 can be reduced with simple manipulations to:

$$\gamma(i, v) = -\ln \frac{1}{\sigma\sqrt{2\pi}} + \frac{(\delta(i) - v)^2}{2\sigma^2} \tag{4.8}$$

The reduction eliminates the potentially costly logarithm operation other than on the constant additive term. An additional reduction is to eliminate the initial constant term completely:

$$\gamma(i, v) = \frac{(\delta(i) - v)^2}{2\sigma^2} \tag{4.9}$$

The additive constant term can be eliminated because it would be added to every path for every level of the tree. Since every path has the same constant added, subtracting it out does not affect the path rankings.

7.2   DURATION MODELING

Duration modeling sets limits on the duration (minimum and maximum) of elements in an MRG. Duration modeling is critical in many applications in

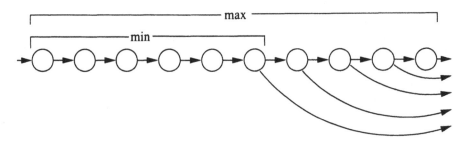

Figure 4.16.   Bounded-duration modeling using MRG vertices.

order to bound the temporal normalization range. There are two approaches to duration modeling: MRG vertex approaches and algorithmic enhancements.

In this section it is assumed that a duration unit is measured in steps equivalent to one visit to an MRG vertex. This step size is equivalent to one step in Algorithm 4.2. MRG modeling approaches convert a vertex incorporating duration modeling to a sequence of vertices. Assume a vertex n with minimum duration min and maximum duration max, $min \leq max$. Figure 4.16 illustrates the construction of an equivalent vertex set implementing duration modeling. This construct is described in Section 5.2.

Expanded MRG duration modeling solutions can significantly increase the size of an MRG. An algorithmic approximation is to maintain with the search tree vertices a count of how many times each vertex parent is associated with the same MRG vertex, which essentially counts how many times that MRG vertex has been repeated. Any loop-back and adjacency edges are disabled prior to the minimum duration. Once the minimum duration is met, adjacency edges and loop-back edges are enabled. Once the maximum duration is met, loop-back edges are disabled. This simple strategy ensures MRG vertex visits meet the duration modeling requirements.

Though this technique is commonly applied to Viterbi's algorithm implementations, it is an approximation and is not equivalent to repeated vertices in the MRG. Figure 4.17 illustrates an algorithmic duration modeling error. The dotted-line path would eliminate the solid-line path at the vertex labeled α because the path weight to that point for the dotted-line path is zero, while the solid-line path weight is one. The problem arises at the next algorithm step, when the comparison for the duration modeled MRG vertex indicates a poor match. The best path in this case would have been the solid-line path, but the dotted-line path is selected due to the previous elimination.

The specific problem in this case is that the optimal substructure of the problem no longer applies in the presence of duration modeling. It no longer makes sense to talk of reaching a vertex by a shorter path, since a vertex now also includes *state*, specifically how long the vertex has been active. Though

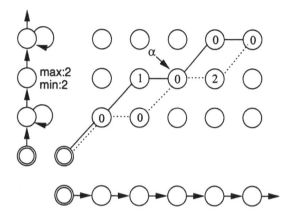

Figure 4.17. Error due to algorithmic duration modeling.

this is clearly a suboptimal solution, it is presented here because it is a common solution in Viterbi implementations and produces good approximate results in speech systems. The specific implementations described in this presentation utilize vertex duplication for duration modeling, not this heuristic algorithm modification.

8. SUMMARY

The primary contribution of this chapter is Algorithm 4.2, a general solution to N-way weighted media representation graph normalization. Though very general, this algorithm is appropriate for a wide variety of problems, including all applications described in this book. The algorithm has significant performance advantages for common special cases of input MRGs.

One of the most important features of Algorithm 4.2 is that it is designed to easily and effectively accommodate pruning, a strategy for limiting the search space in media normalization problems. Media objects are often very large, so even an improved asymptotic running time, as occurs in Algorithm 4.1, the simple application of Dijkstra's algorithm, is not effective in controlling problem size. This is the reason for the uniform path length design of Algorithm 4.2. The many approaches to performance enhancement presented in this chapter can be applied to control problem size and produce tractable solutions. The following chapters illustrate the application of this algorithm to different problems and give evidence of performance in real implementations.

The algorithms presented in this chapter have been implemented as components of the Xtrieve cross-modal information retrieval system. Two implementations of Algorithm 4.2 have been produced, one completely general and one optimized for synchronous application. These algorithms have been applied to several application areas. The implementations are completely media-type blind, in that the media type and the media element comparison strategy are abstract to the implementation. This is an interesting example of how general tools can be devised for multimedia applications.

Notes

1 This book adopts the convention used in Cormen et al. [26] that the symbols V and E in asymptotic notations will unambiguously imply the vertex and edge counts respectively in a graph.

Chapter 5

PARALLEL TEXT ALIGNMENT

An interesting problem in media synchronization is the alignment of *parallel texts*, multiple translations of the same document. Parallel texts are differing presentations of the same content. An alignment among parallel texts is a mapping of content in one text to content in another wherein the subjects of the mapping are translations of the same range in the original text. Discovery of the alignment between the texts allows comparative analysis of translation style and semantics as well as retrieval of content from multiple translations based on a search of an original document or an alternative translation. Two versions of this problem exist: aligning cross-language or aligning intra-language. *Cross-language alignment* is the alignment of two documents which are not in the same language, Spanish to English for example. *Intra-language alignment* is the alignment of two documents in the same language. This chapter specifically addresses the problem of computed intra-language alignment, though a discussion of cross-language alignment is included.

Most previous work in parallel text alignment has focused on cross-language applications. The new problem of intra-language alignment was discovered as part of the *Hear Homer* project at the DEVLAB [73]. One element of the Hear Homer project is the simultaneous presentation of multiple translations of Homeric poems (such as *The Odyssey* and *The Illiad*). Many Homeric poem translations exist and are routinely studied by scholars. Of particular interest is the question of how two or more translators chose to present the same original text. Indeed, presentation choice varies considerably. Some translators choose to translate the content line-by-line in a literal form. Others preserve the poetic structure, but feel no need to correspond verse-for-verse and often increase or decrease the number of lines considerably (George Chapman for example). Still others translate the poems as prose, resulting in a more free-form interpretation (Samuel Butler for example).

An obvious question is: why not just align the Homeric translations to the original Greek? There are several reasons why an English-to-English alignment is more desirable than synchronization to the original language. A quadratic number of language synchronization combinations exist, and little work has been done on ancient Greek, so synchronization to ancient Greek is not well understood at this time. And, of course, Greek base texts do not represent the only application for this technology. Synchronization of translations of works not based on Greek presents the same problem. An English-to-English solution can accommodate all of these requirements, obviating the need for a large collection of cross-language systems. Finally, an English-to-English alignment has no intermediate document, and therefore computes a single level synchronization function. If two translations are aligned to an original document, synchronization between the translations must be a composition of the alignment for one and the inverse alignment for the other, potentially compounding synchronization errors and granularity.

This chapter presents a solution for the intra-language parallel text synchronization problem. The solution is based on Algorithm 4.2 and the general model for multiple media correlation. An interesting characteristic of this work is that the solution is not restricted to pair-wise application; simultaneous N-way normalization of multiple documents is also possible. The utility of N-way alignment is an open question at this time and deserves further study.

Intra-language parallel text alignment has many additional applications aside from scholarly study. Automatic synchronization of parallel texts allows for cross-modal retrieval of content, the searching of one text for content in another. As an example, translators independently choose to translate or modify names. Samuel Butler does not use the name "Pallas" in his translation of Homer's *Odyssey*, though George Chapman uses this name routinely in place of "Minerva." A search for "Pallas" in the George Chapman translation can be converted to a Samuel Butler cross-modal result wherein the alternative name is used, but the individual intended is the same. Chapter 7 describes the Xtrieve cross-modal information retrieval system, a system supporting cross-modal queries and browsing. Other possible uses include the alignment of multiple textual narratives describing the same sequence of images, for example a picture tour of the Louvre museum. The relation of tours by a curator and an art historian is useful to a museum administrator who wishes to present alternative views in parallel in a multimedia tour system.

Given two or more documents representing the same underlying base content, the goal of multiple media correlation in this application is the computation of synchronization data among the documents. Application of Algorithm 4.2 to a specific problem requires the definition of a media element comparison method and translation of the media objects to media representation graphs. Section 2. describes the general problem formulation. Section 3. then describes the media element comparison method and Section 4. the MRG construction strategy. Section 5. discusses experimental evaluation of the approach. Section 6. discusses some additional issues and future research directions. Section 1. describes related work in the field of parallel text alignment.

1. RELATED WORK

Although the alignment of intra-language content is new, it is closely related to cross-language alignment. There has been considerable work in this area including work with domain knowledge (lexical information) and without [15, 24, 28, 79]. The system described in this chapter utilizes WordNet, a comprehensive linguistic knowledge base for scoring word similarity. Rigau and Agirre [108] use WordNet in conjunction with a cross-lingual dictionary to build a cross-language lexicon for information retrieval and alignment. Other researchers have focused on discovering this knowledge directly from the text data.

Fung and McKeown [43] utilize dynamic time warping (DTW), a causal alignment technique to align feature vectors of words in alternative translations based on the restrictive assumption that translated terms are approximately the same distance apart. Best matching word vectors indicate related terms. These terms are used to create anchor points between the documents which are traced on a 2D diagram with a shortest line to compute the alignment.

Kabir, in an earlier DEVLAB project, determined points of similarity among documents using many simultaneous tools including synonyms and problem specific knowledge hints such as equivalent names [64]. These points are used to construct a line aligning the texts.

A common focus of many of the parallel text approaches is the location of *features* that indicate specific alignment points. These features include character n-grams, matching words, or related sentences and paragraphs. The technique described in this chapter seeks to utilize all non-syntactic words in the documents as features rather than attempting to discover a limited set of important words.

Given varying granularities (characters, words, sentences, etc.) of feature vectors, computation of a best alignment path varies from the simple shortest line approach described above to image-based approaches advocated by Church [24]. The image-based approaches construct a *dot plot*, a square image of size $(n_1+n_2)^2$. Feature correspondences are plotted in this image and line detection is used to find a path. Church plots coincidental characters in an attempt to discover a lexicon with no examination of the actual words. Fung and Church [42] apply the same technique to matching word pairs with more general results, particularly when one of the languages is non-Roman. These approaches suffer from quadratic scaling problems in that they are based on image sizes that are $\Omega(n_1 n_2)$.

Detailed comparison of this work to cross-language alignment results is difficult. Cross-language alignment evaluation is typically performed on literal translations with known alignments, such as the official record of the European Parliament. Results are described at varying granularities. It is most common that the results are a presentation of the discovered lexicon, a graphical representation of alignment, or cross-language retrieval statistics on standard databases. Section 5.2 presents some example results from other systems for comparison.

2.   PROBLEM FORMULATION

Let μ_1 and μ_2 be two translations óf an original (and potentially unknown) document μ_0. These translations may be literal, implying close local relationships to the original document, or not. This chapter uses, as examples, two translations of *The Odyssey* by Homer. Many translations of *The Odyssey* exist. The translations that are described are by Samuel Butler [59] and George Chapman [60]. The Chapman translation is a literal line-by-line transformation of the ancient Greek. The Butler translation is a highly embellished prose translation. Table 5.1 is an example from Book 1 of *The Odyssey* illustrating the differences in the translation approaches[1]. The example selection was chosen from a computed alignment using the techniques described in this chapter.

Table 5.1 also illustrates many of the problems associated with this application. Though these passages are discussing the same topic, they differ considerably. Table 5.2 lists the number of words in each book for the two translations. The Chapman book translations are considerably larger than the Butler translations, with the exception of Book 9. Even names, an expected alignment point, have been found to change. Butler refers to "Minerva," Chapman to "Pallas" and "Minerva." These differences are common throughout the books. Indeed, it has been found that hand-alignment of these translations is quite difficult.

In spite of these differences, both translations are related to the same source material and do share many common words and names. Some of these terms have been underlined in Table 5.1. In addition, the similarity is increased when synonym relationships, such as that of "sire" and "father" are taken into account.

This document set is meant as an example only. The concepts and algorithms presented in this chapter are completely general and applicable to a large class of translation problems.

2.1   SOLUTION GRANULARITY

The problem solution is assumed to have some granularity. An exact word-for-word alignment between two documents is not possible due to the large

Table 5.1. Two translations of Homer's *Odyssey.*

Butler Translation:

Then Minerva said, "Father, son of Saturn, King of kings, it served Ægisthus right, and so it would any one else who does as he did; but Ægisthus is neither here nor there; it is for Ulysses that my heart bleeds, when I think of his sufferings in that lonely sea-girt island, far away, poor man, from all his friends. It is an island covered with forest, in the very middle of the sea, and a goddess lives there, daughter of the magician Atlas, who looks after the bottom of the ocean, and carries the great columns that keep heaven and earth asunder."

Chapman Translation:

Pallas, whose eyes did sparkle like the skies, answer'd: "O Sire! Supreme of Deities, Ægisthus past his fate, and had desert to warrant our infliction; and convert may all the pains such impious men inflict on innocent sufferers to revenge as strict, their own hearts eating. But, that Ithacus, thus never meriting, should suffer thus, I deeply suffer. His more pious mind divides him from these fortunes. Though unkind is piety to him, giving him a fate more suffering than the most unfortunate, so long kept friendless in a sea-girt soil, where the sea's navel is a sylvan isle, in which the Goddess dwells that doth derive Her birth from Atlas, who of all alive the motion and the fashion doth command with his wise mind, whose forces understand the inmost deeps and gulfs of all the seas, who (for his skill of things superior) stays the two steep columns that prop earth and heaven."

Table 5.2. Word counts for twelve books of two *Odyssey* translations.

Book	Butler	Chapman
1	4,279	6,370
2	4,364	5,871
3	4,880	6,335
4	8,276	10,630
5	4,858	6,462
6	3,597	4,986
7	3,511	4,596
8	5,780	7,597
9	5,985	5,287
10	5,879	6,806
11	6,210	7,992
12	4,765	6,155
Total	62,384	79,087

variation in translation approaches. Also, any variation in length seems to limit that possibility. Synchronization is desired for presentation, retrieval, and study of these documents. It is unlikely that any of these functions are necessary at the word level. More likely, an alignment that allows for good contrast of lines, sentences, paragraphs, or stanzas is more appropriate semantically.

The first step in the alignment process is the normalization of the causal ordering of the words in the documents. From this computed normalization the inter-media synchronization is readily derived. The best normalization is one that brings related words as close as possible to each other in the normalized coordinate system.

Chapter 7 describes how the Xtrieve cross-modal information retrieval system makes uses of retrieval granularity in relation to text-to-text alignment in order to present logical retrieval units.

2.2   MONOTONICITY AND ENDPOINT CONSTRAINTS

An important assumption is that a normalization should be monotonic, presenting the same content in the same basic order. This does not imply strict monotonicity in local word order, however. The Table 5.1 examples include the phrases "heaven and earth" and "earth and heaven" which are equivalent above the word level. Since granularity at the word level is not considered to be important, an alignment that places "heaven and earth" and "earth and heaven" next to each other is more than sufficient. The only known work in parallel-text alignment that does not assume monotonicity is the Smooth Injective Map Recognizer (SIMR) system by Melamed (1996) [78]. SIMR allows small local groups of size k, $6 \leq k \leq 9$, to be non-monotonic, primarily in support of local word order variations. The approach presented in this chapter could be modified to allow local non-monotonicity using a post-processing phase that determines the local window match terms.

It is assumed that both translations begin and end together, implying the endpoint constraint. The Chapman translation does have additional "arguments" (short poetic introductions) preceding the translation body that do not relate to the Butler translation. These are clearly indicated and are best simply omitted from the synchronization process.

3.   MEDIA ELEMENT COMPARISON

Application of Algorithm 4.2 requires definition of a media element comparison function ρ, a function that compares media elements corresponding to vertices in a media representation graph and computes a score for the match. Lower value scores indicate better matches than higher values. Perfect alignment of identical words should, ideally, score a match of zero.

The first question is what media elements to choose. Though the obvious choice seems to be words, this is not the only option. Church advocates aligning at the character level — essentially, discovering common n-grams between the texts [24]. Bonhomme and Romary are examples of the more common opposite extreme, the alignment of multi-word units, typically sentences or paragraphs [15]. Much of that work has focused on cross-language applications and testing on large, highly literal translation corpuses. Classics translations tend to have less sentence and paragraph correspondence due to the varied approaches to translation: prose, lyric, or verse. Also, discovery of sentence and paragraph structure is difficult in many applications due to loss of punctuation or uncertainty about sentence structure [124]. Examination of the texts required for the Hear Homer project indicates word-based alignment is most effective. Direct correspondence between sentences or between paragraphs/stanzas seems to be rare.

3.1   WINDOWED TEXT COMPARISON

Strict word alignment is very difficult to do. The simple example of word order reversal leads to an unsolvable problem if absolute word alignment monotonicity is assumed. What is prefered is a means of scoring this alignment well, even if the words do not strictly align. Figure 5.1 illustrates two segments of text. Forcing the word correspondences to align perfectly in this figure would be very difficult. In the left translation there are only two words between "sufferings" and "lonely", while in the right translation there are seven between the best related matches. The words in between do not match well or are syntactic terms (which are ignored due to application of a stop-list [111]).

An alternative view of Figure 5.1 would be to think of the edges as rubber bands, pulling the translations into a warping that minimizes the total tension. This is, indeed, the model that is used in this work. A word $\mu_1(s_1)$ in media object μ_1 is compared to a *window* surrounding the point s_2 in media object μ_2. A fixed range parameter w sets a window width $2w + 1$ such that words within the window are indexed by $s_w \in [s_2 - w, s_2 + w]$. Each word $\mu_2(s_w)$ is compared to $\mu_1(s_1)$ using a distance measure $d(\mu_1(s_1), \mu_2(s_w))$. This measure is referred to as the *word score* and is discussed in the next section. The word score is weighted using an energy function $e = \frac{(s_w - s_2)^2}{(w+1)^2} \xi_\emptyset$, where $\xi_\emptyset$ is the weight for a null match, the score for words which do not match at all. The minimum adjusted score is the score used for the entire window comparison. This example assumes two media objects under correlation. However, the problem is easily extended to N objects by simply adding all of the scores from each combination $\{1, i\}, i = 2, ..., N$. A complete formula for ρ is given in Equation 5.1.

when	a
I	fate
think	more
of	suffering
his	than
sufferings	the
in	most
that	unfortunate
lonely	so
sea-girt	long
island	kept
far	friendless
away	in
poor	a
man	sea-girt
from	soil
all	where
his	the
friends	sea's
It	naval
is	is
an	a
island	sylvan
covered	isle

Figure 5.1.   Word comparisons as a rubber band.

$$\rho(s_1, ..., s_N) = \sum_{i=2}^{N} \left(\min_{s_w = s_i - w, ..., s_i + w} d(\mu_1(s_1), \mu_i(s_w)) + \frac{(s_w - s_i)^2}{(w+1)^2} \xi_\emptyset \right)$$

(5.1)

The result of Equation 5.1 is referred to as the *window score*. Figure 5.2 is a plot of the word score equation assuming pair-wise comparison and a single matching term. The plot assumes the match term is moved back and forth in one document relative to the other by a distance plotted as the word distance. In this figure the window parameter is set to $w = 5$. The curve within the match range is parabolic, approaching the value of $\xi_\emptyset$ at the end of the window, where the worst case score is limited to $\xi_\emptyset$.

This approach is asymmetrical in that every word in μ_1 participates in the window score, while only selected choices in $\mu_i, i > 1$ participate. However, this is rarely an issue in practice. Figure 5.3(a) shows two text segments. The bar represents a rubber band. As the two text segments are moved relative to each other, the rubber band is stretched. The important observation is that if μ_1

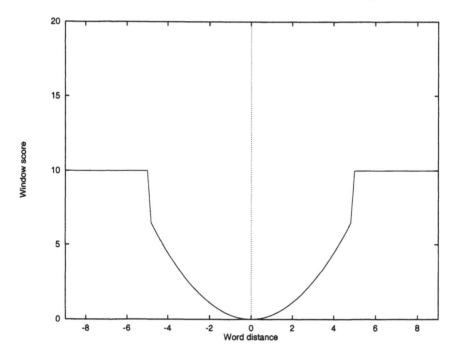

Figure 5.2.   Plot of window score for pair-wise alignment and a single matching term.

is assumed to be the left text, the rubber band attachment is "sea-girt" in the left text and in the right window as long as the distance between the words is within the window range. If μ_1 is assumed to be the right text segment instead, a rubber band with the same stretch characteristics will attach to "sea-girt" on the right and find "sea-girt" in the window on the left. "soil" would not participate in the score if μ_1 is the text on the left, because words in μ_1 all match to other words in μ_2. Effectively, the word could be omitted and the match remain the same. But if "soil" does participate in a score assuming the alternative application of the window, there would have to be a word in the window range on the left it matched against, which would have been found when the word was indexed by s_1 with μ_1 on the left, *assuming the word did not find a better alternative.*

Figure 5.3(b) shows a example where the two cases differ. If the window is applied to the right text segment, only one rubber band exists, attaching to only one of the matching elements. If the window is applied to the segment on the left, both occurrences of "sea-girt" result in connections (rubber bands), the effect being a bit stronger pull for this media segment (a lower score over the segment). This is rarely an issue, since it requires more than one occurrence of matching words in a small window range (typically five or less), a relatively

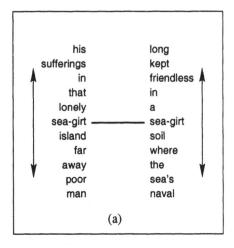
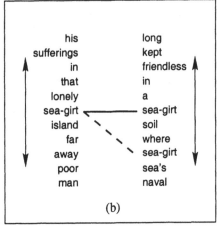

Figure 5.3.   Window match characteristics as alignment moves.

rare occurrence. Also, both cases *favor matching of these text segments*, the desired result.

3.2   WORDNET AND WORD COMPARISON

The window score mechanism described above assumes a mechanism for generating a word score for pair-wise word comparisons. The word scoring approach used in this chapter is based on the WordNet lexical database of the English language [11, 81]. WordNet is an on-line implementation of a *linguistic network*, a data structure indicating relationships between and information about words. WordNet supports many inter-word relationships including synonyms and antonyms.

The score for an exact match is denoted ξ_{exact}. The most obvious word score for ξ_{exact} is 0.

It has been found to be very common that translators vary considerably in word usage. For cross-language applications, this variation is taken care of by the existence or discovery of a cross-language translation dictionary, but for English-only applications another approach is required. The primary relationship of value in word comparison beyond simple equality is *synonymy*, similarity of meaning. Two words are considered to be related through synonymy if one of the words has the other as a member of its synonym list. Since WordNet is structured as a semantic net, all synonym relationships are reciprocated; if β is a synonym of α, then α is a synonym of β, i.e. the synonym relationship is a symmetrical relationship.

The word score for synonym relationships in this application, $\xi_{synonym}$, should not be 0, since an exact match should be favored over an approximate match. A synonym relationship is not a guarantee of identical usage. "Race" and "run" are synonyms, but "race" may be a noun usage implying an event in one document, and "run" a verb implying moving quickly in the other document. If a probabilistic view of the problem is taken, an exact match could be considered a probability 1 match. A detailed study of the use of synonyms in translation documents could assess a probability that a synonym is expressing the same concept. However, considerable variation exists in this distribution among many document categories and different translators, so an estimated probability of 0.5 is used in this application. Probabilistic scores must be converted to weights, so a weight of $\xi_{synonym} = -\ln(0.5) = 0.693$ is utilized as the score for a synonym match.

The WordNet database is divided into four *senses*: nouns, verbs, adjectives, and adverbs. An obvious question is if the match weight should be modified relative to the senses in which the synonym relationship exists. However, the pair-wise usage of the two synonymous terms may or may not represent the same sense and it does not matter in this application if additional senses for a word exist, since only one sense can apply to a word instance. Consequently, word sense is ignored. A more complex approach might attempt to determine sense using natural language processing (NLP). However, it is doubtful if that is a useful contribution, because translations routinely choose different sense usage for the same term. As an example, "I think of his <u>sufferings</u>..." and "a fate more <u>suffering</u> than..." from Table 5.1. The first usage is as a noun, the second an adjective.

A *morphological relationship* between two words is a relationship through modification of a base word. The most common example is the addition of "s" to the end of a word to form a plural. WordNet supports morphological relations as part of the database front-end processing, rather than as a component of the database itself. The morphological analysis tool is applied to all terms during the search process to determine if the term is in the database as a base term. The same tool is applied in the problem solution described here to discover morphological relationships between comparison terms. The score for a morphological relationship, ξ_{morph}, was selected as 0.693, the same as for a synonym relationship. While it may appear that a morphological relationship is a stronger relationship than synonymy, this is not necessarily the case in practice. Clearly, plural and singular usages do not mean the same thing in all cases, and some words have multiple alternative bases. The bases for "axes" are "ax" and "axis", for example. Also, the WordNet morphological rules are limited in that they are context-free and do not have knowledge of special terms, proper names, etc.

The score for a bad match, $\xi_{\emptyset}$, should be a larger positive value. A probabilistic approach to the problem would imply that two words that do not match at all have a probability of 0 of alignment. However, this is not at all the case.

The probability that two words align should be non-zero, because words that do not have relatives in the alternative document must still exist in-line. They will align to other, non-matching words because they have been chosen by the translator as part of a concept. Hence, ξ_0 should be larger than ξ_{exact} and $\xi_{synonym}$, but not ∞. The score chosen in this work has been $\xi_0 = 10$. This score was selected as a compromise between maintaining a large margin over the scores ξ_{exact}, $\xi_{synonym}$, and ξ_{morph} and maintaining reasonable total path scores. As long as this score is considerably larger than ξ_{exact}, $\xi_{synonym}$, and ξ_{morph}, the value of ξ_0 becomes inconsequential, since any larger value simply scales all path totals identically.

3.3   STOP-LIST APPLICATION

Syntactic words such as "and", "the", and "do" are not present in the Word-Net database. Syntactic terms convey little information, are not semantically meaningful, and are effectively *noise* in the alignment process. However, the non-existence of a word in the database does not always indicate insignificance; proper names are highly significant, but also not present. The solution to this problem is the application of a "stop-list", a list of 571 common English syntactic words which are ignored in the matching process. The stop-list used in this application is based on the Smart system stop-list [111].

4.   MEDIA REPRESENTATION GRAPH

A textual document is a sequential list of words. However, what does it mean to align two or more text documents? Clearly, the alignment cannot be simply word-to-word since the document lengths may vary. Some mechanism is required that allows for causal warping of the documents relative to each other.

The rate of progression through a text document relative to a causal normalization coordinate system can be varied in two ways: repeating words or skipping words. Word repetition assumes that $\tau_i(s_1) = \tau_i(s_j), \forall 1 < j \leq r$ for some range $s_j \in [s_1, s_1 + r]$, so that the causal normalization function maps a sequential range of causal normalization variables to the same word. Skipping words assumes that some words do not exist in the domain of τ_i. Skipping words is not considered an effective approach, because skipped words do not participate in alignment at all. A skipped-words approach was implemented as an earlier result, but is not presented here. The approach presented in this section models causal normalization entirely through the repetition of words.

Figure 5.4 illustrates a simple causal MRG with words associated with the vertices. Loop-back edges model the repetition of words. Stop-list terms are omitted from the MRG completely and do not participate in the normalization process. Since conversion of a document to an MRG with application of a

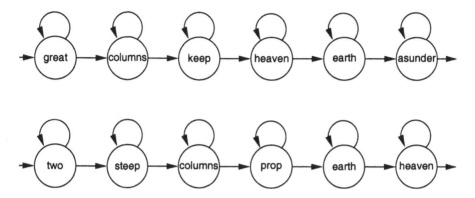

Figure 5.4.   Document media representation graph.

stop-list is a transformation operation, not an equivalence operation, an index for each word is also associated with the vertex. This index allows for the conversion of the computed normalization to word document synchronization information. Additional document content not directly related to the body of the text, such as titles, credit information, and front matter, are omitted.

A supergraph in the presence of these two example causal document MRGs is illustrated in Figure 5.5. Loop-back edges have been omitted from this supergraph even though they are implied by the existence of loop-back edges in all constituent MRGs. As discussed in Chapter 4, loop-back edges in the supergraph are never elements of an optimal solution because optimal solutions are simple paths. Repeating a supergraph vertex simply extends the match length and a shorter path with a weight less than or equal to that of a path including supergraph vertex repetition will always be selected.

One path has been highlighted in Figure 5.5. This is the best path through this supergraph section.

The number of vertices and edges in the supergraph is $O(\prod_{i=1}^{N} c_i)$, where c_i is the number of non-stop-list words in document μ_i. Clearly, it is not practical to construct the supergraph. *The Odyssey* Book 1 synchronization problem would require a $3,265,763$ vertex supergraph and the alignment of the Bible book of *Genesis*, described in Section 5., would require a supergraph with $178,371,808$ vertices. A practical solution to this problem requires application of Algorithm 4.2, which does not build the supergraph, and a pruning strategy as described in Section 5.3. The pruning parameter used in this application has been 1000. Section 5. discusses how the effectiveness of the pruning parameter is assessed. Should an insufficient pruning parameter be selected, the best path could be pruned during algorithm execution. In such a case, a sub-optimal solution is selected.

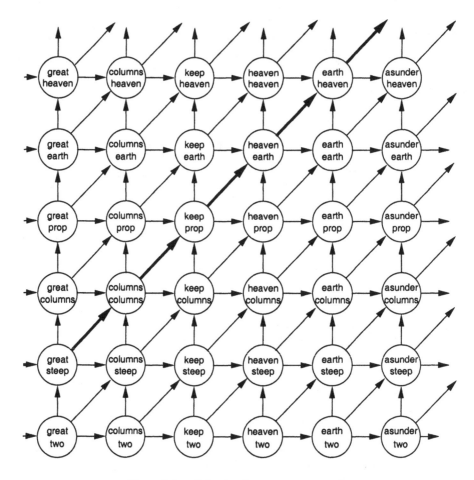

Figure 5.5.   Pair-wise documents supergraph.

5.   EVALUATION

This section describes techniques and criteria for the evaluation of parallel intra-language text alignment. The system described in this chapter has been implemented and all of the evaluation tests described in this section are based on this implementation. The implementation parameterization consists of a word window size of $w = 5$, and match scores of $\xi_\emptyset = 10$, $\xi_{exact} = 0$, $\xi_{synonym} = 0.693$, and $\xi_{morph} = 0.693$. The window width parameter was determined experimentally by evaluating a range of window widths and selecting the most effective width within that range. The pruning parameter was set to 1000.

Evaluation of parallel text alignment is complicated by the lack of ground-truth data. Any known correct alignment is based on either literal translation or hand-marking. This work is the first known attempt to establish test criteria and test data for intra-language text alignment. Two evaluation strategies are applied to the determination of match accuracy: comparison with reference alignments and subjective evaluation of alignment quality. An additional evaluation criterion is retrieval efficacy, the ability to search one translation and find the appropriate result in another, but no known reference corpus exists to support such an evaluation.

5.1   SUBJECTIVE EVALUATION AND AN EXAMPLE

Subjective evaluation is the simple examination of the program results by a human evaluator. The authors and several other users have viewed the Homeric alignments and feel they are accurate at a granularity of at least twenty words. A complete sample alignment of Book 1 of *The Odyssey* is included in Appendix B.

5.2   COMPARISON TO REFERENCE DATA

A more quantitative evaluation is achieved by comparing the computed results to some assume correct alignment. An example dataset with multiple translations and known points of alignment is the Bible. Many different translations of the Bible have been produced, and the verse and chapter structure enforces a fixed alignment among the different translations. This structure is used as a reference for evaluation.

The system was evaluated using several books of the Bible. Each word pair (w_1, w_2), representing the computed alignment between two non-stop-list words in the synchronization result, was converted to a relative verse number (v_1, v_2). A relative verse number is simply a sequential numbering of all verses in a document instance. The verse number corresponding to a word instance is determined by the relative verse in which the word is located. A verse distance error $\epsilon = v_2 - v_1$ is computed. This error indicates a distance between the ideal placement of the word and the computed placement in verse units. As mentioned before, word-for-word synchronization means very little. Verse sizes are a relatively small unit and highly indicative of content structure.

All testing was performed on three standard Bible translations, the *King James Version* (KJV), the *New International Version* (NIV), and the *Revised Standard Version* (RSV). The King James Version was created from contemporary texts and some known original texts in the 1600's. The language is distinctly the King's English. The stop-list was *not* modified to account for this, and words such as "thee", "thou", and "yea" were passed on to the system. The decision not to adapt the system to the additional English text was made deliberately to stress the system. It should also be noted that many archaic terms in the KJV translation are not in the WordNet lexical database, such as the word "appeareth".

The Revised Standard Version was translated in the 1940's and was based on both known texts and revision of the King James Version. The New International Version was translated by a large group of scholars in the 1960's and 1970's and was based entirely on original language texts with no reference to existing translations.

The effectiveness of the Bible as an alignment test might be questioned due to the literal nature of the translations. There is considerable commonality among all of these translations, but there are also considerable differences. As an example, Genesis 42:26 is translated as "And they laded their asses with the corn, and departed thence" (KJV), "They loaded their grain on their donkeys and left" (NIV), and "Then they loaded their asses with their grain, and departed" (RSV). All three translations vary in content within a verse. In some cases, verses are omitted from the later translations due to better knowledge of original texts or new content is included due to the availability of new original texts.

Table 5.3 presents results for several book/translation combinations. Each combination listed includes percentages for error ranges of -2 to $+2$ verses. The word counts listed in the table column "Aligned Words" are after application of the stop-list. The "Max Rank" column is discussed in the next section. An additional column, the "RMS Error" column lists the square root of the average squared character error distance (root-mean-squared or RMS error), where a character error distance is defined as the distance in characters from the first letter of the word to the correct verse. This error measure has been included primarily for comparison with related work, where RMS error measures are common. Note, however, that the RMS error is increased in this result due to the word-based alignment. An error distance is always a multiple of the length of words (plus any inter-word spacing). This result has been adjusted to omit the SGML markup between verses, since that quantity would be an additive amount and is not related to the alignment process.

As can be seen, the synchronization result matched the known correct result very closely. The most common error is a one verse error. The balanced error distribution (similar positive and negative verse error measures) is a result of the symmetrical nature of the algorithm. One verse errors are typified by "hang-over", the overlap of one verse alignment with another. The small RMS error values are an indication that this "hang-over" is usually small, often only one or two words. An example is the alignment of the beginning of Matthew 2:13 (KJV): "And when they departed, behold, the angel of the Lord appeareth...". In the NIV translation, this example overlaps the last word of Matthew 2:12 (NIV): "...by another route. (13) When they had gone, an angel...". It is interesting to observe that "route" would be expected to match "way", the last word of Matthew 2:12 (KJV) except that, "way" is a stop-list term. Often the overlap occurrences are due to a final word in a verse matching not only the

Table 5.3.   Evaluation results for Bible books.

Bible Book	Versions	Aligned Words	Verse Error					RMS Error	Max Rank
			-2	-1	0	+1	+2		
Genesis	KJV,NIV	14,142 12,604	0.01%	3.3%	93.6%	3.1%	0%	5.7	277
Genesis	KJV,RSV	14,142 12,728	0%	1.8%	97.1%	1.1%	0%	3.2	142
Matthew	KJV,NIV	8,226 7,294	0.02%	3.8%	92.7%	3.4%	0.03%	5.6	159
Matthew	NIV,KJV	7,294 8,226	0.01%	3.4%	93.2%	3.4%	0.02%	7.7	129
Matthew	KJV,RSV	8,226 7,004	0%	3.3%	94.5%	2.2%	0%	5.0	134
Ruth	KJV,NIV	911 811	0%	5.2%	92.7%	2.1%	0%	6.6	140

corresponding word in the alternative verse, but also the first one or more words of the next verse. This behavior is due to the loop-back edges in the MRG which allow words to repeat if necessary to slow the presentation relative to the alternative translation.

As mentioned earlier, it is difficult to compare the results for intra-language alignment directly with those for cross-language alignment. However, it is useful to examine how those approaches are evaluated and relate them to the results presented in this work.

The Melamed (1996) Smooth Injective Map Recognizer (SMIR) system was tested on Canadian government data that has been hand-aligned by a panel of 8 judges (the Hansard corpus) [78]. The translations are very literal. Errors are quoted in paragraphs, a somewhat less restrictive alignment criteria than the verse measure presented in this chapter. The quoted errors for two databases are 1.3% and 1.8%, assuming knowledge of bitext correspondences (lexical domain knowledge). Considering that a paragraph granularity is considerably larger than a verse granularity, the results in Table 5.3 are quite comparable.

Melamed (1997) quotes character RMS error distances [79]. It is curious that error reporting in characters has become popular, since it is not indicative of alignment at any meaningful granularity. The quoted RMS errors range from 5.7 characters for literal French/English translations of parliamentary debates to 20.6 for literal translations of technical reports. Church aligns at the character level and quotes an RMS error of 57 characters, based on the Hansard corpus [24]. The results in Table 5.3 are clearly comparable to these results.

5.3   GRAPHICAL RESULTS

Graphical illustrations of alignment functions and alignment examples are common means of presenting parallel text alignment results. Fung and Church present graphical results, example alignments, and example discovered word correspondences [42]. Fung and McKeown present graphical results and example discovered word correspondences [43]. A frequently used graphical illustration is the simple X-Y correspondence plot. Words or other units of alignment in one text are plotted relative to the similar unit in the other text. Figure 5.6 illustrates the computed alignment between the KJV and NIV books of Genesis. The plot presents the alignment of the non-stop-list terms in the books. Some variation from the diagonal can be seen in the image; this variation is enhanced in Figure 5.7, which plots the vertical difference from an exact diagonal in Figure 5.6. This difference represents the difference between the computed alignment and a simple linear interpolation between the two documents. Appendix B presents an X-Y correspondence plot for one book of Homer's *Odyssey*.

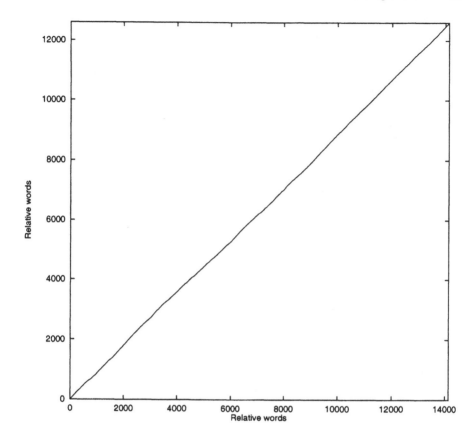

Figure 5.6.   X-Y correspondence plot of Genesis KJV/NIV alignment.

5.4   PRUNING STRATEGY EVALUATION

The efficient performance of this algorithm is dependent upon use of a pruning,strategy. In the evaluation, the pruning width was set to a fixed value of 1000. This parameterization limits the search space for the Genesis KJV/NIV alignment to no more than $15,359,000$ supervertices, or about 8.4% of the available space. Is it effective to so severely limit the search space?

The implementation was instrumented to record the weight rank for every vertex in the search tree for each tree depth s. During the back-tracking phase the maximum (worst case) rank is recorded and is presented in Table 5.3. Since this rank is typically less than a fourth of the pruning parameter value, it is unlikely that a better path was pruned. A worst case path of 277 indicates that the pruning parameter could be set to any greater value and the path would not be pruned. Figure 5.8 is a plot of the rank for the Genesis KJV/NIV best computed normalization path. This plot is indicative that the rank does not exhibit asymptotic growth over time.

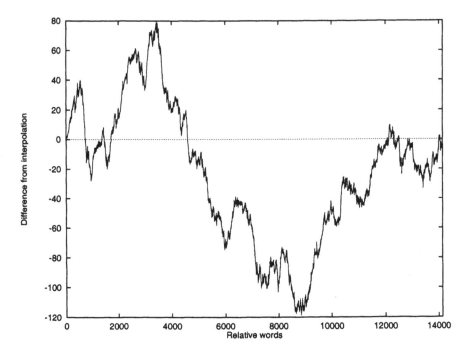

Figure 5.7.   Variation from linear interpolation in Genesis KJV to NIV alignment.

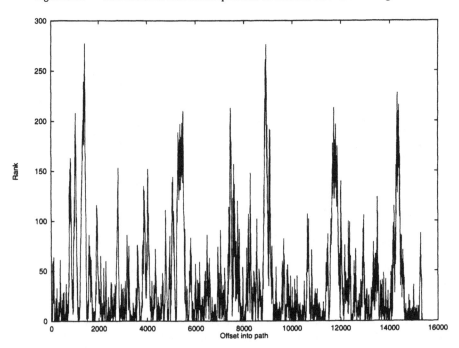

Figure 5.8.   Best path rank plot for Genesis KJV to NIV alignment.

5.5   EXECUTION PERFORMANCE

The algorithm execution time is dependent upon the pruning parameter value and the size of the texts. The implementation discussed in this chapter is highly instrumented and not optimized. Even so, this implementation is able to process approximately 5 synchronization tree levels per second of CPU time on an Alpha processor-based Digital Equipment Corporation DEC 500/333. This is equivalent to $50,000$ media element comparisons per second, which places alignment times for the larger documents in the half hour range. Shorter documents are a bit faster due to the logarithmic factor in the asymptotic running time. (The log factor in the implementation is due to the determination of a supervertex visit using red-black trees [26]). Since alignment computation is a one-time process for a set of texts, longer computation times are not considered a serious factor.

Two implementations of Algorithm 4.2 exist. A completely general implementation is utilized in this application. The text-to-speech application presented Chapter 6 utilizes an implementation that has been optimized to take advantage of the synchronous nature of that application. Several system engineering level modifications to that implementation led to performance improvements in excess of 100 to 1. It is strongly believed that similar performance improvements could be gained in the general implementation.

Memory usage is based on the same parameters. The size of the synchronization tree is bounded by the pruning parameter. In practice, the tree is even smaller due to decreasing tree width for depths less than s at any point in the algorithm execution. Using the entirely general directed graph and tree class libraries supplied by the IMAGECL multimedia development environment, the largest problem required about $100MB$ of memory during execution [90]. Most of the memory was used in the recording of execution statistics and specific optimizations are expected to decrease this usage considerably.

6.   ISSUES AND EXTENSIONS

Experimentation with parallel texts and the application of multiple media correlation has resulted in a solution for a general class of problems in intra-language alignment. In the process several interesting issues have arisen with great potential for future work. Post-processing alignment data in search of a locally non-monotonic alignment is one such issue. The section also discusses N-way alignment and extension of this work to cross-language alignment.

6.1   N-WAY ALIGNMENT

The experimental results described in this chapter assume pair-wise alignment of parallel texts. However, since Algorithm 4.2 is a general N-way solution, the extension of the results in this chapter to 3-way or more alignment is trivial. N-way text alignment advantages need to be researched further and constitute an element for future work. It is expected that an N-way alignment will favor terms co-located in all texts, effectively giving them a stronger pull in the alignment process.

It is also expected that the pruning parameter will have to be increased for N-way applications. The performance will be affected by the $2^N - 1$ out-degree of the supergraph vertices. It is doubtful that problem instances beyond 3-way can be solved efficiently.

6.2   CROSS-LANGUAGE PARALLEL TEXT ALIGNMENT

The focus of this work has been entirely on intra-language alignment. This focus was driven by large digital library projects in the Classics, such as the Hear Homer project, and a perception that intra-language alignment had been overlooked by the parallel text research community. However, the general techniques described here are entirely applicable to cross-language application. A cross-lingual WordNet database can be built using techniques described by Rigau and Agirre [108]. An interesting future project currently being considered is the alignment to ancient Greek, another useful element for the Hear Homer project.

7.   SUMMARY

The alignment of parallel texts provides an interesting example of the application of a general media alignment technology to a specific problem instance. The use of the multiple media correlation framework and an energy minimization model makes this approach to parallel text alignment unique. The use of windowed word comparisons is also a new approach to the problem of local non-monotonicity in translations.

This problem is indicative of the general implementation approach for multiple media correlation. A media element is first chosen, in this case significant words. Next, a method for building a media representation graph for a problem instance is devised. The MRG in this application is the standard causal MRG with vertices having associated words and word indexes. Finally, a media element comparison strategy is determined. In this example that strategy is based on windowed word comparison. In implementation each of these elements is either an application of a standard [MAGE]CL component or a new [MAGE]CL object. Given the standard [MAGE]CL media correlation tools, the application required only a new module for the media element comparisons.

An interesting characteristic of this work is the emphasis on intra-language alignment. Intra-language alignment solutions are particularly useful to experts in classic literature who are interested in studying how different translators interpreted the same original text. The automatic synchronization of parallel texts also provides a new mechanism for indexing and cross-modal retrieval.

Notes

1 The George Chapman translation is in verse form. It is presented here without the line breaks specified by Chapman in order to permit columnar presentation of the material.

Chapter 6

TEXT-TO-SPEECH ALIGNMENT

Text-to-speech alignment is the alignment of a textual transcript to an audio stream. The computed synchronization data is a mapping from words in the text transcript to temporal intervals in the audio. This alignment provides a basic tool that facilitates many applications and has wide-spread general applicability.

A major application for text-to-speech alignment is database indexing. Speech-based media, is content such as video or audio primarily consisting of speech. Speech-based media is one of the largest classes of media data. As large multimedia databases develop, technologies for searching those databases become critically important. If both a textual transcript and synchronization data relating the transcript to intervals in the audio exist, the speech audio can be searched indirectly by searching the text and presenting an equivalent audio result. This technique allows for accurate and fine-grained searching of speech-based media.

The obvious questions are: when do transcripts exist, and why do they not already have associated alignment? Why must the alignment be computed? In researching this problem it was discovered that large classes of data exist where unaligned transcripts and speech-based audio both exist. Examples include legal depositions, court testimony, broadcasting, talking books, and dramatic presentations. This class of data has been termed *script-light content* and is described in more detail in Section 1.1 [97].

Searching content in one media type or modality and presenting results in an alternative media type or modality is called *cross-modal information retrieval* [98]. Chapter 7 describes cross-modal information retrieval in more detail and illustrates the application of text-to-speech computed synchronization in the Xtrieve cross-modal information retrieval system.

Another major application for text-to-speech alignment is *captioning*, the addition of captions to video or film. *Closed-captioning* is the inclusion of text with the video signal, which requires special decoding for presentation on the screen. *Open-captioning* is the direct presentation of the caption text on the screen. Closed-captioning is common in broadcast television in support of the hearing disabled. Open-captioning is used in learning materials and for alternative language film captioning. Section 7.2 describes the use of text-to-speech alignment in caption applications in more detail.

Text-to-speech synchronization is the alignment of two media streams: μ_1, the text stream, is aligned to μ_2, the audio. This alignment is easily invertible to provide speech-to-transcription retrieval or captioning location information if necessary (i.e., given a location in the audio, find the equivalent location in the transcription). The system presented in this chapter uses Algorithm 4.2 to compute an alignment to a normalization coordinate system s that coincides with the indices for media elements in the audio. Section 1. describes related work in the fields of text-to-speech alignment, speech recognition, automatic text transcription, and searching speech-based content. Application of Algorithm 4.2 requires the definition of a media element comparison technique and of a technique for constructing the media representation graphs, as discussed in Chapter 4. Section 2. describes the general problem formulation. Section 3. describes the MRG construction strategy and Section 4. the media element comparison method. This application utilizes many of the Algorithm 4.2 enhancements described in Chapter 4. Section 5. describes the application of the algorithm and the enhancements. Section 6. discusses experimental evaluation of this approach to text-to-speech alignment. Section 7. discusses some additional issues and future research directions.

1.   RELATED WORK

Most previous work on text-to-speech alignment has been concerned with automatic corpora labeling, the accurate location of sound elements such as phones in speech audio [3, 125, 130]. The process is applied to very short audio segments and is used to generate standard training and testing data. These systems are designed for precise alignment of very short segments of audio, not for entire texts. They are not designed to effectively recover from alignment failures or to scale to hours of content.

The importance of alignment of text to speech audio has been recognized in the Informedia [53] and News-on-demand [52, 80] projects at CMU. The Informedia project seeks to index speech-based audio using automatic transcription. Whenever possible, they have taken advantage of the availability of transcript data. However, their approach to synchronization is to perform automatic transcription on the audio without knowledge of the transcription and then align the text transcripts based on word matching, hoping for some minimal recognition performance. The News-on-demand project utilizes close-captioned digital video, but has observed that the caption content can lead or lag the video by up to 20 seconds.

Most approaches to searching speech content assume no available transcription data. Of particular interest is work at Cambridge University [16] and the Swiss Federal Institute of Technology [113]. A good introduction to speech recognition technologies can be found in [102]. Cole, et al. describe recent developments in the field [25].

2.   PROBLEM FORMULATION

Speech-based audio can be viewed as the sequential presentation of units of sound that, taken as a whole, represent words. These units of sound represent the possible sounds than can be produced by the human vocal system. Alone, they convey very little information; it is only when they are combined into aggregates that they gain meaning. The specific solution to the problem of text-to-speech alignment presented in this chapter attempts to classify these small units of sound and discover a causal warping of the transcription that creates a contextual best fit to the audio.

Linguistic research has determined that speech can be modeled using a small set of units of pronunciation. The most common sub-word speech unit is the *phoneme*. There are several standard phoneme sets including the International Phonetic Alphabet (IPA), WorldBet, and OGIbet. These phoneme sets differ in coverage of sounds, but mostly overlap. This work uses the WorldBet phonemic labeling set as a standard. The elements of WorldBet utilized in this work are included as Appendix A. As an example, the word "the" can be considered to be the WorldBet phonemes "D ^", where "D" is the "th" sound, as in "<u>th</u>y" and "^" is the "ah" sound as in "ab<u>o</u>ve." Many words have alternate pronunciations. "The" can also be pronounced using the phonemes "D i:", where "i:" is the "ee" sound as in "b<u>ee</u>t." It is common in the literature to use the term *phone* either interchangeably with phoneme or as a representation of an actual sound rather than a class of sounds.

A problem with phonemic representations is the co-articulatory effect of speech. Speech is not well modeled as only a series of phonemes. While phonemes attempt to model physical states of the vocal system, in real speech these states are only reached momentarily and the transition between the states is very important. There are many approaches to accommodating these co-articulatory effects. Glass, et al. treat speech as a dynamic process using time warping of speech patterns, which include the phonetic representations [49]. However, the most common approach is to consider phonemes in context, typically either a biphone or triphone context. A *triphone context* considers each phoneme in the context of the phonemes preceding and following it. This is the approach used in the CMU Sphinx-II speech recognition system [104]. A *biphone content* models transitions into and out of context-free phoneme states.

Basically, the period of a phoneme is modeled as a beginning (left context), middle (context independent), and end (right context). The beginning period is when the phone is transitioning from the previous sound to the new sound, and when the new phone is dominant. The middle period models the part of the phone that is stable. The end period models the transition out of the phoneme and to the next phoneme. Biphones are used in the Oregon Graduate Institute speech tools [112].

The biphone has been selected as the contextual sound unit in this work because effective tools are available, and because it represents a good compromise between effective context modeling and search space size. Strict phoneme-based systems compromise context modeling in favor of a minimized search space. Triphone systems have very large sound modeling spaces. While the transcript-based system described in this chapter is more tolerant of large search spaces than conventional automatic transcription systems, a very large space does impact execution time. A possible direction for future work is to classify the relative merits of using phones, biphones, or triphones as the sound unit in this application.

Biphones in this chapter are notated as a<b for a *left context of b transitioning from a*, b>c for a *right context of b transitioning to c*, and <b> for the *context independent period of b*.

Text-to-speech alignment utilizes 53 of the WorldBet phonetic labels. Modeling all biphone combinations would require $53 \times 52 + 53 \times 52 + 53 = 5565$ possible sound states, a large and potentially unreasonable number. Fortunately, many transition states are not necessary because they are either too short or are indistinguishable. Hence, a subset is used. As an example all transitions from or to any of "9r 3r &r", the *retroflexes* and a *glide*, are considered identical and are represented by a single biphone; i.e., 9r<f, 3r<f, and &r<f are all considered to be the same sound. In the implementation described in this chapter, a subset of 536 biphone elements is used.

Each word is translated into phonemes, which are, in turn, translated into biphones. The biphone translation represents a sequence of sound states that can be used to present the word. As an example, the word "note" translates to the phoneme sequence "n oU th", then to biphones "<n> n>oU n<oU <oU> oU>th oU<th <th>", omitting any (unknown) entering and leaving context. Speech sound units are expected to reproduce this biphone string.

A major characteristic of sound modeling that is omitted in this example is *duration*. Duration is modeled in one of two ways. Dynamic time warping adjusts the sound model duration to match that of the utterance [49]. An alternative approach, and the one utilized in this work, is to model duration by simply repeating biphone units relative to fixed duration sound frames. Sound is segmented into fixed (10 millisecond) time frames and biphone elements are repeated to model duration in 10 millisecond steps.

Speech recognition systems are not capable of absolutely recognizing a sound frame as a particular biphone in isolation. Were systems capable of doing this, the problems of speech recognition and automatic transcription would be trivial. Real systems must deal with considerable uncertainty: audio is corrupted by noise, many biphone elements have similar sounds, and human speech is not at all perfect. Coughs, pauses, alliterations, etc. are all common distortions in speech audio. Hence, what speech system feature recognition components attempt to do is to *classify* sounds by computing an estimate of the probability of observance of each biphone element. In this application the probability estimates consist of a vector of 536 real-valued estimates for each audio frame. The probability estimates are denoted $\hat{p}(y_i)$. This sequence of vectors represents an observable stochastic process.

Biphone models of words (or larger units of speech) impose a state structure onto this sequence of vectors. A sequence of biphone states, $< s_1, ..., s_N >$ is *valid* if it is a representation of some presentation of the word (implying sequential presentation of the biphone elements of the word with repetition for duration modeling). The value computed by the classifier is the estimated probability $\hat{p}(y_t = b)$ of observing biphone b at time t. This value is independent of state because the state has no influence on the classifier (an independence assumption). The probability that state s_i is a state containing biphone b is denoted $p(s_t = b)$. The value of this probability can be 1 or 0 only. Finally, the probability of being in state s_t is $p(s_t)$. Due to the independence assumption, $\hat{p}(y_t|s_t) = \hat{p}(y_t = b \cap s_t = b)p(s_t) = \hat{p}(y_t = b)p(s_t = b)p(s_t)$, which means [36]:

$$\hat{p}(y|s) = \prod_{t=1}^{N} \hat{p}(y_t|s_t) \qquad (6.1)$$

Equation 6.1 provides a tool for assessing the "goodness" of a state sequence. Better state sequences are indicated by a greater probability that the state sequence predicts the observation sequence. In an isolated word recognition system, the goal is to choose a word and a state sequence through the word that maximizes Equation 6.1. Techniques for doing so are commonly called *maximum likelihood* or *maximum a priori* techniques.

The assumption of independence is commonly made in the literature, though it is not strictly true. In actuality, the biphone classifier does have some contextual input, such that each observation is dependent upon the most recent one or more observations. However, the dependence is minimal and only complicates the problem, so it is routinely ignored. This chapter also assumes independence.

Often, the probabilities of a particular state sequence are based on a first order Markov process. The fundamental property that must be obeyed for a process to be first order Markovian is:

$$p(s_t|s_t - 1, ..., s_1) = p(s_t|s_t - 1) \qquad (6.2)$$

This property is the "past forgetting" property of a Markov process. Assuming the state sequences are modeled using a Markov process, Equation 6.1 is equivalent to:

$$\hat{p}(y|s) = \prod_{t=1}^{N} \hat{p}(y_t = b)p(s_t = b)p(s_t|s_{t-1}) \qquad (6.3)$$

In practice, the result of Equation 6.3 is subject to numeric underflow problems due to the large product size (100 per second of audio). By converting the problem to a summation, the numerical underflow problem is avoided:

$$\ln \hat{p}(y|s) = \sum_{t=1}^{N} (\ln (\hat{p}(y_t = b)p(s_t = b)) + \ln p(s_t|s_{t-1})) \qquad (6.4)$$

A sign change converts the problem to a minimization problem rather than a maximization problem and converts all values to non-negative values:

$$- \ln \hat{p}(y|s) = \sum_{t=1}^{N} - (\ln (\hat{p}(y_t = b)p(s_t = b)) - \ln p(s_t|s_{t-1})) \qquad (6.5)$$

This is now a problem that fits well into the context of the multiple media correlation model. One media representation graph is created to model the possible sound transitions of the transcript, and another to model the sequences of probability estimates.

3.   MEDIA REPRESENTATION GRAPHS

This application of Algorithm 4.2 requires two media representation graphs. μ_1 models all of the possible sound transitions, creating a context model for the entire text. μ_2 models the synchronous computation of probability estimate vectors. This section describes the construction of these two MRGs.

3.1   THE TRANSCRIPTION MRG

μ_1, the transcription MRG, represents possible transitions of sound. μ_1 is built in a four-step process. The words are converted to a *words MRG*, a sequential presentation of the words. In the second step the words are expanded to phonemic translations, adding additional paths where necessary

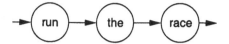

Figure 6.1. Words MRG for "...run the race...".

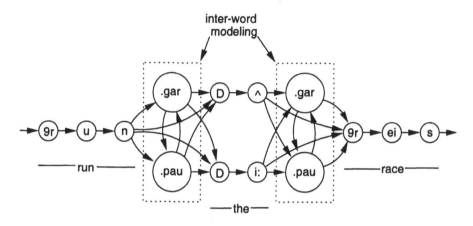

Figure 6.2. Phonemic MRG for "...run the race...".

to model alternative pronunciations, creating a *phonemic MRG*. This step also adds modeling for inter-word events such as pauses and noise. The third step adds any specialty modeling, such as insertion and deletion support edges. In the fourth step, the phonemic MRG is expanded to a *biphonemic MRG*. A biphonemic MRG adds modeling of context.

Assume the text "...run the race..." as a fragment of a transcription. Figure 6.1 illustrates the words MRG fragment for this text. This is a simple conversion of the sequential word presentation to a sequential vertex representation. Associated with each vertex is an index value indicating the word's position in the original document in order to simplify the synchronization inversion process.

Figure 6.2 illustrates the expansion from a words MRG to a phonemic MRG. The translation of words to phonemes is done using a lookup dictionary containing about 100,000 words. This dictionary is based on a standard dictionary made available by CMU that has been translated to WorldBet and expanded in DEVLAB use. Words and proper names not found in the dictionary are translated using standard pronunciation rules developed by the U. S. Naval Research Laboratory [86]. Multiple pronunciations in the MRG are represented using parallel paths. Duration modeling in the phonemic MRG is implemented using loop-back edges, which are omitted in the figures for clarity.

It is impossible to accurately predict when speakers will pause between words or when additional noises may intervene between words. For this reason, the phonemic MRG must model all possible combinations and rely on the media

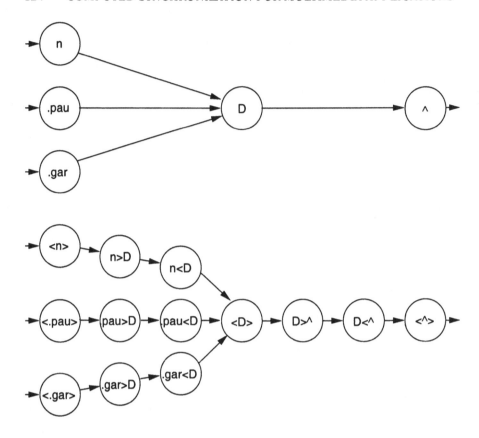

Figure 6.3.   Biphonemic MRG segment for "...run the race...".

correlation process to discover from the audio what combination has actually occured. As is seen in Figure 6.2, two extra vertices are inserted between every word pair. The vertices are labeled ".pau" and ".garbage" (abbreviated to ".gar" in figures to conserve space). ".pau" models silence events, ".garbage" non-speech sounds. Every possible combination of bypassing inter-word modeling, pausing, alternating pause and garbage, etc. is supported by this mechanism.

The inter-word modeling vertices in Figure 6.2 also provide the anchor points for insertion and deletion modeling edges, as described in Section 6.. In the system implementation, deletion and insertion bypass edges are incident on the ".pau" and ".garbage" vertices. The cross-combination (".pau" bypass to ".garbage" and vice versa) is not supported in order to decrease the edge loading and because error tolerance easily accommodates an extra inter-word modeling vertex in-line.

The final step in the transcription MRG building process is to expand phonemes to biphones. Figure 6.3 illustrates this process for a single phoneme. The phoneme is replaced with the context-independent biphone, then left and right context vertices are added. It is common that some left and right and even context-independent vertices are missing. In such cases, the missing vertex is simply spliced out.

An obvious MRG reduction strategy is to eliminate duplicate parallel paths in the MRG. Duplicate paths are common when words have alternative pronunciations. The current implementation does not support this feature, which is expected to decrease MRG size by about 20%.

The MRG is meant to represent a Markov model after the application of the $-\ln(p)$ function to all probabilities. In practice, the probability distribution for the transitions is not known. One assumption that can be made is that the probability of duration modeling (loop-back) on a vertex is equal to the probability of proceeding in the model and all other alternative paths are equally likely. It is observed that alternative paths in the model typically have a similar number of vertices, since pronunciation differences are usually local. If no insertion or deletion modeling edges are taken, all simple paths through the MRG — i.e. paths that do not include a loop-back edge — have nearly the same number of vertices, approximated by some value n. The number of total vertices in the path actually taken, including loop-back edges, is determined by $m - n$, where m is the number of audio frames. If parallel paths are equally probable, the weights for the parallel paths are the same. Likewise, the number of duration modeling edges are also the same. Hence, a correct solution that maximizes the path remains a correct solution if all edge weights are set to zero under these assumptions.

In practice, it is common that an unknown transition state hidden Markov model is used with either no transition probabilities or with transition probabilities that violate the probabilistic framework. A configuration of OGI speech tools for multiple word spotting uses probabilities of 1.0 for alternative paths in lexical search trees, even though these probabilities do not add to 1.0 [112]. Again, the difference translates to scaling of the numerical result, not a different optimum choice.

Experiments were performed using edge weights carefully designed to meet all probabilistic requirements. The results were equivalent to those without edge weights and the increased complexity was deemed unnecessary.

Edge weights are applied to the insertion and deletion edit modeling edges. These edges increase the search space considerably, and without some penalty, matching becomes unconstrained. The penalty used in practice is 8.25. This value was determined by computing the average good-match per-vertex weight and the average bad-match per-vertex weight for a large set of test data. Good-match data was captured using exact transcripts and no edit modeling. Bad-match data was captured using invalid transcripts (transcripts not matching the audio) and no edit modeling. The good-match value is 3.42, the bad match value 3.75. The similarity of these two values is due to the imprecision of the speech feature recognition processing and the general unconstrained nature of the audio test data. The difference between these two values is 0.33. Edits need to incur a penalty that can be effectively spread over some period of time. One second, or 100 audio frames, was chosen as that period. The penalty should not move a good match to a bad match, so $\frac{0.33}{4} = 0.0825$ per-vertex penalty was considered acceptable. Spread over 100 frames, the resulting edit modeling edge weight is 8.25. This weight is used for both hierarchical and heuristic edit modeling edges in the transcription MRG.

3.2   THE AUDIO MRG

The construction of the audio MRG consists of converting speech audio to sound unit probability estimates. It should be noted that this MRG is not actually built. Since Algorithm 4.2 is a synchronous algorithm and the audio MRG is also synchronous, only one vertex of the audio MRG is built at a time. This is a major savings in memory usage. A complete audio MRG for 30 minutes of audio would require $771MB$ of memory.

The sound unit in this application is biphones, so speech recognition tools are used to convert audio frames into a sequence of biphone probabilities. The complete process is beyond the scope of this presentation, but is described in detail in Rabiner and other sources [102]. This section includes only a simple summary of the process.

Figure 6.4 illustrates the steps necessary to convert speech audio to biphone likelihoods. This process is repeated for each 10 millisecond audio frame.

The first step is removal of any *DC-offset*. A DC-offset is an additive value in the signal and is generally considered a remnant of the recording process. DC-offset removal is accomplished using a simple high-pass filter.

Perceptual linear prediction (PLP) reduces audio waveforms to a minimal set of numbers representing frequency concentrations and densities [54]. The technique used in this application is RASTA-PLP (RelAtive SpecTrAl), a technique developed by Hermansky et al. [55]. Short-time Fourier analysis is used to estimate a frequency spectrum for the signal. This spectrum is then warped (re-mapped) onto the *Bark* frequency spectrum, a spectrum distribution believed to better represent human hearing. A Fletcher masking curve is convolved with this response and sampled to create a limited set of spectral samples with spectral characteristics related to human auditory system spectral characteristics. These samples represent maximum coverage of the human hearing range in a minimum set of numbers. The logarithm of these samples is taken. RASTA filtering is a band-pass filter applied to the spectral estimates. Long term spectral changes appear in the logarithms of the spectral coefficients as additive terms. The high-pass element of the filter cancels those terms, effectively normalizing the spectral response. The low-pass element of the filter helps to cancel high frequency aliasing artifacts and noise.

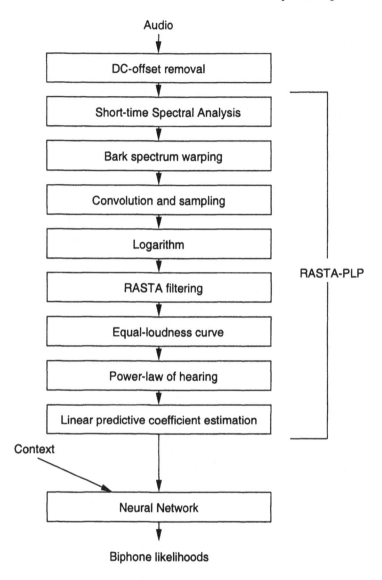

Figure 6.4. Speech audio to biphone likelihoods process.

An equal-loudness preemphasis function is applied next. The earlier steps focused on normalizing out the human hearing spectral frequency response; this step focuses on normalizing out the differing sensitivities of human hearing to varying frequencies. Then the cube root of all samples is taken (multiplication of the logarithm by 0.33). The cube root is a close approximation of the power law of hearing, a non-linear ratio between intensity and perceived loudness. Finally, autoregression analysis is used to estimate the parameters for an all-pole linear prediction model. A predictive model is a filter that, given past audio samples, closely approximates predicting future audio samples. One view of linear prediction models is that they attempt to approximate the characteristics that make the sound (the vocal tract) rather than the sound itself. The goal of the linear prediction process is to create a filter that can predict the normalized and processed audio data.

The output of the RASTA-PLP process in this implementation is 8 PLP coefficients. These and some additional recent frame coefficients (some additional context) are used as input to a neural network classifier. The use of context allows for greater accuracy in the classification process. The network is a feed-forward neural network that has been trained on the TIMIT corpus [44], which consists of 630 speakers representing 8 major dialect divisions of American English each speaking 10 sentences selected for phonetic richness.

The output of the neural network is 535 biphone likelihoods. The ".garbage" biphone is not an actual biphone and the network is not trained with its value. It is assumed that beyond a certain ranking in the likelihood results, the biphone likelihood estimates mean very little. In practice this number is typically about 10% of the space. Beyond these top ranking candidates, the numbers are more likely to be simply garbage. A common technique for modeling noise between speech units is to select a likelihood ranking at around this level and assign it to a biphone named ".garbage". In this application, a ranking of 50 has been used. Some experimental manipulation of this value was performed and it is believed that this number is an effective choice. The net effect of this approach to noise modeling is that noise induces smaller delineations between the top and 50th ranked estimates than valid biphonemic content. Hence, noise results in matches closer to the highest ranking choice. When combined with context (biphones are recognized in context, not in isolation), this technique effectively models noise and non-speech sounds. No effort was made in this application to model the WorldBet specialized non-speech sound items such as background noise (.bn), cough (.cough) or sneeze (.sneeze).

The actual implementation of the speech feature recognition system is based on the Oregon Graduate Institute CSLU-C toolkit [112] in combination with the ImageCL multimedia algorithm development system [90].

4.   MEDIA ELEMENT COMPARISON

The other component required for application of Algorithm 4.2 is a media element comparison method. Given vertices for the two media representation graphs, the media element comparison in this application is trivial. The transcription MRG vertices have an associated index indicating the biphone for the vertex. This index is used to directly look up the biphone likelihood estimate in the vector of biphone likelihoods associated with the audio MRG vertex.

5.   APPLICATION OF MULTIPLE STREAM CORRELATION

Algorithm 4.2 proceeds synchronously in this application. The implementation simply requests a new audio MRG vertex for every new value of s.

The use of a pruning parameter is essential in this application. The red-headed.league evaluation data-set described in Section 6., for example, generates a transcription MRG with 188,990 vertices. The audio duration is 248,413 frames (41 minutes and 40 seconds). Use of a Viterbi-style implementation with no pruning would require 4^{10} media element comparison operations and an estimated 8 terabytes of memory.

5.1   ENFORCED INTERPOLATION

The implementation employs causal variation on the transcription MRG as described in Section 7.1. The specific parameter chosen (empirically) is a value of $\sigma = 5000$. This is equivalent to an average of one minute of MRG content. This use of a causally varying MRG allows for *enforced interpolation*. If the audio quality degrades so far as to be unable to discriminate matches, enforced interpolation keeps an alignment estimate advancing. The presence of insertion and deletion edges provides a search space for resynchronization when audio quality improves.

The goal of enforced interpolation is to interpolate an alignment over bad audio so as to allow users the ability to retrieve as closely as possible the desired content. This technique has been used to effectively locate elements in music selections as discussed in Section 6.3, even though most music is too wide-band and complex for the speech recognition system to classify.

5.2   SOLUTION GRANULARITY

The granularity of solutions in this application is considerably finer than would be expected. Since the system is aligning sub-phonemic elements, the recall is at the sub-phonemic level, and is, therefore, of very high accuracy. The exceptions to this accuracy are transitions to and from noise and the use of hierarchical deletion or insertion modeling.

Audio transitions of speech to or from noise can cause the beginning or end of a biphone to be extended into the noise region, particularly if the noise is easily mistaken by the speech system for a vocal sound. In experimentation, it was found that bird sounds often were interpreted as the opening of the "T" or the sound. A simple heuristic post-processing of the synchronization data could be devised to estimate a correction for this problem. The practical concern is whether the correct content will be retrieved and, in this case, that would be so, albeit with a few bird sounds at the beginning or end of the selection.

The penalty for using a bounded out-degree hierarchical deletion and insertion modeling structure is that the system cannot match insertions and deletions exactly. Fortunately, the vast majority of edits seem to be either limited local changes or heuristic units such as paragraphs and sentences. However, for deletions not matching these criteria, some additional words are inserted in the match as the system resynchronizes. As an example, the following is quoted from a reading of the short story "The Red-Headed League" by Sir Arthur Conan Doyle, as read by Ben Kingsly.

...when in judicial moods. Mr. Jabez Wilson here has been good enough to call...

The actual text reads:

...when in judicial moods. "I know, my dear Watson, ..." (163 words deleted) Now, Mr. Jabez Wilson here has been good enough to call...

The actual deletion from the text is 169 words. The computed synchronization selected the following words. The misaligned inserted words are underlined.

...when in judicial <u>know of bizarre and by to go to than any for</u> enough to call upon me...

The modeling requires 11 words to handle a rather large deletion of 169 words. (inserted words are bounded by $2 \log_2 D$, to allow for reaching the largest step, then stepping back down). The net effect when viewing a synchronized presentation of the text and the audio is the system jumping through text to catch up as quickly as possible. Note that the 11 words were inserted in the period of time that Ben Kingsly spoke only 7 words. This was the worst-case example in the test data of a large, unconstrained deletion.

5.3   MONOTONICITY AND ENDPOINT CONSTRAINTS

Enforcement of the endpoint constraint is not necessary in this application. Indeed, failing to align to the end of the transcript is typically an indication of a deletion at the end of the transcript. Termination is guaranteed by the synchronous processing of the audio MRG vertices. The number of algorithm steps is exactly the number of audio frames.

Monotonicity is assumed to apply in this example. Insertion modeling edges can violate monotonicity, but only while recovering from an insertion. The backtracking phase of the algorithm is modified for this application to enforce monotonicity by eliminating any non-monotonic steps. When backtracking, it is expected that the causal normalization function is monotonically non-increasing. When the causal normalization function is found to increase (when viewing in reverse order), all values are ignored until a new, lower, value is found. Figure 6.5 illustrates this truncation process.

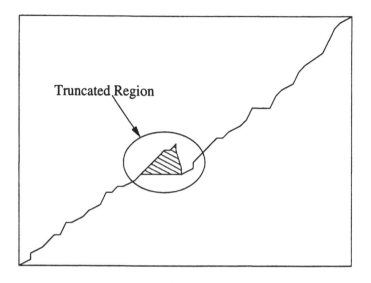

Figure 6.5.   Enforcement of monotonicity on causal normalization.

6.   EVALUATION

This section describes techniques and criteria for the evaluation of the text-to-speech alignment system, that has been implemented as an element of the Xtrieve system. Various configurations have been tested, so parameterization is discussed in context. The pruning parameter was bounded at 6000, although smaller values were occasionally used in testing for performance reasons. However, a smaller pruning parameter will not increase accuracy. A discussion of the pruning parameter choice is included in Section 6.6. Edit modeling edges were configured for a minimum bypass distance of 2 so as to avoid single word false deletions which tend to be common when a minimum bypass of 1 is utilized (mostly due to very short words). The bypass edge penalty used is 8.25.

Three approaches have been taken in the evaluation of this system. A significant quantity of material has been used for *subjective evaluation*, the evaluation of alignment results by observation. The Xtrieve system described in Chapter 7 utilizes text-to-speech alignment as a primary cross-modal index tool. Section 6.3 describes Xtrieve content experiences. *Hand-alignment* has been used to create a limited set of test materials. Hand-alignment is the labor intensive process of assigning a text-to-speech alignment by hand. A major goal of hand-alignment has been to create test materials representative of real-world content. Section 6.4 describes hand-alignment testing. Finally, a set of test data has been built using the *TIMIT Corpus*, a standard speech system training and testing data-set of utterances (short sentences) with precise alignment information. These utterances have been used to build a larger alignment test data-set. This dataset is particularly useful for the demonstration of noise tolerance. Section 6.5 describes the use of the TIMIT corpus as a text-to-speech alignment evaluation tool. The evaluation data-set is described in Section 6.2.

6.1   EVALUATION CRITERIA

Many measures of alignment accuracy are possible. The evaluation criteria presented in this chapter are designed to emphasize features important to the major applications of this technology: cross-modal information retrieval and automatic captioning. The techniques used in this chapter closely parallel those of Chapter 5. An evaluation set is a 4-tuple $\{\mu_1, \mu_2, S_{test}, S_{ref}\}$. μ_1 is the document and μ_2 the audio file. S_{test} is a synchronization data-set under test. S_{ref} is a reference synchronization data-set assumed to be correct. This set may be hand-aligned, computed from standard reference data, or may not exist at all other than in the mind of a subjective evaluator.

A synchronization data-set assigns each word w a location in time in μ_2 (in seconds) and a relative index r in the synchronization data-set. The relative index is a sequential numbering of the words which actually exist in the data-set. Words which do not exist in the data-set are assigned a relative index of nil. This criterion was chosen so as not to inflate word distance errors in the presence of deletions. Consequently, a relative index is not assumed to correspond between two synchronization data-sets.

Deletion errors are measures of effectiveness of deletion modeling. If a word exists in S_{test} but not in S_{ref}, a *missed deletion error* has occured. The word should have been recognized as a deletion and was not. If a word exists in S_{ref} but not in S_{test}, a *false deletion error* has occured. Insertion modeling results are indicated by the accuracy of the alignment, since inserted content in the audio is not assigned to words in S_{ref}.

The alignment distance δ_w for a word is the difference between the associated location of w in S_{test} and S_{ref} (assuming no deletion errors). Given a vector of M alignment distances, $< \delta_1, ..., \delta_M >$, the mean error $\bar{\delta}$ is defined as:

$$\bar{\delta} = \frac{1}{M} \sum_{i=1}^{M} \delta_i \tag{6.6}$$

The standard deviation s is computed as [58]:

$$s = \frac{(M) \sum_{i=1}^{M} \delta_i^2 - \left(\sum_{i=1}^{M} \delta_i\right)^2}{M(M-1)} \tag{6.7}$$

The mean error is primarily indicative of general offsets in the hand-marking process due to individual word boundary estimation. This measure tends to be small in most testing of the system due to the averaging of positive and negative errors over a large number of words. Consequently, the standard deviation is often very similar in value to the root-mean-squared error (RMS). RMS error statistics are common in the measurement of parallel-text alignment systems. However, it is felt in this evaluation that the standard deviation is a more general tool. The RMS error measure is:

$$RMS = \frac{1}{M} \sum_{i=1}^{M} \delta_i^2 \qquad (6.8)$$

Local distance measures such as the mean and standard deviation are useful for measuring fine-grain accuracy of a computed alignment. However, they mean very little in retrieval and captioning applications. The real question in those applications is how accurately the content is retrieved. A more valuable measure, then, is how accurate the alignment is relative to retrieval and presentation granularities. All retrieval and presentation is assumed to begin and end at word boundaries, so a measure of how accurately words are selected is more indicative of system performance. This is especially true when the large variation in word presentation durations is considered. An identical alignment error is more noticeable around a shorter word than a longer word.

Given a word w that exists in both S_{test} and S_{ref}, let $r_{correct}$ be the relative index for the word in S_{ref} and t_{test} be the computed word start time in S_{test}. Each word in S_{ref} has an associated range that is assumed to start with the word start time in S_{ref} and end with the start time of the next word in S_{ref}. This range is different from the actual word duration in that it assumes the range extends until the next word. However, the larger range allows assignment of word relative indices to all time intervals in S_{ref}. Let r_{actual} be the relative index for some word in S_{ref} such that the associated range for the word contains t_{test}. The *word distance error* δ_w is defined as:

$$\delta_w = \begin{cases} r_{actual} - r_{correct} & \text{if } r_{actual} \geq r_{correct} \\ r_{actual} - r_{correct} + 1 & \text{otherwise} \end{cases} \qquad (6.9)$$

Figure 6.6 illustrates the word distance error mechanism. Assume $w =$ "was" and that the figure presents a sequential presentation of S_{ref}. Computed alignment (c) is within the range of the word, so an error value of zero is appropriate. (d) represents a placement beyond the correct placement. $r_{actual} \geq r_{correct}$, so the computed error is 1. (b) represents the case of $r_{actual} < r_{correct}$. The word is computed at a location slightly early, but is not an entire word distance in error, so an error value of zero is also appropriate. (a) represents an error distance of -1.

6.2   EVALUATION MATERIAL

Table 6.1 lists the material used for system evaluation. Each evaluation segment is indicated in this section using the segment ID. The word count is

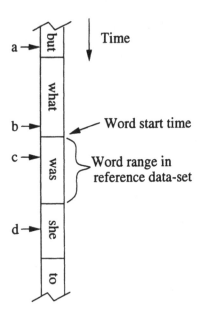

Figure 6.6.   Word distance error definition.

the number of words actually subject to synchronization, and does not include mark-up, front matter, titles, and comments. The MRG size is the number of vertices in the biphonemic media representation graph. For this data collection, the ratio of words to MRG size averages 1 : 19.7. The "Dur." field lists the duration of the audio. The ratio of duration to MRG size varies considerably in the collection from a high of 1 : 77.7 for man.with.twisted.lip to a low of 1 : 8.9 for nights.satin. man.with.twisted.lip is a talking book that is read very quickly. nights.satin is a song with long instrumental sections. The number of speakers is the number of distinct individuals speaking in the segment. "Ref. Data" is an indication of the existence of reference comparison data. "NO" indicates no comparison data is available and the segment is evaluated subjectively. "HM" indicates content with a hand-marked reference synchronization data-set. "GT" indicates content with assumed correct ground-truth data.

The "Del.", "Ins.", and "Sub." columns indication deletions, insertions, and substitutions in the audio content relative to the transcript. Deletions and insertions are listed in the form occurrences/words. Occurrences is the total number of incidents, words is the total number of words involved. Only the word count is listed for substitutions.

cnn.polpot.0401898

The segment cnn.polpot.041898 is a recording of a story presented on CNN news on April 18, 1998. This is a produced story about the cremation of Pol Pot, the former leader of the Khmer Rouge in Cambodia. One of the speakers

Table 6.1. Evaluation material for text-to-speech alignment.

Segment ID	Words Count	MRG Size	Dur.	Speakers	Ref. Data	Del.	Ins.	Sub.
cnn.polpot.041898	422	7,534	2:41	4	HM	0/0	2/5	2
hal	31	612	0:12	2	HM	0/0	0/0	0
hamlet.a1.s2	767	12,180	4:10	4	NO	17/269	1/5	3
late.lament	79	1,442	1:22	1	HM	0/0	0/0	0
man.with.twisted.lip	9,303	186,628	40:01	1	HM	74/1,550	12/13	39
nights.satin	246	3,883	7:15	1	NO	0/0	0/0	0
parrot.sketch	486	7,759	3:35	2	HM	1/1	3/3	6
red-headed.league	9,201	188,990	41:04	1	NO	61/1,209	25/33	38
thisweek-execpriv0419	1,862	35,742	10:01	5	NO	2/2	19/21	2
timit-core	1,570	29,029	9:42	24	GT	0/0	0/0	0

on this segment is a Cambodian native. This segment includes an insertion of foreign language content which continues simultaneously with a vocalized translation.

hal

The segment hal is a 12 second excerpt from the motion picture "2001: A Space Odyssey." This is a short segment used extensively during the development and testing of Xtrieve and deserves inclusion in this set.

hamlet.a1.s2

hamlet.a1.s2 is a segment from act 1, scene 2 of the motion picture *Hamlet* staring Mel Gibson, directed by Franco Zefferilli, an adaptation of the William Shakespeare play. The script for this segment is from the original play, not the Zefferilli adaptation and, consequently, has considerable edits including over 35% deletions. The largest deletion is 40 words.

late.lament

late.lament is the poem "Late Lament" by Graeme Edge, as performed by the Moody Blues. This presentation is interesting as test data for several reasons. The poem is presented over incidental music. The presentation is dramatic and includes wide variations in volume. The end of the poem is followed by 37 seconds of orchestral music.

man.with.twisted.lip

Two talking-book presentations are included in this collection. Both are readings of works by Sir Arthur Conan Doyle: "The Man With The Twisted Lip", and "The Red-Headed League". The stories are read by Ben Kingsley. These segments are meant to be representative of talking-book content. They are also longer-form content which helped ensure robustness. An interesting characteristic of these segments is how much content is deleted. man.with.twisted.lip has 74 deletions for 1,550 words. The largest deletion is 161 words.

nights.satin

nights.satin is the song "Nights in White Satin", as performed by the Moody Blues. Speech tools in general do not perform well on songs. Though the text-to-speech alignment system is more robust than recognition systems, it also does not perform well on this segment. However, the segment is included to illustrate two important characteristics of the system, enforced interpolation and recovery ability.

parrot.sketch

Xtrieve and the text-to-speech alignment system have been demonstrated on many occasions. A common question has been "have you tried it on any Monty Python?" parrot.sketch is the "Dead Parrot" sketch as digitized from the motion picture *And Now For Something Completely Different*. This segment includes highly exaggerated British accents and rapid enunciation. The speech feature recognition system has been trained entirely on American dialects of the English Language. Speech systems meant for application to British English are normally trained in that dialect.

red-headed.league

This is the second talking book selection. The largest deletion in "The Red-Headed League" by Arthur Conan Doyle is 169 words.

thisweek-execpriv0419

thisweek-execpriv0419 is a segment of the program "This Week" from ABC news recorded on April 19, 1998. This program differs from cnn.polpot.041898 in that "This Week" is a live presentation, so the commentators are not reading from script and are not able to correct errors they make other than to repeat words or just go on. Extraneous word insertions are very common in this segment. Insertion examples included repeated words as large as "observed". This segment also has five instances of overlapping content, content where two people are speaking simultaneously.

6.3   SUBJECTIVE EVALUATION

The Xtrieve cross-modal IR system has been used as a demonstration of cross-modal retrieval and text-to-speech alignment. Consequently, a considerable amount of content has been aligned for inclusion in the Xtrieve system. The main criterion for test material is that it fall in the speech-light class, implying the availability of an electronic transcription. Many sources for such material have been found.

Experience with different content sources has led to some interesting observations. Edits in presented content are quite frequent. The most common edit is deletion, the presence of content in the transcript that is not included in the audio. Talking books have been found to have large amounts of deleted content, up to multiple paragraphs in some cases. Dramatic performances also commonly delete lines and speeches.

Single word substitutions are common in all content types. Experience with the system seems to indicate that this error type is easily accommodated. Two word substitutions, typically evidenced by word reversals, are also common and cause little problem. Large scale substitutions seem to be rare.

The most common insertion types are non-verbal utterances and alliterations between words. These insertion types are rarely a problem even without insertion modeling. Larger insertions are accommodated by the insertion modeling system.

One of the test segments, nights.satin, is a 7:15 long recording of the song "Nights in White Satin". This segment was included to observe the results of application of the system to a song. Two specific concerns are tested: enforced interpolation (Section 5.1) and the ability of the system to recover following loss of synchronization. The segment late.lament, another test segment, is a part of nights.satin. late.lament is known to align with high accuracy, as discussed in Section 6.4. nights.satin consists of three verses with choruses between. The chorus is repeated at the end, then followed by late.lament. Interestingly enough, the system is able to accurately synchronize to the first two lines of each of the verses. The synchronization then appears to decay. As the speech feature recognition becomes overwhelmed by the rich spectrum of the music, the system reverts to interpolation, and moves the synchronization over the content linearly. The valuable observation is that at three locations and at the beginning of late.lament the system returns to synchronization.

An interesting future research question is alignment of music and sung content. Music is very different from noise, in that the rich spectrum is not random, but is clustered in much the same way that voice is. Compensating for musical background will likely require suppression of the music as much as possible. Chong and Togneri discuss using neural network approaches to extract speech content in the presence of music, though their work is based on single instruments [23]. Expansion to full performances is an open problem.

6.4   HAND-ALIGNED CONTENT

A quantitative approach to testing synchronization results is to compare the computed results with reference data hand-marked by a human operator. Hand-marking experience has typically required investments of time at least ten times the duration of the content to be hand-marked. The process that has been used begins with a computed alignment. The choice of starting the hand alignment process with a computed alignment is a pragmatic one, but not at all unprecedented. The alignment of the DARPA TIMIT corpus was initially computed, then hand verified and corrected [44]. Parallel-text corpus material has also been created in this way [78]. Starting the process with a computed alignment minimizes the range of manual changes.

Figure 6.7 illustrates the Xtrieve synchronization editor. The Xtrieve synchronization editor is a user tool for the creation of hand-marked reference data. An operator is presented with both audible presentations of the speech and a waveform display. Selection of word start and end points is done using the mouse. The user interface has been designed for rapid selection of the appropriate points.

Five hand-marked selections are currently available, as indicated in Table 6.1. The longest of these is the 40 minute talking book man.with.the.twisted.lip. The accuracy of the hand-marked content is considered by the author to be very good based on the same measures of performance discussed for the text-to-speech alignment system, particularly word distance errors. It is often difficult to specify a boundary between two words, particularly when the words are close and have similar phonemes on their ends. Boundary placement may vary in such cases, but the word distance error will be zero.

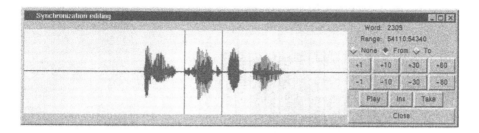

Figure 6.7.   Xtrieve synchronization editor.

Table 6.2 presents evaluation results for the hand-marked content. Word errors are presented in the range -3 to $+3$ and are presented as a percentage and the actual number of occurrences. The mean and standard deviation values are in milliseconds.

The mean error varies considerably, as much due to human variation as to the system variation. However, the largest value of 46 ms is not significant. Standard deviations also vary considerably. Both late.lament and parrot.sketch are noisy presentations, and an observed system behavior is a tendency to lock onto words early when sound effects or music are present. This tendency causes larger relative distance errors, without impacting the word error statistic.

The word error statistics vary from perfect alignment for the hal and cnn.polpot.041898 segments to 78% for the parrot sketch. The cnn.polpot.041898 result is actually somewhat surprising, given that the segment includes a non-native speaker of English, considerable background noise, and translation over a background speaker. However, this result is influenced by the high production quality of the segment.

The worst word error statistics are evidenced for the parrot.sketch segment. This segment includes an exaggerated accent and the British English dialect. It should be noted, though, that nearly 90% of the words have errors distances of one or less. Though this is not a perfect result, it still allows for high quality retrieval of content in the segment. Examination of the synchronization results indicates the system jumped ahead on some occasions for an entire sentence, significantly impacting the word error statistics.

Edit modeling is only an issue for the man.with.twisted.lip segment. The only other segment including deletions is parrot.sketch and the one word deletion in that segment is less than the minimum bypass edge, so it was falsely included. The actual deletion in that case is "No, no, <u>no</u>, I've definitely 'ad enough of this." The computed synchronization placed the additional "no" in the space between the second "no" and "I've", as expected. The 72 missed deletions in man.with.twisted.lip are nearly all words traversed during deletion modeling. Heuristic modeling accounts for a significant percentage of the deletions in the segment with perfect deletion detection. However, many deletions

Table 6.2.   Hand-marked reference evaluation. See Table 6.1 for details on the test data-sets.

	cnn.polpot.041898	hal	late.lament	man.with.twisted.lip	parrot.sketch
Mean error	9.26 ms	0.84 ms	31.08 ms	7.74 ms	46.88 ms
Standard deviation	31.54 ms	61.66 ms	364.49 ms	172.64 ms	759.54 ms
-3 word errors	-	-	-	7 0.1%	3 0.6%
-2 word errors	-	-	1 1.3%	19 0.2%	10 2.1%
-1 word errors	-	-	3 3.8%	49 0.6%	20 4.2%
No error	422 100%	31 100%	71 91.0%	7408 96.1%	375 78.0%
+1 word errors	-	-	3 3.8%	47 0.6%	36 7.5%
+2 word errors	-	-	-	23 0.3%	8 1.7%
+3 word errors	-	-	-	11 0.1%	5 1.0%
Missed deletions	-	-	-	72	5
False deletions	-	-	-	135	1

are not based on sentence or paragraph boundaries, and require the general purpose deletion modeling described in Section 6.. This model requires a logarithmically bounded number of words in the deletion path, and these additional words appear in the statistics as missed deletions.

The false deletions are minimum sized deletions detected falsely in the audio. The minimum size bypass edge in the experiment is two and nearly all of these false deletions are a local bypass of two words. This behavior is more common in the talking book content than any other, possibly because the content is read faster and shorter words (such as "the", "a", etc.) are run together, causing the bypass to become a lesser-weight path. In all instances the skipped words were within sentence boundaries, so retrieval or caption presentation of content would not be impacted and the false deletions represent less than 2% of the words in the content. However, the elimination of this anomalous behavior is a subject of future research.

6.5 COMPARISON TO REFERENCE DATA

The TIMIT corpus is a standard acoustic-phonetic continuous speech corpus consisting of 6,300 utterances (sentences) by 630 speakers from 8 major dialect divisions of the United States [44]. Associated with each utterance is precision alignment information at the word and phonemic level. This alignment information was determined by an automatic phonemic alignment system and then hand evaluated and adjusted by linguistic experts [130]. The utterances average three seconds each.

As a point of comparison with the work presented in this chapter, the TIMIT corpus alignment was restricted to segments averaging three seconds long, not 40 minutes or more. Also, the transcription at both the word and phonemic levels is 100% accurate, so edit modeling and recovery are not an issue.

A test segment timit-core was built using the recommended TIMIT *core test set*. The core test set consists of 8 utterances by each of 24 speakers. The utterances and speakers have been chosen for phonemic and dialect diversity. Also, none of the utterances or speakers in this set are used as training data in recognition systems or in the speech feature recognition used in this chapter. 8 of the speakers are female, 16 are male. The ground-truth data supplied with the TIMIT corpus was used to create a reference synchronization data-set. The segment has 1,570 words and is 9:42 long.

The TIMIT corpus consists of cleanly recorded content by speakers asked to speak smoothly and clearly. Consequently, the computed alignment of timit-core is very accurate. Table 6.3 presents results for simple alignment including edit modeling.

An important characteristic of any speech system is tolerance of noise. The larger context model available in text-to-speech alignment should be more tolerant of noise. To test this hypothesis, experiments were performed using

Table 6.3.   Segment timit-core evaluation.

Mean error		21.0 ms
Standard deviation		42.4 ms
-1 word errors	0.1%	2
No error	99.8%	1563
+1 word errors	0.01%	1
Missed deletions		N/A
False deletions		4

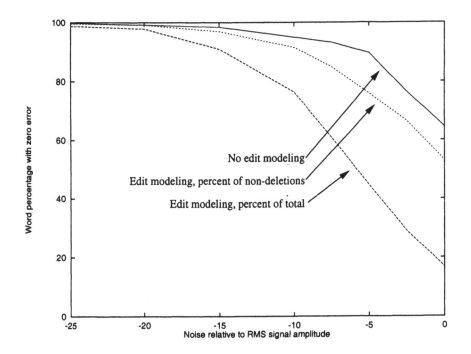

Figure 6.8.   Word error performance in the presence of noise.

the timit-core segment and Gaussian noise mixed with the audio during the alignment process. Tests were performed using 8 noise amplitudes ranging from $-25dB$ to $0dB$ relative to the root-mean-squared (RMS) amplitude of the timit-core audio. The specific amplitude for a v decibel noise injection is:

$$RMS_{noise} = 10^{\log(RMS_{timit\text{-}core})+v/20} \qquad (6.10)$$

Figure 6.8 presents the word error performance of the system in the presence of noise. The line labeled "No edit modeling" is the total percentage of words in the test set that have a zero alignment error. The line labeled "Edit modeling, percent of total" is the equivalent value with edit modeling in place.

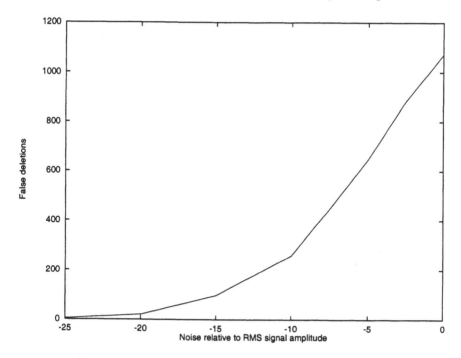

Figure 6.9.   False deletion performance in the presence of noise.

Figure 6.9 plots the false deletion rate as a function of noise. As noise amplitude increases, local content becomes indistinguishable from noise and is more likely to be deleted. This is clearly illustrated in this figure. Deletions were more common for some of the speakers than others, partly due to variation in speaker amplitudes. Figure 6.8 includes a line labeled "Edit modeling, percentage of non-deletions". This line plots the percentage of non-deleted words that have zero alignment error. Given the large number of deletions as noise increases, this value is more indicative of alignment performance in that it is a measure relative to the words actually aligned. Even at a 0dB noise level, better than 50% of the aligned words have zero error (although this is only about 17% of the total words.)

No specific noise cancelation or compensation has been included in this design. Many strategies exist which could be added to the speech feature recognition component of the system for even better noise performance. See Moreno for a good overview and some interesting new approaches [82]. The RATZ (Multivariate-Gaussian-Based-Cepstral-Normalization) family of algorithms are quoted in that work to have recognition accuracies of around 40% at $-5dB$ Gaussian noise injection. It is not reasonable to compare recognition accuracy to alignment accuracy directly, but it is interesting to note that the ap-

Table 6.4.   Maximum ranks for evaluation segments.

Segment	Max rank
cnn.polpot.041898	135
hal	111
hamlet.a1.s2	532
nights.satin	1193
timit-core, No noise	1367
timit-core, -15dB noise	1647
timit-core, 0dB noise	1365

plication of RATZ improves performance in the Sphinx-II recognition system from near zero accuracy at that $-5dB$ noise injection level.

6.6   PRUNING STRATEGY EVALUATION

As with the parallel-text synchronization system described in Chapter 5, efficient performance of text-to-speech alignment is dependent upon use of a pruning strategy. In the evaluation, the pruning width was set to fixed values ranging from 2000 to 6000. The larger width was employed with segments requiring significant edits and in the higher noise injection examples.

The implementation was instrumented to record the weight rank for every vertex in the search tree for each tree depth s. During the back-tracking phase the maximum (worst case) rank is recorded and is presented for some examples in Table 6.4. A worst case path of 1647 indicates that the pruning parameter could be set to any greater value and the paths would not be pruned.

6.7   EXECUTION PERFORMANCE

The execution performance of the system is closely related to the pruning parameter. An Alpha processor-based Digital Equipment Corporation DEC 500/333 with a pruning parameter of 5000 requires a 7.1 : 1 ratio of processor time to audio duration. Smaller pruning parameters decrease this value almost linearly. A common pruning parameter when the content quality is good has been 2000, which reduces the ratio to about 2.5 : 1. This is based on a highly instrumented and very general purpose implementation. Performance improvements of at least one order of magnitude are believed possible in a highly optimized implementation.

An alternative measure of performance is the number of MRG vertices examined per audio frame. As an example, for the timit-core segment with a pruning parameter of 5000, an average of 12, 418 MRG vertices are examined per audio frame. Ravishankar lists the number of hidden Markov models (HMM) evaluated per frame for the Sphinx-II speech recognition system [104].

The processing requirement for HMM evaluation is very similar to that for an MRG vertex examination. For two different tasks (with differing dictionary sizes), the average HMMs evaluated per frame for the Sphinx-II system are $15, 985$ and $29, 272$. $12, 418$ MRG vertex examinations in the system presented in this chapter compares very favorable with these values.

7.   ISSUES AND APPLICATIONS

This section discusses issues related to text-to-speech alignment and some additional applications for this technology. An important issue is the placement of alignment technologies relative to transcription technologies. Neither is intended as a replacement for the other. The additional applications discussed include captioning systems and talking books.

7.1   RELATION TO AUTOMATIC TRANSCRIPTION

Text-to-speech alignment is a very different process than automatic transcription. Automatic transcription attempts to discover words by monitoring audio. Word recognition cannot be completely unconstrained; for example, it is not sufficient to recognize the beginning of "airplane" as "air". However, nothing is special about word beginnings and endings in isolation. The solution for this problem is *context*: rather than looking for words, systems attempt to find sequences of words, with boundaries determined by the boundaries in the sequences. Bigram or trigram word sequences are common examples. The problem with word sequences is that the number of N-grams is exponential in N, so typically context is limited to three words.

This is a significant difference from text-to-speech alignment. In the system presented in this chapter, context is the entire transcription. The possibility of insertions or deletions does confuse that issue a bit, but fundamentally, the next word searched for on any candidate path follows the previous word. This is a significant decrease in uncertainty.

At any point in time, text-to-speech alignment is searching for an alignment with a limited number of words. This is in contrast to conventional automatic transcription wherein the number of words searched for at any time is in the tens of thousands. Search resources are concentrated on expected words, not a large vocabulary. It should be noted that the vocabulary for text-to-speech alignment is exactly the words in the transcript. The unknown-words problem is not an issue in this application.

7.2   CAPTIONING APPLICATIONS

A major potential application area for text-to-speech alignment is captioning [109]. Captioning is the placement of text on a movie or television image in support of the hearing impaired or alternative language viewer. There are two approaches to captioning content. In live applications, a steno-captioner provides a real-time transcription of the content as it is being generated. The techniques in this chapter are not likely to be useful in that application. For pre-recorded applications, including movies, television programs, and most news programs, off-line captioning is utilized. Off-line captioning is an extremely time-consuming process requiring the selection of exactly when and where every caption should appear.

In the presence of a text-to-speech alignment, the question of "when" is solved (for same language applications). The captioning computer program can be pre-loaded with all caption start times. The operator can then adjust these locations so as to improve placement where desired. Sentence granularity, the amount of text to place on the screen at one time, can be estimated heuristically and verified by an operator before placement. The remaining issue is where to put the caption on the screen. This is often a complicated decision, involving indicating the speaker and guarding screen regions from coverage. Many possible solutions for seeding this process are possible, though it is assumed that an operator will fine-tune the result.

Captions are opaque and cover content completely. *Guarding* is protecting content from coverage. Some content may be permanent and marked off-limits at the beginning of the operation. A common example is the "bug" or station identification in the corner of the screen. Motion can be detected using differencing techniques. Regions of the screen with little are no motion are less likely to be hampered by caption placement. The concept of speaker identification discussed in Chapter 8 can provide cues to proper caption placement such that the captions are identified with the speaker. All of these heuristics should be combined in a framework that minimized the variation of caption location so as to avoid forcing the user's vision to bounce around the screen.

7.3   TALKING BOOK APPLICATIONS

A major source of test data for Xtrieve and text-to-speech alignment has been talking books. Talking books are vocal presentations of books, usually provided for the vision impaired or for use while driving or when the eyes cannot be distracted. A problem with talking books is that they do not have an index, so it is hard to locate specific content. However, talking books fall into the script-light category and can be aligned using text-to-speech alignment. A small amount of computed index data can be used to move directly to a point on a CD-ROM for story playback. Indexing can be done using the techniques described in Chapter 7 in relation to the Xtrieve system. Queries can be entered with a keyboard and results presented audibly.

8.   SUMMARY

This chapter describes the application of multiple media correlation to text-to-speech alignment. Text-to-speech alignment promises to provide solutions for a wide variety of information retrieval and captioning problems still too complex for automatic transcription technologies. The large and narrow language model limits uncertainty, allowing faster, more accurate solutions.

Text-to-speech alignment has been implemented and evaluation results are presented. Text-to-speech alignment is the premier component of the Xtrieve cross-modal information retrieval system, making possible simple and fast query-based retrieval of multimedia content.

Chapter 7

THE XTRIEVE CROSS-MODAL INFORMATION RETRIEVAL SYSTEM

This book develops a new framework for computed synchronization and demonstrates it within the context of several applications. A major contribution of this research is the development of a cross-modal information retrieval (CMIR) system that can serve as a test-bed for application of computed synchronization technologies: the Xtrieve cross-modal information retrieval system. Xtrieve provides infrastructure in support of media alignment technologies and is the implementation environment for the solutions presented in Chapters 5 and 6. Xtrieve also provides a tool for exploring the use of computed synchronization technologies in information retrieval applications.

Cross-modal information retrieval is the querying of one media type in search of content in another. Xtrieve allows for cross-modal retrieval in a database of multimedia material. Several cross-modal pairings have been developed in Xtrieve, including text-to-audio, text-to-video, and text-to-text. Browsing facilities are included for additional future pairings. Query processing in Xtrieve uses a keyword-based text retrieval system.

In a large multimedia database system, documents may represent transcripts for long form programming such as plays or complete newscasts. An important issue is the size (typically duration) of retrieved elements. *Granularity control* in Xtrieve allows the result size to be adjusted to sub-document sizes that are more effective for presentation of continuous media such as video or audio. Retrieval granularity is adjustable to several levels, including sentence and paragraph levels. In addition to text searching, Xtrieve supports media browsing, the viewing of video or audio segments with automatic presentation of cross-modal equivalent selections. Inversion of computed synchronization functions allows location of text content from speech audio or location of the appropriate slide in a presentation video.

This chapter gives an overview of the Xtrieve system. Section 1. discusses the concept of cross-modal information retrieval. The general operation of Xtrieve is described in Section 2., while Section 3. details the internal structure of the system. One benefit of building systems such as Xtrieve is that new questions, ideas, and issues are often discovered during the development process. Section 4. discusses some of these issues and the Xtrieve approach to their solution. Section 5. summarizes what has been learned in the development and testing of Xtrieve.

1.   CROSS-MODAL INFORMATION RETRIEVAL

Cross-modal information retrieval is the searching of one media object for content in another [98]. The query is applied to a *query media object*. The query result is a *target media object*. A key idea behind cross-modal retrieval is that some media types are much easier to search than others. As an example, text is much easier to search than audio. Also, some media types may represent richer information media than others. For example, when parallel texts exist, a search for a name in one text document may yield clues to an alternative name usage in the other.

Causal synchronization, as introduced in Chapter 2, facilitates causal or temporal cross-modal results, the location and duration of a result in the target media ordering space. Some applications also require spatial localization. An example is the location of a speaker's lips in an image sequence. This process requires not only the temporal synchronization of the query to the image sequence, but also the spatial location of the lips in the frames. Most applications of cross-modal retrieval that have been explored have been predominantly causal, though some, particularly the fMRI data analysis application described in Chapter 8, are also spatial in nature.

The primary mechanism for cross-modal retrieval is *computed synchronization*. Given a query media object μ_q and a target media object μ_t, cross-modal retrieval requires, as a minimum, a causal synchronization τ that maps the causal ordering space of μ_q to that of μ_t. A query result is an ordered set of intervals $<< s_1, e_1 >, < s_2, e_2 >, ..., < s_n, e_n >>$ such that each interval includes a starting causal index s_i and an ending causal index e_i. The target segment in μ_i is, then, $\tau(s_i)$ to $\tau(e_i)$. As an example, a text-to-speech cross-modal query result determines intervals of word indices in a text document. A computed causal synchronization is then used to translate these intervals to ranges of an audio media object.

This discussion has assumed a single target object. In many applications multiple targets may exist. A simple example is a digital video target, wherein an associated digital audio sound track will usually exist. Any video query result can be presented in both media. It is possible that a mapping from a query media object to a final target media object will require composition of multiple synchronization functions (or functional representations of synchronization data objects). An example is the location of the description of a given projected slide in a recorded lecture presentation. Presentations often use projected slides to highlight or present important points. These slides can be scanned or, given the popularity of presentation software packages such as PowerPoint, may already exist in electronic form. Since slides are highly condensed summaries of the material in the presentation and are limited in number, they are an ideal browsing medium. A user may select slide 13 and wish to know what was said about the slide. A computed or stored synchronization can locate the time when the slide was presented in a video recording of the presentation. This is the first level of cross-modal retrieval. Given the location in the video, the user may prefer to read a transcript of this portion of the presentation rather than viewing the speaker. A second cross-modal retrieval operation is used to find the associated interval in the transcript. Two causal synchronization functions, slides-to-video and text-to-speech, are required for this query, with the result determined by the composition of these functions. This process is illustrated in Figure 7.1.

1.1   SPEECH-BASED MEDIA TYPES

The Xtrieve system supports speech-based media as a major data type. Speech-based media, digital media that include or are predominantly speech audio, is one of the largest categories of media data. Speech is the most common form of communication and databases are accumulating massive quantities of broadcast programming, interviews, legal proceedings, speeches, and much more. As this data accumulates, high quality search tools that permit the location of specific content are becoming critically important. The *Speak Alexandria* project, an on-going DEVLAB research project, is specifically interested in the retrieval of speech-based multimedia content.

The general problem of searching speech-based databases necessarily requires large-vocabulary speech recognition tools. This technology is improving, but is still far from ideal and may remain so for some time to come. Therefore, it is useful to examine the problem area in search of a constraint that allows fast and accurate searching of a significant subset of that content.

A result in this work has been alignment of text-based and speech-based media objects. Xtrieve has an indexing core designed for rapid retrieval of textual content. The cross-modal IR capabilities of Xtrieve allow for the conversion of a text document query result to equivalent content in a speech-based media object. The result is fast, accurate, and efficient retrieval of speech-based media, provided a transcript is available.

Speech-based media can be divided into three classes of content, referred to as script-less, script-tight, and script-light content. Figure 7.2 illustrates the three classes of speech-based content with examples. *Script-less* content

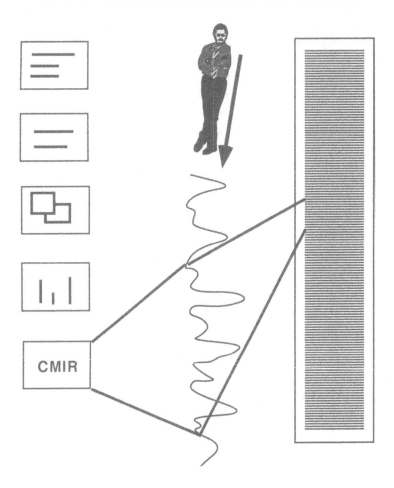

Figure 7.1.   Two level cross-modal retrieval example.

is media for which no transcription exists (live recordings, etc.). The only reasonable solutions to information retrieval in script-less content are based on large-vocabulary speech recognition tools and are beyond the scope of this volume.

Script-tight content is speech audio for which a temporally aligned transcription exists. The most common example of such content is closed-captioned television broadcasting. The ViewStation project at MIT demonstrated searching broadcast programming based on closed-caption data [68]. Compared to speech recognition technologies, this technique is trivial to implement and as accurate as the captioning. It has been noted, however, by researchers at Carnegie Mellon University that closed-caption data is not always sufficient for information retrieval purposes due to the fact that the alignment error may

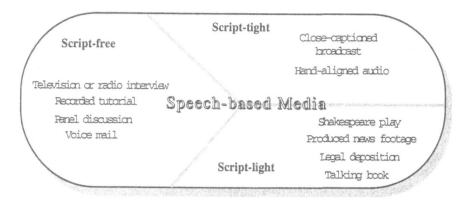

Figure 7.2.   Three classes of speech-based media.

be up to 25 seconds [53]. Consequently, closed-captioned content is some-times considered script-light content and subjected to an alignment process to improve the quality of the captioning alignment.

Script-light content is speech-based audio content for which an unaligned (unsynchronized) transcription exists. This is a surprisingly large category of content. Most broadcasting is produced from a script, though only what is aired is closed-captioned. Recordings of dramatic productions are of great interest to researchers in the arts and nearly always have scripts available. Legal proceedings are commonly recorded and transcribed. Services such as Lexis-Nexis routinely transcribe major political speeches, debates, and proceedings. In fact, closed-captioning often begins as script-light content that is then hand aligned by a human operator [109]. The ability to retrieve such content through a fast and accurate mechanism is essential in many applications.

There is a significant advantage to applying cross-modal information re-trieval to script-light content rather than using the same techniques used for script-less content, i.e., automatic transcription technologies. The script repre-sents the actual content and can drive computed synchronization tools with the words that exist in the content rather than attempting to automatically recognize the text and produce a new transcription. Much higher accuracy is possible using the CMIR approach.

1.2   CROSS-MODAL BROWSING

The Xtrieve query processing engine is text-based. One reason for this em-phasis on text and speech content is that little is known about query processing beyond text. Query-based retrieval of audio, images, and video remains an open problem with only limited general results [56, 85, 117].

An alternative to query-based retrieval is the mechanism of *browsing*, the facilitated exploration of a media object [7, 27, 118, 129]. Given a media object, browsing provides tools for exploring the object's contents as quickly as possible. Common tools include VCR-like controls and the ability to jump about in the object. More complex browsing tools can include summaries, storyboards, decreased resolution representations, key frames, and salient stills (composed images representative of a video sequence) [7, 122].

Xtrieve supports cross-modal browsing, a new browsing approach. Two media objects have a cross-modal relationship if media synchronization data exists between them. Cross-modal browsing implies the simultaneous presentation of browsing results in a related media object.

2.   XTRIEVE OPERATION OVERVIEW

Xtrieve has been designed to facilitate exploration of the capabilities and advantages of cross-modal retrieval. An additional design objective of the Xtrieve system has been the development of effective user interfaces for cross-modal retrieval and cross-modal browsing.

Figure 7.3 shows the main interface window for the Xtrieve system following a query. This image has been labeled to indicate the major components of the user interface. The query is the term "ex-parrot." Section 3.4 describes the search engine in more detail. Both text and video results have been returned in response to this query. Query results are presented at varying granularities in Xtrieve. In this example the granularity has been selected as "Paragraph/Speech/Stanza." Granularity is an important feature in a multimedia database, particularly when results can be presented temporally. Presenting results as complete media objects typically produces a result too large for effective user examination.

Two types of results are indicated in the window. Those with an associated score, a numeric value between 0.00 and 1.00, are direct results of the textual search mechanism. The score indicates the quality of the match between the query and the text. The second result type, indicated by an Xtrieve logo icon in place of the score, is a cross-modal result. Cross-modal results always follow the related query result.

To the left of each of the results is an icon indicating the result media type. Xtrieve currently supports audio, video, and text media objects. Video objects are assumed to have associated audio tracks. Clicking on an icon activates the appropriate *media browser*. Xtrieve has media browsers for all supported data types. Figure 7.4 is the Xtrieve SGML document browser, Figure 7.5 is the Xtrieve audio media browser, and Figure 7.6 is the Xtrieve video media browser. Each of the temporal media browsers includes a *temporal results bar*. The bar illustrates the range of a selection and the current location in the range. Clicking on the bar moves the current playback location to anywhere in the

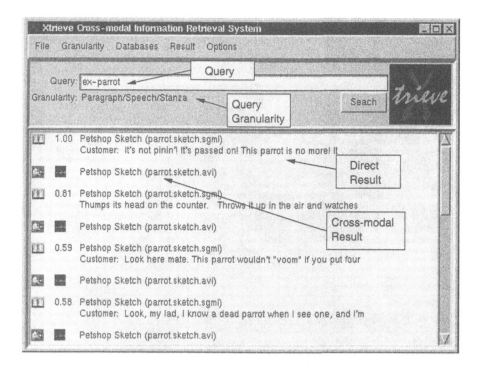

Figure 7.3.   Xtrieve system main window.

media object. Dragging the mouse within the bar allows rapid examination of digital video frames or digital audio. The VCR-like controls allow playback of the selected range as well as content in the vicinity of the selected range or anywhere else in the media object. A query often directs a user only to the neighborhood of the desired result in the media data. The result in then located manually using browsing. The default option is for audio and video playback to commence immediately upon activation of the appropriate media browser. Text results are highlighted in the SGML document browser.

In all of the Xtrieve browsers it is possible to select a range of content. If a cross-modal result exists in another open browser window, the cross-modal equivalent of the selection is selected in that window as well. This allows for playback of desired speech audio based on a text selection, for example, or the study of equivalent translated content. Xtrieve browser windows can be placed side-by-side on the screen for rapid examination of cross-modal selections.

It is assumed in Xtrieve that all content browsing begins with a query-based selection. Some applications may not support a query-based search at all, particularly cross-modal applications involving only images, audio, or video. In such cases it is assumed that a starting media object must be reached through the query mechanism in some way. In Xtrieve the assumption is

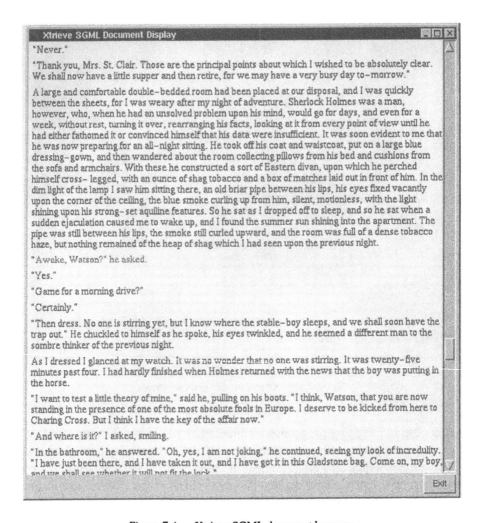

Figure 7.4. Xtrieve SGML document browser.

Figure 7.5. Xtrieve audio browser.

that annotation text is available to allow selection of a media object. As an example, annotation text can lead to an image collection that enjoys a cross-modal relationship with a video object. A text-based query is used to find the image collection (which would actually be contained in a document in Xtrieve)

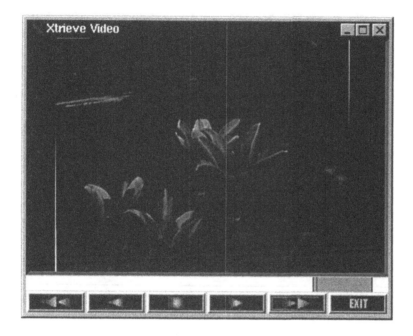

Figure 7.6.   Xtrieve video browser.

and the video is automatically presented as a cross-modal result. Content-based query mechanisms using existing image and video search technologies are a future area of research for Xtrieve development.

3.   SYSTEM STRUCTURE

Figure 7.7 illustrates the major components of the Xtrieve system with major connections roughly indicated. This section describes each of these components.

3.1   IMAGETCL

IMAGETCL is the development platform for Xtrieve [72, 93, 90, 94]. Figure 7.7 has an outer box labeled "IMAGETCL" that contains all other components. This is an illustration of the relation of Xtrieve to the IMAGETCL multimedia development system [90]. In many ways, IMAGETCL has formed the system foundation for the development of computed synchronization techniques.

A more detailed description of IMAGETCL can be found in Owen (1997) [90]. Briefly, IMAGETCL creates a *data-flow* model of computation, wherein media data is processed by vertices in a directed multi-graph (*objects*) and passed on to additional vertices via edges (connections) [83]. The IMAGETCL objects can have attachments called *modules* that enhance or provide specific features for an

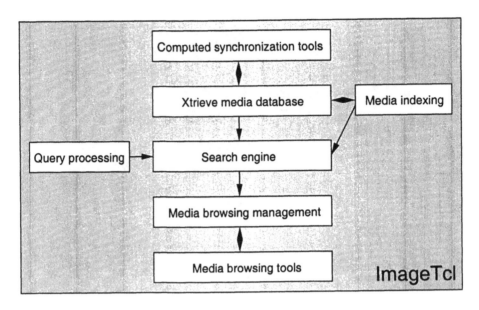

Figure 7.7.   Xtrieve system block diagram.

object. As an example, Algorithm 4.2 has been implemented in IMAGETCL as the object `itsyncgeneral`. The inputs to the object are media representation graphs (several types exists in IMAGETCL). A module is attached to provide a specific media element comparison tool.

Media synchronization has been a major design goal as IMAGETCL has been developed. Consequently, many synchronization related tools are standard IMAGETCL components. Table 7.1 lists some of the IMAGETCL components utilized by Xtrieve. Standard IMAGETCL components such as image viewers and common media processing objects are omitted. Each component is prefixed with **it** or **xt**. A prefix of **it** is an indication that the component is a core IMAGETCL component. A prefix of **xt** indicates that the component is a custom Xtrieve component. A unique feature of IMAGETCL is that custom components (written in C++) are easy to develop and integrate into the system. Each component has a listed type. A *class* (technically an *option* in IMAGETCL) is a C++ superclass providing general functionality. Additional components are built upon these classes. Objects are the vertices in the IMAGETCL data-flow model. *Modules* are attachments to objects. Items labeled *data* are the data types passed along the edges between objects. IMAGETCL supports a large set of standard media data types including images, audio, video, and generic matrix and vector types. Data types not specific to this application are omitted from the table.

Figure 7.8 presents an IMAGETCL data-flow diagram for the text-to-speech application presented in Chapter 6. The majority of the figure components are objects, with arrows representing data-flow connections. `xtbiphonecompare`

Table 7.1. ĪMAGEȚCL components used by Xtrieve.

Component	Type	Description
itaudioresample	object	Audio sample rate conversion.
itaudiowaveform	object	Audio waveform display for hand-marking support.
itmediaelement	class	Superclass for media elements.
itmediafilein	object	General purpose media file input.
itmediagraphmodify	object	General MRG modification object.
itmediarepgr	class	Superclass for media representation graphs.
itmgmodbypass	module	Edit modeling MRG modification module.
itsgml	object	SGML processing in ĪMAGEȚCL .
itsgmlwordgraph	object	SGML to words MRG conversion.
itsgmlwordindex	object	SGML to indexing support file conversion.
itsgmltk	object	SGML document browser.
itsynccompute	object	Algorithm 4.2 optimized for synchronous applications.
itsyncfile	object	Synchronization data file support.
itsyncgeneral	object	Algorithm 4.2 general implementation.
ittemporal	object	Temporal synchronization management. Used by browsers.
itwordgraphconnect	data	Words MRG data type.
xtaviplay	object	Digital video browser for Xtrieve.
xtbiphonecompare	module	Comparison module for biphones.
xtbiphoneprobabilities	object	Speech front-end processing.
xtindexcreate	object	Text IR index construction tool.
xtindexsearch	object	Text IR query processing.
xtmediadb	object	The Xtrieve media database.
xttgbiphoneexpand	object	Phoneme and biphone expansion in a transcription MRG.
xttrangraphconnect	data	Transcription MRG data type.
xtwgtotg	object	Words MRG to Transcription MRG conversion.
xtwordcompmod	module	WordNet-based words comparison module.

is a module attached to `itsynccomp` that provides the media element comparison function. Similar data-flow diagrams exist for many of the components in Xtrieve. In ĪMAGEȚCL, data-flow graphs are routinely constructed, modified, and destroyed as necessary, so no single diagram exists for the entire Xtrieve system.

ĪMAGEȚCL is structured as a set of components and a Tcl interpreter [87]. The Tcl interpreter provides a scripting language for indicating the connections between the components (sometimes called *glue*). During the course of Xtrieve development many custom scripts were produced which provided intermediate results for evaluation and presentation, tested software components in isolation, and produced indexing, reference, and graphic files. An advantage of the development approach used by ĪMAGEȚCL is that these script-based tools have access to all of the Xtrieve components and run under the same executable as

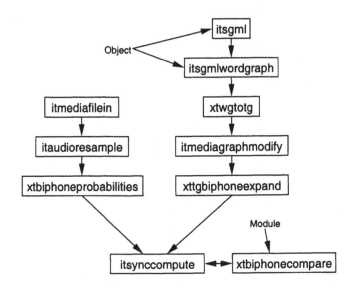

Figure 7.8.   IMAGETCL data-flow diagram of text-to-speech alignment application.

Xtrieve itself. The specific Xtrieve functionality is provided by IMAGETCL scripts (approximately 3,500 lines of code).

3.2   COMPUTED SYNCHRONIZATION TOOLS

The major computational components of Xtrieve are the computed synchronization tools. As an experimental system, these tools are run off-line using IMAGETCL scripts (though, as discussed in the previous section, only one Xtrieve-enhanced IMAGETCL executable exists). A final system would build this functionality into the overall user interface. However, as a research system, these tools have been highly instrumented in order to gather statistics and to gauge system and algorithm performance.

Two general purpose IMAGETCL objects, itsyncgeneral and itsynccompute, implement two variations of Algorithm 4.2, the multiple media correlation algorithm. The itsyncgeneral implementation is a completely general implementation as the algorithm is presented. The itsynccompute implementation has been optimized for pair-wise synchronous applications such as text-to-speech alignment. Note that neither implementation is aware in any way of the media type. Both implementations use a system of "plug-in" comparison modules and are supplied with generic media representation graphs as input (the synchronous application only processes one synchronous MRG vertex for each algorithm step, however).

3.3   MEDIA DATABASE

The Xtrieve media database is implemented as a simple relational database with four major relations. The first of these is the set of multimedia data objects. Xtrieve manages text, audio, and video media types (an additional "other" type is supplied for future expansion). The other relations manage sets of SGML DTDs, DSSSL Style Sheets, and computed synchronization data. These components are discussed in detail in this section.

The use of SGML has been found to be critically important in the design of Xtrieve as is discussed in Section 4.1. All text documents in Xtrieve are in SGML format. SGML is a language for describing a *markup format* for a text document. Markup is the addition of distinct syntactic elements (tags) to a document to indicate the structure of the document. *Document Type Definitions* (DTDs) are associated with SGML documents, and define the markup format in use for a particular document instance [5, 116]. A DTD defines a major document type. Xtrieve has DTDs for plays, religious works, news programming, and a standard DTD, TEI (Text Encoding Initiative) [57], used in the study of classic literature.

SGML is a general mechanism for describing the structure of a document. It is specifically meant to divorce document structure from presentation format. Some additional mechanism is required to associate format with an SGML DTD, relating the generalities of SGML document structure with the specifics of page layout, fonts, and text styles. Xtrieve uses the *Document Style Semantics and Specifications Language* (DSSSL) to associate format with structure [62]. DSSSL is an international standard for precisely describing the appearance of an SGML document when displayed. Xtrieve also extends the uses of DSSSL to associating indexing granularity and analysis with structure. Section 4.2 describes these advanced issues.

The text index in Xtrieve is *structured*. It allows retrieval at varying granularities. Different levels of granularity are defined by different levels of tag nesting in SGML. A DSSSL style sheet is used to specify the meaning of the various levels of nesting.

Finally, Xtrieve maintains a database of all computed synchronization data. Synchronization data is only computed once for any media object pair. Once computed, the data serves as a cross-modal index in Xtrieve.

All synchronization data in Xtrieve are assumed to be pair-wise and are stored as a set of *range associations*. A range association is a range in one media object and an associated range in the other. Figure 7.2 presents some example range associations using an excerpt from a real synchronization data file. The left two columns represent the range in a text file. In this alignment example, extracted from a text-to-speech alignment data file, the text document range is always exactly one word index. The right two columns present the

Table 7.2.   Synchronization data example.

μ_1 range		μ_2 range	
322	322	430	610
328	328	620	740
333	333	750	1050
337	337	1060	1470
346	346	1480	1520

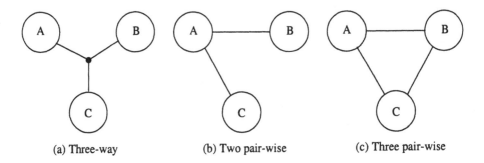

(a) Three-way   (b) Two pair-wise   (c) Three pair-wise

Figure 7.9.   Pair-wise equivalence of three-way synchronization computation.

equivalent ranges in an audio file. The values are in milliseconds relative to the beginning of the file and represent the start and end of the word presentation.

The path compression implementation used by itsyncgeneral and itsync-compute selects a minimal set of range associations such that synchronization resolution is maintained. Details of path compression are omitted here.

The general implementation of Algorithm 4.2 in itsyncgeneral allows specification of input media representation graph (MRG) pairs that result in synchronization data-files. A three-way synchronization operation can be represented as two or three pair-wise synchronization data objects. Figure 7.9 illustrates two equivalent representations of a three-way normalization. In this example, three media objects, labeled A, B, and C, have synchronization relationships. The relationships are shown undirected in this figure because Xtrieve assumes synchronization data is invertible. Figure 7.9(b) is the simple scenario taking advantage of the transitive relationship to allow synchronization between B and C. This transitive relationship is an approximation, and each level of synchronization can result in error accumulation. Figure 7.9(c) illustrates pair-wise selection of all results.

Synchronization data may not always be invertible, as discussed in Section 6.6. Xtrieve assumes invertibility of all synchronization data though application of the following heuristic. Let $q = (\alpha_2, \beta_2)$ be a range defined on media object μ_2. The cross-modal range in media object μ_1 is determined by selecting all synchronization ranges overlapped by q in μ_2 and computing a minimum range that contains all translated ranges in μ_1. As an example, referring to the Figure 7.2 data, a range in μ_1 of 328–333 maps directly to a range of 620–1050 in μ_2. A range of 700–1100 in μ_2 overlaps the ranges 620–740, 750–1050, and 1060–1470. These ranges correspond to the ranges 328–328, 333–333, and 337–337 in μ_1. A minimum range in μ_1 containing these translated ranges would be 328–337.

3.4   MEDIA INDEXING

Media indexing is the support structure for conversion of queries to results in a multimedia database. Xtrieve is meant to provide a test-bed for cross-modal retrieval of multimedia content. Consequently, the text indexing development was limited to application of existing code, specifically a modified version of the indexing core of Automatic Site Markup Language (ASML) [92]. This code creates an inverted word index for a document collection in a B-tree form that can be searched very quickly. The multi-granularity indexing features of Xtrieve were implemented by simply creating a unique index for each level.

The advantages of the ASML indexing engine include availability and very fast retrieval from large collections. However, it is primitive by modern IR standards. An interesting future enhancement of Xtrieve is the inclusion of a more advanced IR indexing core, possibly through an adaptation of the Smart system [111].

As a word-based retrieval system, Xtrieve has a deterministic behavior and will retrieve the desired result provided the keywords are indicative of that result. Basically, search performance in Xtrieve is as good as the text IR system used for searching and the quality of the computed synchronization results. Computed synchronization result evaluation has been discussed in Chapters 5 and 6. Text IR technologies are a different research focus than this work.

3.5   QUERY PROCESSING AND SEARCH ENGINE

Xtrieve accepts queries and dispatches them to the search engine. The search engine initially searches the selected text index, testing each query result against the available cross-modal synchronization data. A cross-modal result is supplied if a textual solution translates to a valid range in the cross-modal media object. This may not always be the case — content in a text document may have been deleted in presentation and may not have a cross-modal equivalent.

3.6   MEDIA BROWSING

Media browsing management in Xtrieve assigns media objects to browsing windows. This assignment is designed to provide a user friendly interface that allows simultaneous presentation of multiple modalities. When browsing, any synchronization relationships between browsing windows are used to cross-highlight or display results. As an example, highlighting content in one text document automatically cross-highlights the equivalent selection in an alternative text document or plays the appropriate segments of an equivalent audio or video media object.

An interesting user interface issue in media browsing is the granularity of selections (as opposed to queries as discussed earlier), both in the original document and in the cross-modal result. Xtrieve allows for user control of this granularity. Selections can optionally be expanded to granularity boundaries (sentences or paragraphs for example). For many applications, particularly parallel-text alignment, word-level alignment means very little, while sentences, paragraphs, or stanzas mean considerably more. In such applications a mouse click or drag selects not the word or words, but the granularity unit containing the words. Likewise, Xtrieve allows the cross-modal result to be expanded to granularity boundaries as a user-selected option.

4.   ISSUES

Xtrieve development was a rich source of new problems and solutions regarding both CMIR and multimedia database design. Many issues were raised in the system development. This section describes some of these issues and the approaches chosen in the Xtrieve system design.

4.1   IMPORTANCE OF STRUCTURED DOCUMENT PROCESSING

Media objects often include considerable structural information not relevant to media alignment, such as meta-data in audio and video file formats. Meta-data information is not generally an issue because it is clearly defined and easily ignored. Text-based media objects, on the other hand, are very unconstrained. A script for a news program contains not only what is spoken by the commentator, but also the speaker names, control information such as tape insertion indications or commercial breaks, and major program control data such as times, places, and dates. This additional content shows up as noise in the alignment process and should be avoided for maximum accuracy.

The simple solution for ensuring relevance in the alignment process is to clearly indicate what elements of a document are subject to alignment. For a news program, the elements that are spoken are of interest, not the additional control information. Heuristic approaches such as avoiding capitalized names are not effective in real systems. The solution for this problem in Xtrieve is the use of structured documents. All text documents in Xtrieve are valid SGML documents. Using SGML, spoken lines are clearly indicated. As an example, Table 7.3 is excerpted from the play Hamlet as marked up with the

Table 7.3. SGML markup of Hamlet excerpt.

```
<SPEECH>
<SPEAKER>LORD POLONIUS</SPEAKER>
<LINE>Come, sirs.</LINE>
</SPEECH>
<SPEECH>
<SPEAKER>HAMLET</SPEAKER>
<LINE>Follow him, friends: we'll hear a play to-morrow.</LINE>
<STAGEDIR>Exit POLONIUS with all the Players but the First</STAGEDIR>
<LINE>Dost thou hear me, old friend; can you play the</LINE>
<LINE>Murder of Gonzago?</LINE>
</SPEECH>
```

Xtrieve "Play" DTD. The lines, stage directions, and speaker names are clearly indicated.

Xtrieve is expected to work with content from a variety of sources, and these sources do not always provide the content in an appropriate SGML format. Plays, religious works, and classic literature in the Xtrieve test data were commonly available in SGML markup formats and could be used directly. However, for other content, the most common solution was to create scripts that converted content to SGML. Scripts have been developed to convert raw text documents, transcripts provided by CNN and ABC, and some content from Lexis/Nexis to SGML formats automatically. The scripts are written in the Tcl scripting language, which provides a powerful regular expression substitution capability and fast processing of text content. Content from these sources can be automatically converted and added to the Xtrieve database with no user editing or intervention.

4.2   STRUCTURED DOCUMENT ASSOCIATIONS

DSSSL is a powerful Scheme-based formatting language used in Xtrieve to associate format with SGML document structure. As an example, the play lines in Table 7.3 are displayed with speaker names to the left and lines to the right in the Xtrieve SGML document browser, while stage directions appear in italics. In the Xtrieve development project two very similar issues arose: associating alignment processing with structure and associating indexing granularity with structure. It was decided that the general tool of DSSSL could be adapted to these needs as well.

DSSSL has the ability to ignore content contained in specific tags. This feature is normally used when content is displayed using some other method (the `process-matching-children` function for example) or if the content need not be displayed at all (control information for example). An alternative style sheet simply prevents the processing of undesirable content during the alignment process:

```
(element (SPEECH SPEAKER)
         (empty-sosofo))
```

The empty-sosofo function instantiates an empty *specification of a stream of flow objects*. A flow object describes how content is formatted. The DSSSL function empty-sosofo indicates that content will not be formatted, or displayed, at all. For more details on DSSSL functions, the reader is referred to the DSSSL standards document [62].

The primary function of style sheets in analysis is the omitting of irrelevant content. When associating SGML levels with varying granularities for indexing, the issue becomes indicating the various granularity levels. DSSSL style sheets are used to insert distinctive literal values (which are later recognized by the index processing) into a version of the document. These literal values indicate beginnings and endings of granularity levels.

A complete set of example DSSSL style sheets and a DTD from the Xtrieve system for broadcast news programming is included in Appendix C.

4.3   INDEXING UNDER ALTERNATIVE PRESENTATION

Indexing, analysis, and display processing of SGML documents in Xtrieve utilize alternative style-sheets, so the actual documents displayed or processed are *transformations* of the original document. The alternative representations may not include all word content, much less word and character placement on lines or in files. Xtrieve manages this issue by associating an invariant *index code* with every document word. This code follows the word through processing and ensures that alternative document presentations can exist that reference the same content. The actual index code is related to the byte offset of the word in the original SGML file.

The association of an index code ensures the processed SGML/DSSSL output maintains a semi-equivalence relationship with the original document (semi-equivalence is defined in Section 3.2). The fidelity measure is the ability to reconstruct the original file such that the word index can be recovered for each word. Maintaining a word index in association with each word allows that capability. Semi-equivalence relationships after processing are necessary if the processed document must be related to the original. This is clearly the case given the requirement that alignment or indexing computed on the processed document must be translated to equivalent information for the original document. An index range after DSSSL processing must be translated to an index range in the original document that includes the exact same words.

Table 7.4. Xtrieve search granularity levels.

1	Sentence/Line
2	Paragraph/Speech/Stanza
3	Scene
4	Act
5	Front Matter
9	Document

4.4 TRANSITIVE CROSS-MODAL RESULTS

For each direct result (query or browsing result), Xtrieve attempts to find all possible cross-modal results. This task is accomplished by creating an undirected graph with edges representing direct (single level) synchronization relationships and vertices representing database media objects. Each direct result corresponds to a vertex in this graph. A breadth-first search of the graph locates all available cross-modal results and *the shortest path to the result*. The shortest path is chosen to minimize any cumulative alignment error. Xtrieve makes no attempt to differentiate identical length redundant paths and selects one of the redundant paths arbitrarily.

4.5 MEDIA RETRIEVAL AND GRANULARITY

Retrieval of temporal content requires selection of search granularity. While it is useful to locate a specific text document containing given search terms, it is less useful to locate a 30 minute video segment. Xtrieve uses DSSSL stylesheets to associate search granularity with SGML document entities. The basic Xtrieve search granularities are listed in Table 7.4. Front matter is meta-data included at the beginning of a document. Levels 6 to 8 are reserved for future expansion.

Table 7.4 illustrates that retrieval granularity need not be in strictly hierarchical divisions. Some initial support has been included in the Xtrieve system for retrieval of all content spoken by a single speaker, for example. A "play rehearsal system" that speaks all of the lines in a play except for those of one speaker would be another interesting application.

4.6 DATABASE ISSUES

The database in Xtrieve is a simple flat-file database. Actual media content is stored in original format files with indirect referencing via file names. A future project is to extend Xtrieve to include a full feature relational database management system.

The cross-modal indexing features of Xtrieve require searching of the synchronization data during query time. At this time, Xtrieve uses a simple sequential search of that data and caches synchronization data to accelerate searches. Initial search performance is impacted by this structure, but subsequent searches of similar content are very fast, typically less than one second. Range tree data structures exist that can significantly improve this performance as Xtrieve is scaled to much larger document collections [88]. Again, this is the subject of future work.

5.   SUMMARY

This chapter has introduced the Xtrieve cross-modal information retrieval system. Xtrieve is the first multimedia IR system specifically designed to exploit the value of computed synchronization and is one of the few systems in existence that can accept user queries and produce truly relevant audio and video results.

Xtrieve works by combining conventional text IR and multimedia browsing technologies with computed synchronization data. That data allows the conversion of query results in well understood media such as text to results in complex media such as audio and video. Xtrieve provides demonstration of concept for computed synchronization applications.

The development of Xtrieve brought to light many new questions about multimedia database systems. The granularity of queries must necessarily be of a higher resolution in a multimedia system including temporal content than in a text retrieval system. Also, sensitivity to user interaction with varying granularities is very important. User experience with Xtrieve seems to indicate that retrieval granularity of paragraphs is appropriate much of the time. Expansion of cross-modal selections to the chosen granularity has been found to be useful, since common inter-media alignment errors include omitting a word from the beginning of a selection. This is particularly true for parallel text alignment. The first word in a paragraph or sentence is often in the stop list and omitted from the analysis process.

Unconstrained document formats present problems when analysis is required. A general solution in Xtrieve is to use a standard structured document format and style-sheets to associate indexing and analysis with structured documents. This is the first known use of DSSSL for analysis and indexing support and is a promising problem solution approach.

Chapter 8

APPLICATIONS AND FUTURE WORK

Computed multimedia synchronization and multiple media correlation are new areas of research in multimedia data analysis. As such, the applications and solutions presented in this book are the Genesis of this new research area. This chapter describes many potential applications for multiple media technologies, as well as possibilities for core research in multiple media analysis and computed synchronization. This chapter is representative of planned future work in this field. Some of these applications are already in preliminary development at the DEVLAB and the Michigan State University Media and Entertainment Technologies Laboratory (METLAB), while others represent future research areas proposed or planned.

Chapters 5 and 6 presented applications for multiple media correlation that have been implemented, and Chapter 7 described the Xtrieve system, an information retrieval system that exploits computed synchronization for multimedia database content location. These applications were chosen for generality and immediate usefulness, particularly in the Xtrieve system. However, these applications represent only two of many possible practical uses for multiple media correlation.

The challenge in new applications is applying the synchronization framework. The use of multiple media correlation and, in particular, Algorithm 4.2 for solving media correlation problems requires a methodology for construction of media representation graphs with a semi-equivalence relationship among the media objects and a definition of a media element comparison technique. Media representation graphs are a general tool and a natural representation for many media types and are the standard tool for representing media objects as input to Algorithm 4.2. In most cases the real application complexity is the media element comparison strategy.

1.   SLIDE-TO-PRESENTATION ALIGNMENT

A continuing research topic for many years at the DEVLAB has been multimedia reproductions of conference and classroom presentations [35, 106, 107]. The model for these presentations is nearly always that of a lecturer and slides, where the slides may be projections of a computer display or view-graphs. A considerable number of video and audio recordings of presentations has been collected. An interesting question is how best to search these presentations.

The presentations in question vary from 20 minutes to over an hour in length. Simply shuttling back and forth in the video is ineffective when specific information is desired. The content is script-less (no transcription exists), so the Chapter 6 techniques are not useful in this application (though transcriptions can and have been produced in some previous DEVLAB projects). One key to searching these presentations is the set of presentation slides.

Slides are an interesting summary of a presentation. Most presentations use a small set of slides relative to the quantity of video or audio media data the presentation may produced and slides must be readable from any location in a room. Consequently, slides tend to present topic bullets, tables, complex equations, and other high-density elements of the presentation, but not all of the content of the presentation. They are intended to be, quite literally, visual aids, not the actual presentation. However, they provide a key for finding content in the presentation. Slides are compact, and visually browsing even a large lecture slide set takes very little time. Given the common use of computer presentation tools such as PowerPoint and SliTex, slides often exist in searchable electronic forms.

Multiple media correlation is used in this this application to compute an alignment between the slides and a video of the lecture presentation. The problem is referred to as *slides-to-presentation alignment*. Simply seeking the best slide to associate with each video frame is not an effective method for computing this alignment. Such a solution will likely suffer from noise-induced rapid slide switching, and a resulting illogical presentation sequence. This is a synchronous application in that the video is represented by a synchronous MRG.

1.1   MEDIA ELEMENT COMPARISON

Media element comparison is, of course, the most complicated element of this problem. Slides under presentation are subject to cropping, considerable perspective distortion, significant contrast loss, and other degradations. Figure 8.1 illustrates an original slide image (a) and a degraded slide image taken from video (b). The distortion in the presented slide is obvious.

Preliminary work has been done on this project. Some of the obvious heuristic approaches, such as discovering the slide outline, turn out to be

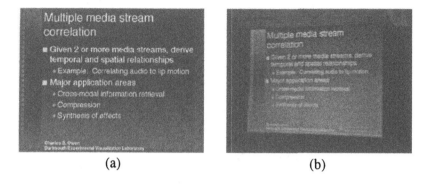

Figure 8.1.   Original and degraded presentation slides.

impractical when compared to the DEVLAB presentation library due to the large number of hand produced slides which do not present a clear rectangular border. Image gradient-based alignment techniques have also been ruled out due to the fact that slides are typically flat shaded and have limited gradient [121]. Indeed, it has been discovered that the only real content in slides is in the edges, so current work focuses on edge and feature point detection followed by feature point correspondence [38, 114]. Specific features are corner points and the end of content lines [119]. A limited set of features that is highly representative of the slide content is desired. Results are too preliminary to report at this time.

1.2   SLIDES MRG

Assuming a slide comparison routine that allows differentiation among slides with local noise and some uncertainty, the prerequisite to effective results in slides-to-presentation alignment is an effective slides media representation graph. The slides MRG should be of the form illustrated in Figure 8.2. "Tween" represents a vertex that does not match any slides, but is between the presentation of slides. "Tween" serves the same purpose as ".garbage" in the text-to-speech alignment application, providing a catch-all for noise not matching any slide, specifically the slide change process.

For Figure 8.2 to be effective, it is absolutely necessary that duration modeling be used for the slide vertices. Section 7.2 discusses duration modeling approaches. In preliminary experimentation, duration modeling has been implemented using sequential identical vertices without loop-back and a final vertex with loop-back. Slides have been required to obey a two second minimum presentation. Without duration modeling, Figure 8.2 allows many simple local cycles.

This application does not assume monotonicity in the slide presentation. It is common that slides are repeated in presentations, particularly near the end of

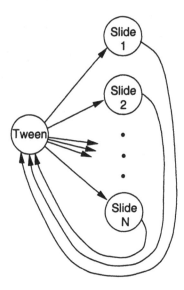

Figure 8.2.   Presentation slides MRG.

the presentation when questions are asked. Heuristic approaches to controlling the estimated slide appearance order are under investigation.

1.3   VIDEO MRG

Video is represented by sequential vectors of media element comparison values, just as speech audio is in the text-to-speech application. As in that application, the video MRG is synchronous, so the synchronous algorithm performance enhancements are available.

Many additional performance enhancements are also possible. Frame differencing, comparing the contents of successive frames of video, is used to detect frame sequences likely to present an identical slide. Cut detection, a common application of frame differencing technologies, is unlikely to be effective given that most presentations are recorded as a single camera sequence, but the general change detection technologies can be effective [2]. When little change is noted, the previous frame scores are repeated. This simple enhancement can eliminate about 80% of all media element comparisons, assuming even groups as small as four frames are common.

2.   FUNCTIONAL MAGNETIC RESONANCE IMAGING

Another application of multiple media correlation currently under joint development in the DEVLAB and the Dartmouth Medical School Brain Imaging Lab is medical diagnostic analysis of functional magnetic resonance imaging (fMRI). fMRI captures image sequences that detail changes in cerebral blood flow, a valuable clue in the search for an understanding of the operation of the brain [9, 41, 40]. fMRI is a non-invasive technique. Subjects can be imaged repeatedly and large studies performed. Early experimentation is underway wherein multiple media correlation is applied to fMRI datasets in order to better understand the human brain. The general goal of the project is to develop rich, immersive multimedia patient stimuli and tools for the correlation of stimuli instances with fMRI datasets. A specific multiple media correlation goal is to precisely classify spatial and temporal characteristics of brain activation in the presence of multimedia stimuli (video and audio), thereby providing a valuable tool for the diagnosis and treatment of disease as well as a better understanding of how the brain functions.

This section describes preliminary work in the application of multiple media correlation to fMRI experiments. The techniques described in this section are closely related to those used in Statistical Parametric Mapping [120].

In the analysis of fMRI data, the two streams ($N = 2$) undergoing correlation are the multimedia subject stimulus μ_1 and the fMRI image sequence μ_2. A subject is placed in the machine, and during a finite period (typically 3 minutes for the GE scanner available for this work) a multimedia stimulus is made available to the subject. Stimuli media formats available in this work include images, video, and audio. It is common that the subject is expected to interact with the stimulus.

During the experiment period, the scanner captures sequential brain volume sets. Each volume set consists of slice images which, as a collection, represent a three-dimensional view of the brain. The recorded activation value at three-dimensional locations in the dataset, referred to as voxels, is tuned to differentiate oxy- and deoxy-hemoglobin. Hence, the temporal changes in the voxel values are an indication of regional cerebral blood flow (rCBF). Positron emission tomography (PET) and fMRI research seem to indicate that variations in rCBF are indicative of local brain activity [39].

After the brain volume set is captured, a motion analysis/cancelation operation is applied to remove subject head motion during the test [120]. The value of a single voxel for each capture period (once every two seconds for example), forms a waveform. If a waveform is available to represent the history of the stimulus delivery, correlation of the two waveforms can help identify areas of the brain related to that activity.

Figure 8.3 is a concrete example of this process. In this experiment a subject was presented with an audio stimulus requesting rapid finger tapping in alternation with rest periods. The box-car waveform in the plot represents the times the subject was requested to tap as maximum values and rest periods as minimum values. This waveform was correlated with all voxel sequences. The voxel sequence that maximally correlated with the stimulus waveform is

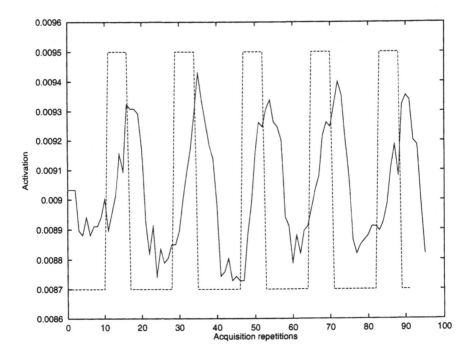

Figure 8.3. fMRI stimulus and activation waveforms.

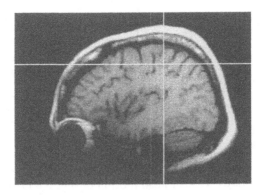

Figure 8.4. Spatial localization for fMRI activation.

plotted in the figure. Figure 8.4 illustrates the localization of this voxel in sagittal slice 4, counting from the left-most slice of 20 slices.

One characteristic obvious in Figure 8.3 is a delay between stimulus and activation. This is expected, given that activation is tracking blood flow, a fluidic activity. This delay represents the *hemodynamic response character-istic* of the brain. This delay characteristic is not well understood and is of considerable interest to researchers. Correlation activity in the Brain Imaging

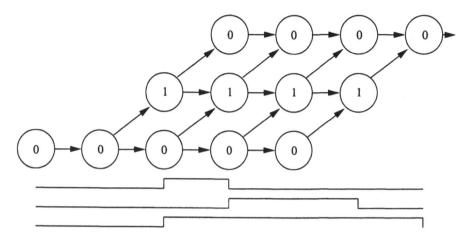

Figure 8.5.   Stimulus MRG example.

Lab accommodates this delay by shifting application of the stimulus waveform during correlation and selecting an offset that maximizes a correlation value. While this approach is effective in discovering global delay characteristics, it is not effective at discovering local characteristics. Also, as stimuli become more complex (immersive multimedia, virtual reality), the potential benefits of accurate alignment of the stimulus to the activation waveforms increase. This is particularly the case when stimulus events are impulses rather than periods. The *MediaStim multimedia experiment management system* currently under development at the Brain Imaging Lab and the DEVLAB particularly stresses the requirements of analysis.

2.1   STIMULUS MRG

As in all previous examples, the current fMRI application of multiple media correlation is based on construction of media representation graphs. The brain activation data MRG is treated as a simple synchronous MRG. The media element value is the brain activation value for each time period. Voxels are treated independently, the process described in this section is used to determine a best alignment and a correlation score. Scores are thresholded to determine voxels considered to be maximally correlated to an activity.

Figure 8.5 illustrates one technique for constructing a stimulus MRG assuming an on/off stimulus pattern. Several paths through the MRG are plotted below the MRG to illustrate the range of variation. This example is, of course, at decreased resolution (real MRGs have more nodes representing smaller temporal intervals). The example accommodates a stimulus delay of up to three units and duration ranges from one to four units. This MRG format is similar to duration modeling, but differs in that it ensures the entire event duration is strictly controlled, so as to not offset future activation patterns.

2.2   MEDIA ELEMENT COMPARISON

The media element comparison technique used in this application is:

$$\rho(\mu_1(s_1), \mu_2(s_2)) = -(\mu_1(s_1) - 0.5)(\mu_2(s_2) - \overline{\mu_2}) \qquad (8.1)$$

μ_1 is the stimulus MRG and $\mu_1(s) \in [0,1], \forall s = 1, ..., |\mu_1|$. μ_2 is the brain activation data MRG. $\overline{\mu_2}$ is the mean of the activation sequences and is pre-computed prior to algorithm application. This function represents an approximation of "anti-correlation", the negative of simple correlation. This element comparison strategy violates the condition that $\rho \geq 0$. However, the MRGs are directed and acyclic, so the supergraph is also directed and acyclic. The reason for preventing negative media element comparison values was to ensure monotonically increasing path scores which, in turn, ensures simple paths in the search tree. However, cyclic paths are not possible in this application, so that constraint can be waived. This is yet another example of a special case problem instance that allows improved or changed performance for Algorithm 4.2. Once an optimum causal normalization of the stimulus waveform is selected using Algorithm 4.2, a score is assigned using the conventional correlation coefficient [58]:

$$\rho_{i,j} = \frac{\sigma_{i,j}}{\sigma_i \sigma_j} \qquad (8.2)$$

3.   ADDITIONAL APPLICATIONS

There are many other applications for computed media alignment. An early media alignment system called WordFit is described in [21] and has been in use in motion picture production for many years. WordFit temporally aligns speech audio to alternative speech audio. It is used to align a newly "dubbed" audio track to the original, where the original is deemed unsuitable due to poor audio quality or bad acting. WordFit is based on alignment of speech to speech. An open problem is the alignment of speech to video, which is useful for for restoration of films where the audio track has been lost and for foreign language dubbing.

Speaker localization is the location in each video frame of the moving lips that maximally correlate to speech-based audio in an image sequence. Speaker localization helps identify the speaker in a sequence, and is a prerequisite technology for lip resynchronization, the re-warping of the lips in an image sequence to better match an alternative sound-track.

Musical score alignment is the alignment of musical scores to a performance. This problem is very similar in structure to text-to-speech alignment, though the media element comparison strategy is considerably different. It is expected that musical score alignment can be performed using *chordal events*, periods of the score represented by a particular combination of fundamental tones. Musical score alignment has applications in performance, music education, and music retrieval.

Degraded media alignment is the realignment of a media object to match an original template of that object. It is assumed that the degraded media may have been skewed temporally or spatially. This problem is of particular interest to the media signatures or watermarks community [34]. A common method for defeating watermarks is to apply local skew. Watermark techniques that assume comparison to an original template are not able to recover from skew attacks unless the degraded copy can be accurately realigned to the original. Multiple media correlation is a promising tool for the realignment of audio applications, though general applicability to images and other 2-D applications is not obvious.

Another future research area is *speech-reading*, utilizing lip motion information derived from image sequences to enhance the recognition of speech [30, 77]. Lip motion can also be derived using sensor techniques [63]. Multiple media correlation and multiple media data analysis have great potential for modeling the detection of correlations between the audio and lip motion streams in this application in order to better identify correlates for input to analysis systems.

An application that requires analysis of multiple media streams simultaneously is the automatic generation of multimedia presentations [8, 18]. Simultaneous analysis of multiple streams is necessary to detect cues for data segmentation and composition. In most application of this sort, media synchronization is known a priori.

Of course, humans are highly multi-modal. Much work seeks to exploit this user characteristic in order to increase the efficiency of human-computer interaction [126, 127]. Multiple media correlation provides a framework for selecting and emphasizing correlates among media objects.

4. FUTURE COMPUTED SYNCHRONIZATION RESEARCH

As a new solution approach, multiple media correlation cannot be assumed to be a final, completely optimal solution. Possible enhancements to the algorithm are sure to exist that will increase performance. In particular, the algorithms and approaches presented in this book tend to be batch approaches designed to be run off-line and often requiring considerable computational resources.

While media processing is commonly a heavy consumer of resources, major advances in performance are always a benefit.

A source for ideas on improving the performance of Algorithm 4.2 is the work in improving speech system and Viterbi approaches. Laface, Vair, and Fissore accelerate the Viterbi algorithm by detecting likely transitions and avoiding search branches in many cases [66]. Their work trades recognition accuracy for execution performance enhancements. However, this tradeoff has not proved useful in computed synchronization applications given the lowered expectation of content quality. Patel describes a lower complexity Viterbi algorithm [100]. However, the Patel approach only improves performance for fully connected models. Fully connected media representation graphs are unlikely to be useful given the $O(N^2)$ edge memory requirement.

The most likely place to look for performance improvements is the large amount of redundancy in MRGs. Words, phrases, and other media element sequences are often repeated. A nested multi-resolution approach to media correlation may be possible that exploits this redundancy to improve performance, though a method of implementing these ideas is not clear.

The edit strategies presented in this volume have proved effective in application, but do not yield the highly accurate edit determination that is often desired. A subject of future research is a two-pass approach to edit modeling that includes a second pass to fine-tune the edit boundaries.

5.   SUMMARY

The many applications presented in this book are an indication that multiple media correlation is a general tool with wide-spread applicability. Multiple media correlation cannot not solve these problems alone; it requires a media element comparison strategy, which can be difficult to define in some applications. However, multiple media correlation provides a strong framework for the definition of problem solutions and algorithms that can solve all of the problems presented in this chapter, given the required basic tools.

These results have proved to be very realizable, having been implemented as a component of the IMAGECL multimedia development system. It is of particular interest that the implementations are completely blind to underlying media components. Multiple applications can share common core elements, and new applications can be tested in minimal time.

As multiple media correlation moves to new vistas, it is hoped that others will examine the ideas presented in this book and carry on this work. Multimedia research has for too long focused only on single modalities. The potential for mining simultaneous content in multiple domains needs to be examined if practical retrieval and automatic presentation systems are to be devised. Xtrieve illustrates that computed synchronization makes possible the fine-grain retrieval of multimedia content in a practical system.

Appendix A
English Phonetic Labels

This book uses phonetic labels based on WorldBet, a standard international phonemic labeling system. This appendix lists the core WorldBet phonetic labels. Also listed in Table A.4 are extensions to the WorldBet label set added to facilitate this work. Closures, sounds preceding words, and diacritics, modifications to labels, are omitted since they play no role in this work.

Some labels included in these tables are not actually used. For example, the specifically British alternative pronunciations such as i& and 5 are not included in training data, pronunciation dictionaries, or pronunciation rules since these were built using the *American English* dialect.

These tables are based on a set of IPA (International Phonetic Alphabet), WorldBet, and OGIbet comparison tables in the OGI speech tools documentation [112].

Table A.1. WorldBet English phonetic labels: non-speech items.

WorldBet	Non-speech Sound Item
.bn	Background noise
.br	Breath noise
.cough	Cough
.ct	Clear throat
.laugh	Laugh
.ln	Line noise
.ls	Lip smack
.ns	Human, but not speech
.sneeze	Sneeze
.tc	Tongue Click

Table A.2.   WorldBet English phonetic labels: vowels.

WorldBet	Example	Category
i:	b<u>ee</u>t	
I	b<u>i</u>t	Front
E	b<u>e</u>t	Vowels
@	b<u>a</u>t	
Lx	ros<u>es</u>	
u_x	s<u>ui</u>t	Central
&	<u>a</u>bove	Vowels
&_O	t<u>o</u> go	
5	p<u>o</u>t	(British)
u	b<u>oo</u>t	
U	b<u>oo</u>k	Back
^	ab<u>o</u>ve	Vowels
>	c<u>au</u>ght	
A	f<u>a</u>ther	
3r	b<u>ir</u>d	Retro-
&r	butt<u>er</u>	flexes
ei	b<u>ay</u>	
aI	b<u>ye</u>	Diph-
>i	b<u>oy</u>	thongs
iU	f<u>ew</u>	
aU	ab<u>ou</u>t	
oU	b<u>oat</u>	
i&	b<u>ere</u>	(British)
e&	th<u>ere</u>	(British)
u&	p<u>oor</u>	(British)

Table A.3.   WorldBet English phonetic labels: consonants.

WorldBet	Example	Category
ph	pan	Voiceless
th	tan	Plosives
kh	can	
b	ban	Voiced
d	dan	Plosives
g	gander	
m	me	Nasals
n	knee	
N	sing	
th_(	writer	Flaps
d_(	rider	
f	fine	
T	thigh	Voiceless
s	sign	Fricatives
S	assure	
h	hope	
v	vine	
D	thy	Voiced
z	resign	Fricatives
Z	azure	
tS	church	Affricate
dZ	judge	
l	lent	Glides
9r	rent	
j	yes	(approxi-
w	went	mants)
m=	bottom	
n=	button	Syllabics
l=	bottle	

Table A.4.   Phonetic labels: non-WorldBet labels.

Label	Non-speech Sound Item
.pau	Pause between words
.garbage	Unknown noise

Appendix B
Odyssey Simultaneous Translations

This appendix presents an example of simultaneous alignment. The specific texts are Book 1 of *The Odyssey* by Homer. The translations are by Samuel Butler, a prose translation, and George Chapman, a verse translation.

The effectiveness of presenting the alignment of two text documents in print is limited. The Xtrieve system provides a more effective user interface for viewing the document correspondence. The following presentation is based on breakdowns of the Butler text on the left with the corresponding Chapman text on the right. In order to most effectively demonstrate the alignment, the Butler text has been cut into smaller pieces. Likewise, the Chapman text is displayed without verse orientation.

Each alignment point was rounded to the nearest sentence or line end. Longer sentences in the Butler text are sometimes broken when they aligned to very large segments of the Chapman text.

Figure B.1 is an alignment plot for this translation. The plot is based on the alignment of media representation graphs and includes only non-stop-list words. The near-diagonal nature of the plot is evidence that segments of the translations have similar ratios of number of words. However, this plot is clearly not an exact diagonal.

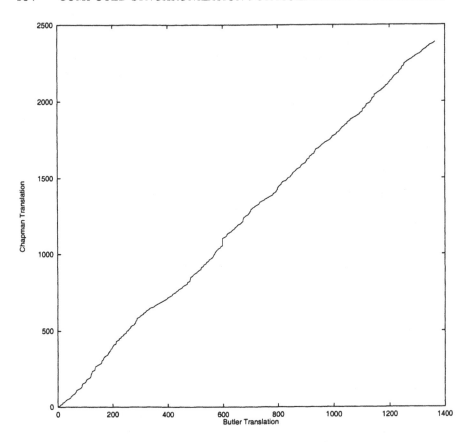

Figure B.1.   Plot of Butler and Chapman translation synchronization.

Samuel Butler Translation:

Tell me, O muse, of that ingenious hero who traveled far and wide after he had sacked the famous town of Troy. Many cities did he visit, and many were the nations with whose manners and customs he was acquainted; moreover he suffered much by sea while trying to save his own life and bring his men safely home;

George Chapman Translation:

The man, O Muse, inform, that many a way wound with his wisdom to his wished stay; that wandered wondrous far, when he the town of sacred Troy had sack'd and shivered down; the cities of a world of nations, with all their manners, minds, and fashions, he saw and knew; at sea felt many woes, much care sustained, to save from overthrows himself and friends in their retreat for home;

but do what he might he could not save his men, for they perished through their own sheer folly in eating the cattle of the Sun-god Hyperion; so the god prevented them from ever reaching home. Tell me, too, about all these things, O daughter of Jove, from whatsoever source you may know them.

So now all who escaped death in battle or by shipwreck had got safely home except Ulysses, and he, though he was longing to return to his wife and country, was detained by the goddess Calypso, who had got him into a large cave and wanted to marry him.

But as years went by, there came a time when the gods settled that he should go back to Ithaca; even then, however, when he was among his own people, his troubles were not yet over; nevertheless all the gods had now begun to pity him except Neptune, who still persecuted him without ceasing and would not let him get home.

Now Neptune had gone off to the Ethiopians, who are at the world's end, and lie in two halves, the one looking West and the other East. He had gone there to accept a hecatomb of sheep and oxen, and was enjoying himself at his festival;

but the other gods met in the house of Olympian Jove, and the sire of gods and men spoke first. At that moment he was thinking of Ægisthus, who had been killed by Agamemnon's son Orestes; so he said to the other gods:

But so their fates he could not overcome, though much he thirsted it. O men unwise, they perish'd by their own impieties, that in their hunger's rapine would not shun the oxen of the lofty-going Sun, who therefore from their eyes the day bereft of safe return. These acts, in some part left, tell us, as others, deified Seed of Jove.

Now all the rest that austere death outstrove at Troy's long siege at home safe anchor'd are, free from the malice both of sea and war; only Ulysses is denied access to wife and home. The grace of Goddesses, the reverend nymph Calypso, did detain him in her caves, past all the race of men

Enflam'd to make him her lov'd lord and spouse. and when the Gods had destin'd that his house, which Ithaca on her rough bosom bears, (The point of time wrought out by ambient years) should be his haven, Contention still extends her envy to him, even amongst his friends. All Gods took pity on him; only he, that girds earth in the cincture of the sea, divine Ulysses ever did envy, and made the fix'd port of his birth to fly.

But he himself solemnized a retreat to th' Æthiops, far dissunder'd in their seat, (In two parts parted, at the sun's descent, and underneath his golden orient, the first and last of men) t' enjoy their feast of bulls and lambs, in hecatombs address'd; at which he sat, given over to delight.

The other Gods in heaven's supremest height were all in council met; to whom began the mighty Father both of God and man discourse, inducing matter that inclined to wise Ulysses, calling to his mind faultful Ægisthus, who to death was done by young Orestes, Agamemnon's son. his memory to the Immortals then

"See now, how men lay blame upon us gods for what is after all nothing but their own folly. Look at Ægisthus; he must needs make love to Agamemnon's wife unrighteously and then kill Agamemnon, though he knew it would be the death of him;

for I sent Mercury to warn him not to do either of these things,

inasmuch as Orestes would be sure to take his revenge when he grew up and wanted to return home.

Mercury told him this in all good will but he would not listen, and now he has paid for everything in full."

Then Minerva said, "Father, son of Saturn, King of kings, it served Ægisthus right, and so it would any one else who does as he did; but Ægisthus is neither here nor there; it is for Ulysses that my heart bleeds, when I think of his sufferings in that lonely sea-girt island, far away, poor man, from all his friends.

It is an island covered with forest, in the very middle of the sea, and a goddess lives there, daughter of the magician Atlas, who looks after the bottom of the ocean, and carries the great columns that keep heaven and earth asunder.

Mov'd Jove thus deeply: "O how falsely men accuse us Gods as authors of their ill, when by the bane their own bad lives instil they suffer all the miseries of their states, past our inflictions, and beyond their fates. as now Ægisthus, past his fate, did wed the wife of Agamemnon, and (in dread to suffer death himself) to shun his ill,

Incurred it by the loose bent of his will, in slaughtering Atrides in retreat. which we foretold him would so hardly set to his murderous purpose, sending Mercury that slaughter'd Argus, our considerate spy, to give him this charge: "Do not wed his wife, nor murder him; for thou shalt buy his life

With ransom of thine own, imposed on thee by his Orestes, when in him shall be Atrides' self renew'd, and but the prime of youth's spring put abroad, in thirst to climb his haughty father's throne by his high acts."

These words of Hermes wrought not into facts Ægisthus' powers; good counsel he despised, and to that good his ill is sacrificed."

Pallas, whose eyes did sparkle like the skies, answer'd: "O Sire! Supreme of Deities, Ægisthus past his fate, and had desert to warrant our infliction; and convert may all the pains such impious men inflict on innocent sufferers to revenge as strict, their own hearts eating. But, that Ithacus, thus never meriting, should suffer thus, I deeply suffer. His more pious mind

Divides him from these fortunes. Though unkind is piety to him, giving him a fate more suffering than the most unfortunate, so long kept friendless in a sea-girt soil, where the sea's navel is a sylvan isle, in which the Goddess dwells that doth derive her birth from Atlas, who of all alive the motion and the fashion doth command with his wise mind, whose forces understand the inmost deeps and gulfs of all the seas, who (for his skill of things superior) stays the two steep columns that prop earth and heaven.

This daughter of Atlas has got hold of poor unhappy Ulysses, and keeps trying by every kind of blandishment to make him forget his home, so that he is tired of life, and thinks of nothing but how he may once more see the smoke of his own chimneys. You, sir, take no heed of this, and yet when Ulysses was before Troy did he not propitiate you with many a burnt sacrifice? Why then should you keep on being so angry with him?"

His daughter 'tis, who holds this homeless-driven still mourning with her; evermore profuse of soft and winning speeches, that abuse and make so languishingly, and possest with so remiss a mind her loved guest, manage the action of his way for home. Where he, though in affection overcome, in judgment yet more longs to show his hopes, his country's smoke leap from her chimney tops, and death asks in her arms. Yet never shall thy lov'd heart be converted on his thrall, austere Olympius. Did not ever he, in ample Troy, thy altars gratify, and Grecians' fleet make in thy offerings swim?

And Jove said, "My child, what are you talking about?

O Jove, why still then burns thy wrath to him?" The Cloud-assembler answer'd: "What words fly,

How can I forget Ulysses than whom there is no more capable man on earth, nor more liberal in his offerings to the immortal gods that live in heaven?

Bold daughter, from thy pale of ivory? As if I ever could cast from my care divine Ulysses, who exceeds so far all men in wisdom, and so oft hath given to all th' Immortals throned in ample heaven so great and sacred gifts?

Bear in mind, however, that Neptune is still furious with Ulysses for having blinded an eye of Polyphemus king of the Cyclopes.

But his decrees, that holds the earth in with his nimble knees, stand to Ulysses' longings so extreme, for taking from the God-foe Polypheme his only eye; a Cyclop, that excelled all other Cyclops, with whose burden swell'd

Polyphemus is son to Neptune by the nymph Thoosa, daughter to the sea-king Phorcys; therefore though he will not kill Ulysses outright, he torments him by preventing him from getting home. Still, let us lay our heads together and see how we can help him to return; Neptune will then be pacified, for if we are all of a mind he can hardly stand out against us."

The nymph Thoosa, the divine increase of Phorcys' seed, a great God of the seas. She mix'd with Neptune in his hollow caves, and bore this Cyclop to that God of waves. For whose lost eye, th' Earth-shaker did not kill erring Ulysses, but reserves him still in life for more death. But use we our powers, and round about us cast these cares of ours, all to discover how we may prefer his wished retreat, and Neptune make forbear his stern eye to him, since no one God can, in spite of all, prevail, but 'gainst a man."

And Minerva said, "Father, son of Saturn, King of kings, if, then, the gods now mean that Ulysses should get home, we should first send Mercury to the Ogygian island to tell Calypso that we have made up our minds and that he is to return.

In the meantime I will go to Ithaca, to put heart into Ulysses' son Telemachus; I will embolden him to call the Achaeans in assembly, and speak out to the suitors of his mother Penelope, who persist in eating up any number of his sheep and oxen;

I will also conduct him to Sparta and to Pylos, to see if he can hear anything about the return of his dear father- for this will make people speak well of him."

So saying she bound on her glittering golden sandals, imperishable, with which she can fly like the wind over land or sea; she grasped the redoubtable bronze-shod spear, so stout and sturdy and strong, wherewith she quells the ranks of heroes who have displeased her, and down she darted from the topmost summits of Olympus, whereon forthwith she was in Ithaca, at the gateway of Ulysses' house, disguised as a visitor, Mentes, chief of the Taphians, and she held a bronze spear in her hand.

To this, this answer made the grey-eyed Maid: "Supreme of rulers, since so well apaid the blessed Gods are all then, now, in thee, to limit wise Ulysses' misery, and that you speak as you referred to me prescription for the means, in this sort be their sacred order: Let us now address with utmost speed our swift Argicides,

To tell the nymph that bears the golden tress in th' isle Ogygia, that 'tis our will she should not stay our loved Ulysses still, but suffer his return; and then will I to Ithaca, to make his son apply his sire's inquest the more; infusing force into his soul, to summon the concourse of curl'd-head Greeks to council, and deter each wooer, that hath been the slaughterer of his fat sheep and crooked-headed beeves,

From more wrong to his mother, and their leaves take in such terms, as fit deserts so great. To Sparta then, and Pylos, where doth beat bright Amathus, the flood, and epithet to all that kingdom, my advice shall send the spirit-advanced Prince, to the pious end of seeking his lost father, if he may receive report from Fame where rests his stay, and make, besides, his own sucessive worth known to the world, and set in action forth."

This said, her wing'd shoes to her feet she tied, Formed all of gold, and all eternified, That on the round earth or the sea sustain'd Her ravish'd substance swift as gusts of wind. Then took she her strong lance with steel made keen, great, massy, active, that whole hosts of men, though all heroes, conquers, if her ire their wrongs inflame, back'd by so great a Sire. Down from Olympus' tops she headlong dived, and swift as thought in Ithaca arriv'd, close at Ulysses' gates; in whose first court she made her stand, and, for her breast's support, leaned on her iron lance; her form impress'd

There she found the lordly suitors seated on hides of the oxen which they had killed and eaten, and playing draughts in front of the house. Men-servants and pages were bustling about to wait upon them, some mixing wine with water in the mixing-bowls, some cleaning down the tables with wet sponges and laying them out again, and some cutting up great quantities of meat.

Telemachus saw her long before any one else did. He was sitting moodily among the suitors thinking about his brave father, and how he would send them flying out of the house, if he were to come to his own again and be honoured as in days gone by.

Thus brooding as he sat among them, he caught sight of Minerva and went straight to the gate, for he was vexed that a stranger should be kept waiting for admittance. He took her right hand in his own, and bade her give him her spear. "Welcome," said he, "to our house, and when you have partaken of food you shall tell us what you have come for."

He led the way as he spoke, and Minerva followed him. When they were within he took her spear and set it in the spear-stand against a strong bearing-post along with the many other spears of his unhappy father, and he conducted her to a richly decorated seat under which he threw a cloth of damask.

There was a footstool also for her feet, and he set another seat near her for himself, away from the suitors, that she might not be annoyed while eating by their noise and insolence, and that he might ask her more freely about his father.

With Mentas' likeness, come, as being a guest. There found she those proud wooers, that were then set on those ox-hides that themselves had slain, before the gates, and all at dice were playing. To them the heralds, and the rest obeying, fill'd wine and water; some, still as they play'd, and some, for solemn supper's state, purvey'd, with porous sponges, cleansing tables, serv'd with much rich feast; of which to all they kerv'd. God-like Telemachus amongst them sat, griev'd much in mind; and in his heart begat

All representment of his absent sire, how, come from far-off parts, his spirits would fire with those proud wooers' sight, with slaughter parting their bold concourse, and to himself converting

The honours they usurp'd, his own commanding. In this discourse, he first saw Pallas standing, unbidden entry; up rose, and address'd his pace right to her, angry that a guest should stand so long at gate; and, coming near, her right hand took, took in his own her spear, and thus saluted: "Grace to your repair, fair guest, your welcome shall be likewise fair.

Enter, and, cheer'd with feast, disclose th' intent that caused your coming." This said, first he went, and Pallas follow'd. To a room they came, steep, and of state; the javelin of the Dame he set against a pillar vast and high, amidst a large and bright-kept armory, which was, besides, with woods of lances grac'd of his grave father's. In a throne he plac'd the man-turn'd Goddess, under which was spread a carpet, rich and of deviceful thread;

A footstool staying her feet; and by her chair another seat (all garnish'd wondrous fair, to rest or sleep on in the day) he set, far from the prease of wooers, lest at meat the noise they still made might offend his guest, disturbing him at banquet or at rest, even to his combat with that pride of theirs, that kept no noble form in their affairs. And these he set far from them, much the rather to question freely of his absent father. A table fairly-polish'd then was spread, on which a reverend officer set bread,

A maid servant then brought them water in a beautiful golden ewer and poured it into a silver basin for them to wash their hands, and she drew a clean table beside them. An upper servant brought them bread, and offered them many good things of what there was in the house, the carver fetched them plates of all manner of meats and set cups of gold by their side, and a man-servant brought them wine and poured it out for them.

Then the suitors came in and took their places on the benches and seats. Forthwith men servants poured water over their hands, maids went round with the bread-baskets, pages filled the mixing-bowls with wine and water, and they laid their hands upon the good things that were before them.

As soon as they had had enough to eat and drink they wanted music and dancing, which are the crowning embellishments of a banquet, so a servant brought a lyre to Phemius, whom they compelled perforce to sing to them. As soon as he touched his lyre and began to sing Telemachus spoke low to Minerva, with his head close to hers that no man might hear.

"I hope, sir," said he, "that you will not be offended with what I am going to say. Singing comes cheap to those who do not pay for it, and all this is done at the cost of one whose bones lie rotting in some wilderness or grinding to powder in the surf. If these men were to see my father come back to Ithaca they would pray for longer legs rather than a longer purse, for money would not serve them; but he, alas, has fallen on an ill fate, and even when people do sometimes say that he is coming, we no longer heed them; we shall never see him again.

And other servitors all sorts of meat (Salads, and flesh, such as their haste could get) serv'd with observance in. And then the sewer pour'd water from a great and golden ewer, that from their hands t' a silver caldron ran. Both wash'd, and seated close, the voiceful man fetch'd cups of gold, and set by them, and round those cups with wine with all endeavour crown'd.

Then rush'd in the rude wooers, themselves plac'd; the heralds water gave; the maids in haste serv'd bread from baskets. When, of all prepar'd and set before them, the bold wooers shar'd, their pages plying their cups past the rest.

But lusty wooers must do more than feast; for now, their hungers and their thirsts allay'd, they call'd for songs and dances; those, they said, were th' ornaments of feast. The herald straight a harp, carv'd full of artificial sleight, thrust into Phemius', a learn'd singer's, hand, who, till he much was urged, on terms did stand, but, after, play'd and sung with all his art. Telemachus to Pallas then (apart, his ear inclining close, that none might hear) in this sort said: "My guest, exceeding dear,

Will you not sit incens'd with what I say? These are the cares these men take; feast and play. Which eas'ly they may use, because they eat, free and unpunish'd, of another's meat; and of a man's, whose white bones wasting lie in some far region, with th' incessancy of showers pour'd down upon them, lying ashore, or in the seas wash'd naked. Who, if he wore those bones with flesh and life and industry, and these might here in Ithaca set eye on him return'd, they all would wish to be either past other in celerity of feet and knees, and not contend t' exceed in golden garments. But his virtues feed the fate of ill death; nor is left to me the least hope of his life's recovery, no, not if any of the mortal race should tell me his return; the cheerful face

And now, sir, tell me and tell me true, who you are and where you come from. Tell me of your town and parents, what manner of ship you came in, how your crew brought you to Ithaca, and of what nation they declared themselves to be–

for you cannot have come by land. Tell me also truly, for I want to know, are you a stranger to this house, or have you been here in my father's time? In the old days we had many visitors for my father went about much himself."

And Minerva answered, "I will tell you truly and particularly all about it. I am Mentes, son of Anchialus, and I am King of the Taphians. I have come here with my ship and crew, on a voyage to men of a foreign tongue being bound for Temesa with a cargo of iron, and I shall bring back copper.

As for my ship, it lies over yonder off the open country away from the town, in the harbour Rheithron under the wooded mountain Neritum. Our fathers were friends before us, as old Laertes will tell you, if you will go and ask him. They say, however, that he never comes to town now, and lives by himself in the country, faring hardly, with an old woman to look after him and get his dinner for him, when he comes in tired from pottering about his vineyard.

Of his return'd day never will appear. But tell me, and let Truth your witness bear, who, and from whence you are? What city's birth? What parents? In what vessel set you forth? And with what mariners arrived you here? I cannot think you a foot passenger. Recount then to me all, to teach me well

Fit usage for your worth. And if it fell in chance now first that you thus see us here, or that in former passages you were my father's guest? For many men have been guests to my father. Studious of men his sociable nature ever was." On him again the grey-eyed Maid did pass

This kind reply: "I'll answer passing true all thou hast ask'd: My birth his honour drew from wise Anchialus. The name I bear is Mentas, the commanding islander of all the Taphians studious in the art of navigation; having touch'd this part with ship and men, of purpose to maintain course through the dark seas t' other-languag'd men; and Temesis sustains the city's name for which my ship is bound, made known by fame for rich in brass, which my occasions need, and therefore bring I shining steel in stead, which their use wants, yet makes my vessel's freight,

That near a plough'd field rides at anchor's weight, apart this city, in the harbour call'd rethrus, whose waves with Neius' woods are wall'd. Thy sire and I were ever mutual guests, at either's house still interchanging feasts. I glory in it. Ask, when thou shalt see Laertes, th' old heroe, these of me, from the beginning. He, men say, no more visits the city, but will needs deplore his son's believed loss in a private field; one old maid only at his hands to yield

They told me your father was at home again, and that was why I came, but it seems the gods are still keeping him back, for he is not dead yet not on the mainland.

It is more likely he is on some sea-girt island in mid ocean, or a prisoner among savages who are detaining him against his will I am no prophet, and know very little about omens,

but I speak as it is borne in upon me from heaven, and assure you that he will not be away much longer; for he is a man of such resource that even though he were in chains of iron he would find some means of getting home again.

But tell me, and tell me true, can Ulysses really have such a fine looking fellow for a son? You are indeed wonderfully like him about the head and eyes, for we were close friends before he set sail for Troy where the flower of all the Argives went also. Since that time we have never either of us seen the other."

"My mother," answered Telemachus, tells me I am son to Ulysses, but it is a wise child that knows his own father. Would that I were son to one who had grown old upon his own estates, for, since you ask me, there is no more ill-starred man under heaven than he who they tell me is my father."

Food to his life, as oft as labour makes his old limbs faint; which, though he creeps, he takes along a fruitful plain, set all with vines,

Which husbandman-like, though a king, he proins. But now I come to be thy father's guest; I hear he wanders, while these wooers feast. And (as th' Immortals prompt me at this hour) I'll tell thee, out of a prophetic power, (not as profess'd a prophet, nor clear seen at all times what shall after chance to men) what I conceive, for this time, will be true: The Gods' inflictions keep your sire from you.

Divine Ulysses, yet, abides not dead above earth, nor beneath, nor buried in any seas, as you did late conceive, but, with the broad sea sieged, is kept alive within an isle by rude and upland men, that in his spite his passage home detain. uet long it shall not be before he tread his country's dear earth, though solicited, and held from his return, with iron chains;

For he hath wit to forge a world of trains, and will, of all, be sure to make good one for his return, so much relied upon. But tell me, and be true: Art thou indeed so much a son, as to be said the seed of Ithacus himself? Exceeding much thy forehead and fair eyes at his form touch; for oftentimes we met, as you and I meet at this hour, before he did apply his powers for Troy, when other Grecian states in hollow ships were his associates. But, since that time, mine eyes could never see.renown'd Ulysses, nor met his with me."

The wise Telemachus again replied: "You shall with all I know be satisfied. My mother certain says I am his son; I know not; nor was ever simply known by any child the sure truth of his sire. But would my veins had took in living fire from some man happy, rather than one wise,

And Minerva said, "There is no fear of your race dying out yet, while Penelope has such a fine son as you are. But tell me, and tell me true, what is the meaning of all this feasting, and who are these people?

What is it all about? Have you some banquet, or is there a wedding in the family- for no one seems to be bringing any provisions of his own? And the guests- how atrociously they are behaving; what riot they make over the whole house; it is enough to disgust any respectable person who comes near them."

"Sir," said Telemachus, "as regards your question, so long as my father was here it was well with us and with the house, but the gods in their displeasure have willed it otherwise, and have hidden him away more closely than mortal man was ever yet hidden.

I could have borne it better even though he were dead, if he had fallen with his men before Troy, or had died with friends around him when the days of his fighting were done; for then the Achaeans would have built a mound over his ashes, and I should myself have been heir to his renown; but now the storm-winds have spirited him away we know not wither; he is gone without leaving so much as a trace behind him, and I inherit nothing but dismay.

Whom age might see seis'd of what youth made prise. But he whoever of the mortal race is most unblest, he holds my father's place. This, since you ask, I answer." She, again: "The Gods sure did not make the future strain both of thy race and days obscure to thee, since thou wert born so of Penelope. The style may by thy after act be won, of so great sire the high undoubted son. Say truth in this then: What's this feasting here? What all this rout? Is all this nuptial cheer?

Or else some friendly banquet made by thee? For here no shots are, where all sharers be. Past measure contumeliously this crew fare through thy house; which should th' ingenuous view of any good or wise man come and find,

(Impiety seeing play'd in every kind) he could not but through every vein be mov'd." Again Telemachus: "My guest much loved, since you demand and sift these sights so far, I grant 'twere fit a house so regular, rich, and so faultless once in government, should still at all parts the same form present that gave it glory while her lord was here. But now the Gods, that us displeasure bear, have otherwise appointed, and disgrace my father most of all the mortal race. for whom I could not mourn so were he dead,

Amongst his fellow captains slaughtered by common enemies, or in the hands of his kind friends had ended his commands, after he had egregiously bestow'd his power and order in a war so vow'd, and to his tomb all Greeks their grace had done, that to all ages he might leave his son immortal honour; but now Harpies have digg'd in their gorges his abhorred grave.

Nor does the matter end simply with grief for the loss of my father; heaven has laid sorrows upon me of yet another kind; for the chiefs from all our islands, Dulichium, Same, and the woodland island of Zacynthus, as also all the principal men of Ithaca itself, are eating up my house under the pretext of paying their court to my mother, who will neither point blank say that she will not marry, nor yet bring matters to an end; so they are making havoc of my estate, and before long will do so also with myself."

"Is that so?" exclaimed Minerva, "then you do indeed want Ulysses home again. Give him his helmet, shield, and a couple lances, and if he is the man he was when I first knew him in our house, drinking and making merry, he would soon lay his hands about these rascally suitors, were he to stand once more upon his own threshold.

He was then coming from Ephyra, where he had been to beg poison for his arrows from Ilus, son of Mermerus. Ilus feared the ever-living gods and would not give him any, but my father let him have some, for he was very fond of him. If Ulysses is the man he then was these suitors will have a short shrift and a sorry wedding.

Obscure, inglorious, death hath made his end, and me, for glories, to all griefs contend. Nor shall I any more mourn him alone, the Gods have given me other cause of moan. For look how many optimates remain in Samos, or the shores Dulichian, shady Zacynthus, or how many bear rule in the rough brows of this island here; so many now my mother and this house tt all parts make defamed and ruinous; and she her hateful nuptials nor denies, nor will dispatch their importunities, though she beholds them spoil still as they feast all my free house yields, and the little rest of my dead sire in me perhaps intend to bring ere long to some untimely end."

This Pallas sigh'd and answer'd: "O," said she, "Absent Ulysses is much miss'd by thee, that on thee shameless suitors he might lay his wreakful hands. Should he now come, and stay in thy court's first gates, arm'd with helm and shield,

and two such darts as I have seen him wield, when first I saw him in our Taphian court, feasting, and doing his desert's disport; when from Ephyrus he return'd by us from Ilus, son to Centaur Mermerus, to whom he travell'd through the watery dreads, for bane to poison his sharp arrows' heads, that death, but touch'd, caused; which he would not give, because he fear'd the Gods that ever live would plague such death with death; and yet their fear was to my father's bosom not so dear as was thy father's love; (for what he sought my loving father found him to a thought.) If such as then Ulysses might but meet with these proud wooers, all were at his feet but instant dead men, and their nuptials

"But there! It rests with heaven to determine whether he is to return, and take his revenge in his own house or no; I would, however, urge you to set about trying to get rid of these suitors at once. Take my advice, call the Achaean heroes in assembly to-morrow -lay your case before them, and call heaven to bear you witness.

Bid the suitors take themselves off, each to his own place, and if your mother's mind is set on marrying again, let her go back to her father, who will find her a husband and provide her with all the marriage gifts that so dear a daughter may expect.

As for yourself, let me prevail upon you to take the best ship you can get, with a crew of twenty men, and go in quest of your father who has so long been missing. Some one may tell you something, or (and people often hear things in this way) some heaven-sent message may direct you.

First go to Pylos and ask Nestor; thence go on to Sparta and visit Menelaus, for he got home last of all the Achaeans; if you hear that your father is alive and on his way home, you can put up with the waste these suitors will make for yet another twelve months. If on the other hand you hear of his death, come home at once, celebrate his funeral rites with all due pomp, build a barrow to his memory, and make your mother marry again.

Then, having done all this, think it well over in your mind how, by fair means or foul, you may kill these suitors in your own house. You are too old to plead infancy any longer; have you not heard how people are singing Orestes' praises for having killed his father's murderer Ægisthus?

Would prove as bitter as their dying galls. But these things in the Gods' knees are reposed, if his return shall see with wreak inclosed, these in his house, or he return no more; and therefore I advise thee to explore all ways thyself, to set these wooers gone; to which end give me fit attention: to-morrow into solemn council call the Greek heroes, and declare to all (the Gods being witness) what thy pleasure is.

Command to towns of their nativity, these frontless wooers. If thy mother's mind stands to her second nuptials so inclined, return she to her royal father's towers, where th' one of these may wed her, and her dowers make rich, and such as may consort with grace so dear a daughter of so great a race. And thee I warn as well (if thou as well wilt hear and follow) take thy best built sail, with twenty oars mann'd, and haste t' inquire where the abode is of thy absent sire, if any can inform thee, or thine ear from Jove the fame of his retreat may hear, for chiefly Jove gives all that honours men.

To Pylos first be thy addression then, to god-like Nestor; thence to Sparta haste, to gold-lock'd Menelaus, who was last of all the brass-arm'd Greeks that sail'd from Troy; and try from both these, if thou canst enjoy news of thy sire's returned life, anywhere, though sad thou suffer'st in his search a year. If of his death thou hear'st, return thou home, and to his memory erect a tomb, performing parent-rites, of feast and game, pompous, and such as best may fit his fame; and then thy mother a fit husband give.

These past, consider how thou mayst deprive of worthless life these wooers in thy house, by open force, or projects enginous. Thing childish fit not thee; th' art so no more. Hast thou not heard, how all men did adore divine Orestes, after he had slain Ægisthus murdering by a treacherous train his famous father? Be then, my most loved, valiant and manly, every way approved

You are a fine, smart looking fellow; show your mettle, then, and make yourself a name in story. Now, however, I must go back to my ship and to my crew, who will be impatient if I keep them waiting longer; think the matter over for yourself, and remember what I have said to you."

"Sir," answered Telemachus, "it has been very kind of you to talk to me in this way, as though I were your own son, and I will do all you tell me; I know you want to be getting on with your voyage, but stay a little longer till you have taken a bath and refreshed yourself.

I will then give you a present, and you shall go on your way rejoicing; I will give you one of great beauty and value- a keepsake such as only dear friends give to one another."

Minerva answered, "Do not try to keep me, for I would be on my way at once. As for any present you may be disposed to make me, keep it till I come again, and I will take it home with me. You shall give me a very good one, and I will give you one of no less value in return."

With these words she flew away like a bird into the air, but she had given Telemachus courage, and had made him think more than ever about his father. He felt the change, wondered at it, and knew that the stranger had been a god, so he went straight to where the suitors were sitting.

Phemius was still singing, and his hearers sat rapt in silence as he told the sad tale of the return from Troy, and the ills Minerva had laid upon the Achaeans. Penelope, daughter of Icarius, heard his song from her room upstairs, and came down by the great staircase, not alone, but attended by two of her handmaids.

as great as he. I see thy person fit, noble thy mind, and excellent thy wit, all given thee so to use and manage here that even past death they may their memories bear. In mean time I'll descend to ship and men, that much expect me. Be observant then of my advice, and careful to maintain in equal acts thy royal father's reign."

Telemachus replied: "You ope, fair guest, a friend's heart in your speech, as well express'd as might a father serve t' inform his son; all which sure place have in my memory won. Abide yet, though your voyage calls away, that, having bath'd, and dignified your stay with some more honour, you may yet beside delight your mind by being gratified with some rich present taken in your way, that, as a jewel, your respect may lay up in your treasury, bestow'd by me, as free friends use to guests of such degree."

"Detain me not," said she, "so much inclined to haste my voyage. What thy loved mind commands to give, at my return this way, bestow on me, that I directly may convey it home; which more of price to me

the more it asks my recompence to thee." This said, away grey-eyed Minerva flew, like to a mounting lark; and did endue his mind with strength and boldness, and much more made him his father long for than before; and weighing better who his guest might be, he stood amaz'd, and thought a Deity was there descended; to whose will he fram'd his powers at all parts, and went so inflam'd amongst the wooers, who were silent set, to hear a poet sing the sad retreat the Greeks perform'd from Troy; which was from thence proclaim'd by Pallas, pain of her offence. When which divine song was perceived to bear that mournful subject by the listening ear of wise Penelope, Icarius' seed, who from an upper room had given it heed, down she descended by a winding stair, not solely, but the state in her repair two maids of honour made. And when this queen

When she reached the suitors she stood by one of the bearing posts that supported the roof of the cloisters with a staid maiden on either side of her. She held a veil, moreover, before her face, and was weeping bitterly.

"Phemius," she cried, "you know many another feat of gods and heroes, such as poets love to celebrate. Sing the suitors some one of these, and let them drink their wine in silence, but cease this sad tale, for it breaks my sorrowful heart, and reminds me of my lost husband whom I mourn ever without ceasing, and whose name was great over all Hellas and middle Argos."

"Mother," answered Telemachus, "let the bard sing what he has a mind to; bards do not make the ills they sing of; it is Jove, not they, who makes them, and who sends weal or woe upon mankind according to his own good pleasure. This fellow means no harm by singing the ill-fated return of the Danaans, for people always applaud the latest songs most warmly. Make up your mind to it and bear it;

Ulysses is not the only man who never came back from Troy, but many another went down as well as he. Go, then, within the house and busy yourself with your daily duties, your loom, your distaff, and the ordering of your servants; for speech is man's matter, and mine above all others- for it is I who am master here."

of women stoop'd so low, she might be seen by all her wooers. In the door, aloof, entering the hall grac'd with a goodly roof, she stood, in shade of graceful veils, implied about her beauties; on her either side, her honour'd women. When, to tears mov'd, thus she chid the sacred singer: "Phemius, you know a number more of these great deeds of Gods and men, that are the sacred seeds, and proper subjects, of a poet's song, and those due pleasures that to men belong, besides these facts that furnish Troy's retreat, sing one of those to these, that round your seat they may with silence sit, and taste their wine; but cease this song, that through these ears of mine conveys deserv'd occasion to my heart of endless sorrows, of which the desert in me unmeasur'd is past all these men, so endless is the memory I retain, and so desertful is that memory, of such a man as hath a dignity so broad it spreads itself through all the pride of Greece and Argos." To the queen replied

inspired Telemachus: "Why thus envies my mother him that fits societies with so much harmony, to let him please his own mind in his will to honour these? For these ingenious and first sort of men, that do immediately from Jove retain their singing rapture, are by Jove as well inspir'd with choice of what their songs impell, Jove's will is free in it, and therefore theirs. Nor is this man to blame, that the repairs the Greeks make homeward sings; for his fresh muse men still most celebrate that sings most news.

And therefore in his note your ears employ: For not Ulysses only lost in Troy the day of his return, but numbers more the deadly ruins of his fortunes bore. Go you then in, and take your work in hand, your web, and distaff; and your maids command to ply their fit work. Words to men are due, and those reproving counsels you pursue, and most to me of all men, since I bear

She went wondering back into the house, and laid her son's saying in her heart. Then, going upstairs with her handmaids into her room, she mourned her dear husband till Minerva shed sweet sleep over her eyes. But the suitors were clamorous throughout the covered cloisters, and prayed each one that he might be her bed fellow.

Then Telemachus spoke, "Shameless," he cried, "and insolent suitors, let us feast at our pleasure now, and let there be no brawling, for it is a rare thing to hear a man with such a divine voice as Phemius has; but in the morning meet me in full assembly that I may give you formal notice to depart, and feast at one another's houses, turn and turn about, at your own cost.

If on the other hand you choose to persist in spunging upon one man, heaven help me, but Jove shall reckon with you in full, and when you fall in my father's house there shall be no man to avenge you."

the rule of all things that are managed here." She went amaz'd away, and in her heart laid up the wisdom Pallas did impart to her lov'd son so lately, turn'd again up to her chamber, and no more would reign in manly counsels. To her women she applied her sway; and to the wooers he began new orders, other spirits bewray'd than those in spite of which the wooers sway'd. And (whiles his mother's tears still wash'd her eyes, till grey Minerva did those tears surprise with timely sleep, and that her wooers did rouse
Rude tumult up through all the shady house, disposed to sleep because their widow was) Telemachus this new-given spirit did pass on their old insolence: "Ho! you that are my mother's wooers! Much too high ye bear your petulant spirits; sit; and, while ye may enjoy me in your banquets, see ye lay these loud notes down, nor do this man the wrong, because my mother hath disliked his song, to grace her interruption. 'Tis a thing honest, and honour'd too, to hear one sing numbers so like the Gods in elegance, as this man flows in. By the morn's first light, I'll call ye all before me in a Court, that I may clearly banish your resort, with all your rudeness, from these roofs of mine. Away; and elsewhere in your feasts combine. Consume your own goods, and make mutual feast at either's house. Or if ye still hold best, and for your humours' more sufficed fill, to feed, to spoil, because unpunish'd still, on other findings, spoil; but here I call

Th' Eternal Gods to witness, if it fall in my wish'd reach once to be dealing wreaks, by Jove's high bounty, these your present checks to what I give in charge shall add more reins to my revenge hereafter; and the pains

The suitors bit their lips as they heard him, and marvelled at the boldness of his speech. Then, Antinous, son of Eupeithes, said, "The gods seem to have given you lessons in bluster and tall talking; may Jove never grant you to be chief in Ithaca as your father was before you."

Telemachus answered, "Antinous, do not chide with me, but, god willing, I will be chief too if I can. Is this the worst fate you can think of for me? It is no bad thing to be a chief, for it brings both riches and honour. Still, now that Ulysses is dead there are many great men in Ithaca both old and young, and some other may take the lead among them; nevertheless I will be chief in my own house, and will rule those whom Ulysses has won for me."

Then Eurymachus, son of Polybus, answered, "It rests with heaven to decide who shall be chief among us, but you shall be master in your own house and over your own possessions; no one while there is a man in Ithaca shall do you violence nor rob you. And now, my good fellow, I want to know about this stranger.

What country does he come from? Of what family is he, and where is his estate? Has he brought you news about the return of your father, or was he on business of his own? He seemed a well-to-do man, but he hurried off so suddenly that he was gone in a moment before we could get to know him."

Ye then must suffer shall pass all your pride ever to see redress'd, or qualified." At this all bit their lips, and did admire his words sent from him with such phrase and fire; which so much mov'd them that Antinous, Eupitheus' son, cried out: "Telemachus! The Gods, I think, have rapt thee to this height of elocution, and this great conceit of self-ability. We all may pray, that Jove invest not in this kingdom's sway thy forward forces, which I see put forth a hot ambition in thee for thy birth."

"Be not offended," he replied, "if I shall say, I would assume this empery, if Jove gave leave. You are not he that sings: 'The rule of kingdoms is the worst of things'. Nor is it ill, at all, to sway a throne; a man may quickly gain possession of mighty riches, make a wondrous prize set of his virtues; but the dignities that deck a king, there are enough beside in this circumfluous isle that want no pride to think them worthy of, as young as I, and old as you are. An ascent so high my thoughts affect not. Dead is he that held desert of virtue to have so excell'd. But of these turrets I will take on me to be the absolute king, and reign as free, as did my father, over all his hand

left here in this house slaves to my command." Eurymachus, the son of Polybus, to this made this reply: "Telemachus! The girlond of this kingdom let the knees of Deity run for; but the faculties this house is seised of, and the turrets here, thou shalt be lord of, nor shall any bear the least part off of all thou dost possess,

As long as this land is no wilderness, nor ruled by out-laws. But give these their pass, and tell me, best of princes, who he was that guested here so late? From whence? And what in any region boasted he his state? His race? His country? Brought he any news of thy returning father? Or for dues of moneys to him made he fit repair? Now suddenly he rush'd into the air, nor would sustain to stay and make him known!

"My father is dead and gone," answered Telemachus, "and even if some rumour reaches me I put no more faith in it now. My mother does indeed sometimes send for a soothsayer and question him, but I give his prophecyings no heed.

As for the stranger, he was Mentes, son of Anchialus, chief of the Taphians, an old friend of my father's." But in his heart he knew that it had been the goddess.

The suitors then returned to their singing and dancing until the evening; but when night fell upon their pleasuring they went home to bed each in his own abode.

Telemachus's room was high up in a tower that looked on to the outer court; hither, then, he hied, brooding and full of thought. A good old woman, Euryclea, daughter of Ops, the son of Pisenor, went before him with a couple of blazing torches. Laertes had bought her with his own money when she was quite young; he gave the worth of twenty oxen for her, and shewed as much respect to her in his household as he did to his own wedded wife, but he did not take her to his bed for he feared his wife's resentment.

She it was who now lighted Telemachus to his room, and she loved him better than any of the other women in the house did, for she had nursed him when he was a baby.

He opened the door of his bed room and sat down upon the bed; as he took off his shirt he gave it to the good old woman, who folded it tidily up, and hung it for him over a peg by his bed side, after which she went out, pulled the door to by a silver catch, and drew the bolt home by means of the strap.

His port show'd no debauch'd companion." He answer'd: "The return of my lov'd sire is past all hope; and should rude Fame inspire from any place a flattering messenger with news of his survival, he should bear no least belief off from my desperate love. Which if a sacred prophet should approve, call'd by my mother for her care's unrest, it should not move me. For my late fair guest, he was of old my father's, touching here

from sea-girt Taphos, and for name doth bear Mentas, the son of wise Anchialus, and governs all the Taphians studious of navigation." This he said, but knew it was a Goddess. These again withdrew

To dances and attraction of the song; and while their pleasures did the time prolong, the sable Even descended, and did steep the lids of all men in desire of sleep.

Telemachus, into a room built high of his illustrious court, and to the eye of circular prospect, to his bed ascended, and in his mind much weighty thought contended. Before him Euryclea (that well knew all the observance of a handmaid's due, daughter to Opis Pisenorides) bore two bright torches; who did so much please Laertes in her prime, that, for the price of twenty oxen, he made merchandize of her rare beauties; and love's equal flame to her he felt, as to his nuptial dame, yet never durst he mix with her in bed, so much the anger of his wife he fled.

She, now grown old, to young Telemachus two torches bore, and was obsequious past all his other maids, and did apply her service to him from his infancy.

His well-built chamber reach'd, she op'd the door. He on his bed sat, the soft weeds he wore put off, and to the diligent old maid gave all; who fitly all in thick folds laid, and hung them on a beam-pin near the bed, that round about was rich embroidered. Then made she haste forth from him, and did bring the door together with a silver ring, and by a string a bar to it did pull.

But Telemachus as he lay covered with a woollen fleece kept thinking all night through of his intended voyage of the counsel that Minerva had given him.

He, laid, and cover'd well with curled wool woven in silk quilts, all night employ'd his mind about the task that Pallas had design'd.

Appendix C
News DTD and Style Sheets

This appendix includes example support files for the broadcast news programming SGML markup format utilized in the Xtrieve system. The DTD is relatively simple in this application. Three DSSSL style sheets are provided for display, indexing, and analysis.

For reasons of clarity and brevity, the files presented in this Appendix have been simplified somewhat from the production versions in the Xtrieve system.

1. NEWS DTD

The news DTD is actually quite simple. It allows the definition of a news story, a set of stories, or a program consisting of stories.

```
<!-- DTD for News by Charles B. Owen -->
<?stylesheet href="news.dsl" type="text/dsssl">

<!ENTITY amp "&">
<!ENTITY lt "<">
<!ENTITY gt ">">

<!ELEMENT news      - - (title, fm, (program | story)+)>
<!ELEMENT title     - - (#PCDATA)>
<!ELEMENT fm        - - (p+)>
<!ELEMENT p         - - (#PCDATA)>
<!ELEMENT program   - - (title?, speaker*, story+)>
<!ELEMENT story     - - (title?, speaker*, (direction | segment)*)>
<!ELEMENT speaker   - - (#PCDATA)>
<!ELEMENT segment   - - (speaker+, (line | direction)+)>
<!ELEMENT line      - - (direction | #PCDATA)*>
<!ELEMENT direction - - (#PCDATA)>
```

2.   DISPLAY STYLE-SHEET

The only really complicated issue in the display style-sheet is the simultaneous presentation of speakers and story lines. This presentation requires the creation of a two column table.

```
<!DOCTYPE style-sheet
  PUBLIC "-//James Clark//DTD DSSSL Style Sheet//EN" [
<!-- Display support! -->
]>


;;;;;;;;;;;;;;;;;;;;;;;;;;;;;;;;;;;;;;;;;;;;;;;;;;;;;;;;;;;;;;;;;;;;;
; Constants
(define *titleFontSize*          18pt)
(define *reporterFontSize*       16pt)

(define *fmFontSize*             (/ *titleFontSize* 2))
(define *fmIndent*               3cm)
(define *fmSpaceBefore*          .5cm)

(define *textFontSize*           10pt)
(define *textSpaceBefore*        (/ *textFontSize* 2))
(define *textFontFamily*         "Times New Roman")

(define *sectFontSize*           14pt)
(define *sectsubFontSize*        12pt)

(define *speakerWidth*           4cm)


;;;;;;;;;;;;;;;;;;;;;;;;;;;;;;;;;;;;;;;;;;;;;;;;;;;;;;;;;;;;;;;;;;;;;

(root
  (make simple-page-sequence
        ; margins
        left-margin:         2cm
        right-margin:        2cm
        top-margin:          2cm
        bottom-margin:       2cm

        ; default font
        font-size:           *textFontSize*
        line-spacing:        *textFontSize*
        (process-children))
)


;;;;;;;;;;;;;;;;;;;;;;;;;;;;;;;;;;;;;;;;;;;;;;;;;;;;;;;;;;;;;;;;;;;;;
; Major news elements

(element (NEWS TITLE)
  (make paragraph
```

```
      quadding:                'center
      font-size:               *titleFontSize*
      line-spacing:            *titleFontSize*
      font-weight:             'bold
      keep-with-next?:         #t
      (process-children)))

(element (NEWS REPORTER)
  (make paragraph
      quadding:                'center
      font-size:               *reporterFontSize*
      line-spacing:            *reporterFontSize*
      font-weight:             'bold
      keep-with-next?:         #t
      (process-children)))

;;;;;;;;;;;;;;;;;;;;;;;;;;;;;;;;;;;;;;;;;;;;;;;;;;;;;;;;;;;;;;;;;;;;;;;;
; Front matter

(element (FM)
  (make paragraph
      font-size:               *fmFontSize*
      line-spacing:            *fmFontSize*
      start-indent:            *fmIndent*
      end-indent:              *fmIndent*
      space-before:            *fmSpaceBefore*
      space-after:             *fmSpaceBefore*
      (process-children)))

(element (FM P)
  (make paragraph
      (process-children)))

;;;;;;;;;;;;;;;;;;;;;;;;;;;;;;;;;;;;;;;;;;;;;;;;;;;;;;;;;;;;;;;;;;;;;;;;
; Programs and stories

(element PROGRAM
  (process-children))

(element (PROGRAM TITLE)
  (make paragraph
      quadding:                'center
      font-size:               *sectFontSize*
      line-spacing:            *sectFontSize*
      font-weight:             'bold
      space-before:            *sectFontSize*
      keep-with-next?:         #t
      (literal "Program: ")
      (process-children)))
```

```
(element (STORY TITLE)
  (make paragraph
        quadding:                  'center
        font-size:                 *sectFontSize*
        line-spacing:              *sectFontSize*
        font-weight:               'bold
        space-before:              *sectFontSize*
        keep-with-next?:           #t
        (literal "Story: ")
        (process-children)))

;;;;;;;;;;;;;;;;;;;;;;;;;;;;;;;;;;;;;;;;;;;;;;;;;;;;;;;;;;;;;;;;;;;;;;;
; direction

(element DIRECTION
  (make sequence
        font-posture:              'italic
        ; surround so not spoken accidentally
        (literal "[")
        (process-children)
        (literal "]")))

  ;;;;;;;;;;;;;;;;;;;;;;;;;;;;;;;;;;;;;;;;;;;;;;;;;;;;;;;;;;;;;;;;;;;;;;;
  ; STORY SEGMENT

(element SEGMENT
  (make table                      ; use a table to accommodate
                                   ; multiple speakers
        space-before:              (/ *textFontSize* 2)
        may-violate-keep-after?:   #t
        (make table-column         ;ensure speaker column is narrow
           column-number:          1
           width:                  *speakerWidth*)
        (make table-cell           ;collect all speakers
           (make paragraph
              (with-mode *segmentSpeaker*
                      (process-matching-children "SPEAKER"))))
        (make table-cell           ;collect all lines and instructions
           (process-children))))

(mode *segmentSpeaker*             ; collect speakers into single column
  (element SPEAKER                 ; separate with ampersands
                                   ; to indicate multiple speakers
        (if (= (child-number) 1)
            (make sequence
               font-posture:   'italic
               (process-children))
            (make sequence
               font-posture:   'italic
               (literal " &amp; ")
```

```
                      (process-children))))
```

```
;;;;;;;;;;;;;;;;;;;;;;;;;;;;;;;;;;;;;;;;;;;;;;;;;;;;;;;;;;;;;;;;;;;;;;;
; SPEAKER
; This has been taken care of in segmentSpeaker mode,
; therefore ignore in normal mode

(element SPEAKER
  (empty-sosofo))
```

```
;;;;;;;;;;;;;;;;;;;;;;;;;;;;;;;;;;;;;;;;;;;;;;;;;;;;;;;;;;;;;;;;;;;;;;;
; Actual lines of a story

(element LINE
  (make paragraph
        (process-children)))
```

3. INDEXING STYLE-SHEET

```
<!DOCTYPE style-sheet
  PUBLIC "-//James Clark//DTD DSSSL Style Sheet//EN" [
<!-- Indexing support only! -->
]>

(define *speaker-beg* "::SPKRBEG")
(define *speaker-end* "::SPKREND")
(define *noindex-beg* "::NOIBEG")
(define *noindex-end* "::NOIEND")
(define *l1-beg* "::L1BEG")
(define *l1-end* "::L1END")
(define *l2-beg* "::L2BEG")
(define *l2-end* "::L2END")
(define *l3-beg* "::L3BEG")
(define *l3-end* "::L3END")
(define *l4-beg* "::L4BEG")
(define *l4-end* "::L4END")
(define *l5-beg* "::L5BEG")
(define *l5-end* "::L5END")
(define *l9-beg* "::L9BEG")
(define *l9-end* "::L9END")

(root
  (make simple-page-sequence
        (make sequence
                (make sequence (literal *l9-beg*))
                (process-children)
                (make sequence (literal *l9-end*))
        )
  )
)
```

```
(define (STANDARD-PARAGRAPH)
  (make paragraph
        (process-children)))

(define (STANDARD-SEQUENCE)
  (make sequence
        (process-children)))

(define (level-two)
  (make sequence
        (make sequence (literal *l2-beg*))
        (process-children)
        (make sequence (literal *l2-end*))))

(define (level-three)
  (make sequence
        (make sequence (literal *l3-beg*))
        (process-children)
        (make sequence (literal *l3-end*))))

(define (level-four)
  (make sequence
        (make sequence (literal *l4-beg*))
        (process-children)
        (make sequence (literal *l4-end*))))

(define (level-five)
  (make sequence
        (make sequence (literal *l5-beg*))
        (process-children)
        (make sequence (literal *l5-end*))))

(element TITLE (level-two))
(element AUTHOR (level-two))
(element FM (level-five))
(element P (level-two))

(element PROGRAM (level-four))

(element STORY (level-three))

(element DIRECTION (STANDARD-PARAGRAPH))
(element SEGMENT (level-two))

(element SPEAKER
  (make sequence
        (make sequence (literal *noindex-beg*))
        (make sequence (literal *speaker-beg*))
        (process-children)
```

```
          (make sequence (literal ": "))
          (make sequence (literal *speaker-end*))
          (make sequence (literal *noindex-end*)))))

(element LINE (STANDARD-SEQUENCE))
```

4.   ANALYSIS STYLE-SHEET

```
<!DOCTYPE style-sheet
 PUBLIC "-//James Clark//DTD DSSSL Style Sheet//EN" [
<!-- Synchronization support only! -->
]>

(root
  (make simple-page-sequence
        (process-children))
)

(element TITLE (empty-sosofo))
(element AUTHOR (empty-sosofo))
(element FM (empty-sosofo))

(element PROGRAM
  (process-children))

(element STORY
  (process-children))

(element DIRECTION (empty-sosofo))

(element SEGMENT (process-children))
(element SPEAKER (empty-sosofo))
(element LINE (make paragraph (process-children)))
```

References

[1] Philipp Ackermann. Direct manipulation of temporal structures in a multimedia application framework. In *ACM Multimedia'94*, pages 51–58, San Francisco, CA, 1994. ACM Press.

[2] Donald A. Adjeroh, M. C. Lee, and Cyril U. Orji. Techniques for fast partitioning of compressed and uncompressed video. *Multimedia Tools and Applications*, 4:225–243, 1997.

[3] Aligner: Automatic speech-text alignment software, http://www.entropic.com/aligner.html, 1996.

[4] George S. Almasi and Allan Gottlieb. *Highly Parallel Computing*. The Benjamin/Cummings Publishing Company, Inc., Redwood City, CA, second edition, 1994.

[5] Liora Alschuler. *ABCD–SGML: A User's Guide to Structured Information*. International Thomson Computer Press, London, 1995.

[6] David P. Anderson and George Homsy. A continuous media I/O server and its synchronization mechanism. *Computer*, October, 1991:51–57, 1991.

[7] F. Arman, R. Depommier, A. Hsu, and M-Y. Chiu. Content-based browsing of video sequences. In *ACM Multimedia'94*, pages 97–103, San Francisco, CA, 1994. ACM Press.

[8] C. Bacher and T. Ottmann. Tools and services for authoring on the fly. In Patricia Carlson and Fillia Makedon, editors, *Proceedings of ED-MEDIA'96*, pages 7–12, Boston, MA, 1996. Association for the Advancement of Computing in Education.

[9] Peter A. Bandettini and Eric C. Wong. *Echo Planar Imaging*, chapter in Echo-Planer Magnetic Resonance Imaging of Human Brain Activation. Springer-Verlag, 1997.

[10] Shahab Baqai, M. Farrukh Khan, and Arif Ghafoor. *The Handbook of Multimedia Information Management*, chapter Multimedia Communications – Synchronization, pages 335–363. Prentice Hall PTR, 1997.

[11] Richard Beckwith, George A. Miller, and Randee Tengi. Design and implementation of the WordNet lexical database and searching software. Report, Princeton University Cognitive Science Laboratory, 1993.

[12] Maurice Bellanger. *Digital Processing of Signals*. John Wiley and Sons, Chichester, 1984.

[13] Claude Berge. *Graphs*. North-Holland, Amsterdam, second revised edition, 1985.

[14] P. J. Bloom. High-quality digital audio in the entertainment industry: An overview of achievements and challenges. *IEEE ASSP Magazine*, 2(4):2–25, 1985.

[15] Patrice Bonhomme and Laurent Romary. The Lingua parallel concordancing project: Managing multilingual texts for educational purposes. In *Proceedings of Language Engineering 95*, Montpellier, France, 1995.

[16] M. G. Brown, J. T. Foote, G. J. F. Jones, K. Spärck Jones, and S. J. Young. Video mail retrieval by voice: An overview of the Cambridge/Olivetti retrieval system. In *Proceedings of the ACM Multimedia'94 Workshop on Multimedia Database Management Systems*, pages 47–55, San Francisco, CA, 1994.

[17] M. G. Brown, J. T. Foote, G. J. F. Jones, K. Spärck Jones, and S. J. Young. Open-vocabulary speech indexing for voice and video mail retrieval. In *Proceedings of Multimedia'96*, pages 307–316, Boston, MA, 1996.

[18] Curtis A. Carver and Clark Ray. Automating hypermedia course creation and maintenance. In Hermann Maurer, editor, *Proceedings of WebNet'96 World Conference of the Web Society*, pages 82–87, San Francisco, CA, 1996. Association for the Advancement of Computing in Education.

[19] Mon-Song Chen, Dilip D. Kanklur, and Philip S. Yu. Optimization of grouped sweeping scheduling (GSS) with heterogeneous multimedia systems. In P. Venkat Rangan, editor, *ACM Multimedia '93*, pages 235–241, Anaheim, California, 1993. ACM Press.

[20] Tsuhan Chen, Hans Peter Graf, and Kuansan Wang. Lip synchronization using speech-assisted video processing. *IEEE Signal Processing Letters*, 2(4):57–59, 1995.

[21] Tsuhan Chen and Ram Rao. Audio-visual interaction in multimedia. *IEEE Circuits and Devices*, 11(6):21–26, 1995.

[22] Jason Chong and Roberto Togneri. Speaker independent recognition of a small vocabulary. Technical Report CP96-03, Centre for Intelligent Information Processing Systems, The University of Western Australia, 1996.

[23] K. Chong and Roberto Togneri. Extraction of speech signal in the presence of a musical note signal using the GRNN. Technical Report CP96-02, Centre for Intelligent Information Processing Systems, The University of Western Australia, 1996.

[24] Kenneth Ward Church. Char_align: A program for aligning parallel texts at the character level. In *Proceedings of the 30th Annual Meeting of the Association for Computational Linguistics, ACL'93*, Columbus, OH, 1993.

[25] Ronald A. Cole, Daniel Burnett, and Vince Weatherill. An evaluation guide for emergent technologies in automatic speech recognition. Technical report, Oregon Graduate Institute of Science and Technology, 1993.

[26] Thomas H. Cormen, Charles E. Leiserson, and Ronald L. Rivest. *Introduction to Algorithms*. The MIT Press, Cambridge, MA, first edition, 1990.

[27] Douglass R. Cutting, David R. Karger, and Jan O. Pedersen. Constant interaction-time scatter/gather browsing of very large document collections. In *SIGIR'93*, pages 126–134, Pittsburgh, PA, 1993. ACM Press.

[28] Ido Dagan, Fernando Pereira, and Lillian Lee. Similarity-based estimation of word cooccurrence probabilities. In *Proceedings of the 32nd Annual Meeting of the Association for Computational Linguistics, ACL'94*, New Mexico State University, Las Cruces, NM, 1994.

[29] Digital Equipment Corporation, Maynard, MA. *Multimedia Services for DIGITAL UNIX Programmers Guide*, 1997.

[30] Paul Duchnowski, Martin Hunke, Dietrich Büsching, Uwe Meier, and Alex Waibel. Toward movement-invariant automatic lip-reading and

speech recognition. In *Proceedings of ICASSP'95, Volume I*, pages 557–560, Detroit, MI, 1995.

[31] Alexandros Eleftheriadis. Flavor: a language for media representation. In *ACM Multimedia'97*, pages 1–9, Seattle, WA, 1997.

[32] James Ford, Chris Langmead, Fillia Makedon, Charles Owen, and Sam Rebelsky. Multimedia-based learning and museums: Issues and enabling tools. In *The Consortium for Computing in Small Colleges Second Annual Northeastern Conference*, Boston, MA, 1996.

[33] James Ford, Fillia Makedon, Charles Owen, and Samuel A. Rebelsky. *Multimedia Tools and Applications*, chapter Interactive Multimedia Publishing Systems. Kluwer Academic Press, 1996.

[34] James Ford, Fillia Makedon, and Charles B. Owen. *The Handbook of Multimedia Computing*, chapter Classification and Characterization of Digital Watermarks for Multimedia Data. CRC Press, Boca Raton, FL, 1998. To appear.

[35] James Ford, Fillia Makedon, and Samuel A. Rebelsky. Resource-limited hyper-reproductions: Electronically reproducing and extending lectures. *Multimedia Tools and Applications*, 6:181–197, 1998.

[36] Lindsey A. Foreman. Generalization of the Viterbi algorithm. *IMA Journal of Mathematics Applied in Business and Industry*, 4:351–367, 1992.

[37] G. David Forney, Jr. The Viterbi algorithm. *Proceedings of the IEEE*, 61(3):268–278, 1973.

[38] Wolfgang Forstner. *Lecture Notes in Computer Science*, volume 801, chapter A framework for low level feature extraction, pages 383–394. Springer-Verlag, Berlin, 1994.

[39] Hans-Immo Friel. *Imaging Systems for Medical Diagnostics*, chapter Nuclear Medical Diagnostics. Siemens Aktiengesellschaft, Berlin, 1990.

[40] K. J. Friston, A. P. Holmes, J-B Poline, P. J. Grasby, S. C. R. Williams, R. S. J. Frackowiak, and R. Turner. Analysis of fMRI time-series revisited. *Neuroimage*, 2:45–53, 1995.

[41] K. J. Friston, P. Jezzard, and R. Turner. The analysis of functional MRI time-series. *Human Brain Mapping*, 1:153–171, 1994.

[42] Pascale Fung and Kenneth Ward Church. K-vec: A new approach for aligning parallel texts. In *Proceedings of the Fifteenth International*

Conference on Computational Linguistics COLING '94, pages 1096–1102, Kyoto, Japan, 1994.

[43] Pascale Fung and Kathleen McKeown. Aligning noisy parallel corpora across language groups : Word pair feature matching by dynamic time warping. In *Proceedings of the first conference of the Association for Machine Translation in the Americas, AMTA-94*, Columbia, Maryland, 1994.

[44] John S. Garofolo, Lori F. Lamel, William M. Fisher, Jonathan G. Fiscus, David S. Pallett, and Nancy L. Dahlgren. DARPA TIMIT: Acoustic-phonetic continuous speech corpus CD-ROM. NIST Speech Disk 1-1.1, National Institute of Standards and Technology, Gaithersburg, MD, 1993.

[45] Simon Gibbs, Christian Breiteneder, and Dennis Tsichritzis. Data modeling of time-based media. In Dennis Tsichritzis, editor, *Visual Objects*, pages 1–21. Centre Universitaire d'Informatique, Geneva, Switzerland, 1993.

[46] Simon Gibbs, Christian Breiteneder, and Dennis Tsichritzis. *The Handbook of Multimedia Information Management*, chapter Modeling Time-Based Media, pages 13–38. Prentice Hall PTR, 1997.

[47] Daniel T. Gillespie. *Markov Processes, An Introduction for Physical Scientists*. Academic Press, Boston, MA, 1992.

[48] Arthur A. Giordano and Frank M. Hsu. *Least Square Estimation with Application to Digital Signal Processing*. John Wiley and Sons, New York, 1985.

[49] James Glass, David Goddeau, Lee Hetherington, Michael McCandless, Christine Pao, Michael Phillips, Joseph Polifroni, Stephanie Seneff, and Victor Zue. The MIT ATIS system: December 1994 progress report. In *Proc. ARPA Spoken Language Technology Workshop*, Austin, TX, 1995.

[50] Rafael C. Gonzalez and Richard E. Woods. *Digital Image Processing*. Addison-Wesley Publishing Company, Reading, Massachusetts, 1992.

[51] Rei Hamakawa and Jun Rekimoto. Object composition and playback models for handling multimedia data. In *ACM Multimedia'93*, pages 273–281. Addison-Wesley, 1993.

[52] Alexander G. Hauptmann and Michael J. Witbrock. Informedia news-on-demand: Using speech recognition to create a digital video library. In *Proceedings of Intelligent Integration and Use of Text, Image, Video*

and Audio Corpora, AAAI 1997 Spring Symposium, pages 120–126, Stanford University, CA, 1997.

[53] Alexander G. Hauptmann, Michael J. Witbrock, Alexander I. Rudnicky, and Stephen Reed. Speech for multimedia information retrieval. In *Proceedings of User Interface Software and Technology, UIST-95,* Pittsburg, PA, 1995.

[54] Hynek Hermansky. Perceptual linear predictive (PLP) analysis of speech. *Journal of the Acoustical Society of America,* 87(4):1738–1752, 1990.

[55] Hynek Hermansky, Nelson Morgan, Aruna Bayya, and Phil Kohn. RASTA-PLP speech analysis. Technical Report TR-91-069, International Computer Science Institute, 1991.

[56] Kyoji Hirata and Toshikazu Kato. Query by visual example. In *Extending Database Technology'92,* pages 56–71, 1992.

[57] Susan Hockey. Text encoding initiative and SGML. In *Proceedings of the Seminar on Cataloging Digital Documents,* 1994.

[58] Robert V. Hogg and Elliot A. Tanis. *Probability and Statistical Inference.* Macmillan Publishing Company, New York, third edition, 1988.

[59] Homer. *The Odyssey.* Translated by Samuel Butler.

[60] Homer. *The Odyssey.* Translated by George Chapman.

[61] John E. Hopcroft and Jeffrey D. Ullman. *Introduction to Automata Theory, Languages, and Computation.* Addison Wesley, Reading, MA, 1979.

[62] ISO/IEC, Genève, Switzerland. *Information technology – Processing languages – Document style semantics and specifications language (DSSSL), ISO/IEC 10179:1996(E),* 1996.

[63] David L. Jannings and Dennis W. Ruck. Enhancing automatic speech recognition with an ultrasonic lip motion detector. In *Proceedings of ICASSP'95, Volume I,* pages 868–871, Detroit, Michigan, 1995.

[64] Ahsan S. Kabir. Identifying and encoding correlations across multiple documents. Student project, 1997.

[65] Wolfgang Klas, Erich J. Neuhold, and Michael Schrefl. Using an object-oriented approach to model multimedia data. *Computer Communications,* pages 204–216, 1990.

[66] P. Laface, C. Vair, and L. Fissore. A fast segmental Viterbi algorithm for large vocabulary recognition. In *Proceedings of ICASSP'95, Volume I*, pages 560–563, Detroit, Michigan, 1995.

[67] Kyuchul Lee, Yong Kyu Lee, and P. Bruce Berra. Management of multi-structured hypermedia documents: A data model, query language, and indexing scheme. *Multimedia Tools and Applications*, 4:199–223, 1997.

[68] Christopher J. Lindblad. A programming system for the dynamic manipulation of temporally sensitive data. MIT/LCS/TR-637, Massachusetts Institute of Technology, 1994.

[69] Thomas D. C. Little and Arif Ghafoor. Spatio-temporal composition of distributed multimedia data objects for value-added networks. *Computer*, pages 42–50, 1991.

[70] Fillia Makedon, James Ford, Michael Kenyon, and Charles Owen. Ancient museum collections and the web. In Hermann Maurer, editor, *Proceedings of WebNet'96 World Conference of the Web Society*, pages 315–329, San Francisco, CA, 1996. Association for the Advancement of Computing in Education. Invited paper.

[71] Fillia Makedon, Peter Gloor, and James Matthew, editors. *Parallel Computation: Practical Implementation of Algorithms and Machines*. Springer Verlag, 1992. 1992 Symposium of the Dartmouth Institute for Advanced Graduate Studies in Parallel Computation (DAGS'92). CD-ROM.

[72] Fillia Makedon and Charles B. Owen. Multimedia data analysis using ImageTcl and applications in automating the analysis of human communication. In *Proceedings of the 3rd Panhellenic Conference with International Participation: Didactics of Mathematics and Informatics in Education*, Patras, Greece, 1997.

[73] Fillia Makedon, Mary Owen, Charles Owen, James Ford, Christina Metaxaki-Kossionides, and Tillman Steinberg. HEAR HOMER: A multimedia-data access remote prototype for ancient texts. In *Proceedings of ED-MEDIA'98*, Freiburg, Germany, 1998. To appear.

[74] Fillia Makedon, Samuel A Rebelsky, Matthew Cheyney, Charles B. Owen, and Peter Gloor. Issues and obstacles with multimedia authoring. In *Proceedings of ED-MEDIA 94, World Conference on Educational Multimedia and Hypermedia*, pages 38–45, Vancouver, BC, Canada, 1994. Invited paper.

[75] J. L. Massey. Foundation and methods of channel encoding. In *Proceedings of the International Conference on Information Theory and Systems*, NTG-Fachberichte, Berlin, 1978.

[76] R. McEliece. On the BCJR Trellis for linear block codes. *IEEE Transactions on Information Systems*, IT-42(4):1072–1092, 1996.

[77] Uwe Meier, Wolfgang Hürst, and Paul Duchnowski. Adaptive bimodal sensor fusion for automatic speechreading. In *Proceedings of the 1996 International Conference on Acoustics, Speech, and Signal Processing, ICASSP'96*, Atlanta, GA, 1996.

[78] I. Dan Melamed. A geometric approach to mapping bitext correspondence. Report 96-22, IRCS, 1996.

[79] I. Dan Melamed. A portable algorithm for mapping bitext correspondence. In *Proceedings of the 35th Conference of the Association for Computational Linguistics, ACL'97*, Madrid, Spain, 1997.

[80] Gene Miller, Greg Baber, and Mark Gilliland. News on-demand for multimedia networks. In *ACM Multimedia'93*, pages 383–392, Anaheim, CA, 1993. ACM Press.

[81] George A. Miller, Richard Beckwith, Christiane Fellbaum, Derek Gross, and Katherine Miller. Introduction to WordNet: An on-line lexical database. CSL Report 43, Princeton University Cognitive Science Laboratory, 1990. Revised August, 1993.

[82] Pedro J. Moreno. *Speech Recognition in Noisy Environments*. Dissertation, Carnegie Mellon University, 1996.

[83] Praveen Kumar Murthy. *Scheduling Techniques for Synchronous and Multidimensional Synchronous Dataflow*. Dissertation, University of California at Berkeley, 1996.

[84] Steven R. Newcomb, Neill A. Kipp, and Victoria T. Newcomb. The "HyTime" hypermedia/time-based document structuring language. *Communications of the ACM*, 34(11):67–83, 1991.

[85] V. Niblack, R. Barber, W. Equitz, M. Flickner, E. Glasman, D. Petkovic, P. Yanker, C. Faloutsos, and G. Taubin. The QBIC project: querying images by content using color, texture, and shape. In *IS&T/SPIE 1993 International Symposium on Electronic Imaging: Science & Technology*, volume 1908, Storage and Retrieval of Image and Video Database, pages 173–187, 1993.

[86] Automatic translation of english text to phonetics by means of letter-to-sound rules. NRL Report 7948, Naval Research Laboratory, Washington, D.C., 1993. Published by the National Technical Information Service as document AD/A021 929.

[87] John K. Ousterhout. *Tcl/Tk Engineering Manual*. Sun Microsystems, 1994.

[88] Mark H. Overmars. Geometric data structures for computer graphics: an overview. *Theoretical Foundations of Computer Graphics and CAD*, F40:21–49, 1987.

[89] Charles B. Owen. Application of multiple media stream correlation to functional imaging of the brain. In *Proceedings of the International Conference on Vision, Recognition, Action: Neural Models of Mind and Machine*, Boston, MA, 1997.

[90] Charles B. Owen. The ImageTcl multimedia algorithm development system. In *Proceedings of the 5th Annual Tcl/Tk Workshop '97*, pages 97–105, Boston, MA, 1997.

[91] Charles B. Owen. The Phedias graphics system: A 3D computer graphics project environment. In *Proceedings of ED-MEDIA'98 World Conference on Educational Multimedia and Hypermedia*, Frieberg, Germany, 1998. To appear.

[92] Charles B. Owen and Fillia Makedon. Asml: Automatic site markup language. *Multimedia Tools and Applications*, 17:113–139, 1997.

[93] Charles B. Owen and Fillia Makedon. Multimedia data analysis using ImageTcl. In I. Balderjahn, R. Mather, and M. Schader, editors, *Data Highways and Information Flooding, a Challenge for Classification and Data Analysis*. Springer-Verlag, 1997.

[94] Charles B. Owen and Fillia Makedon. Multimedia data analysis using ImageTcl (extended version). Technical Report PCS-TR97-310, Dartmouth College, 1997.

[95] Charles B. Owen and Fillia Makedon. Multiple media stream data analysis: Theory and applications. In I. Balderjahn, R. Mather, and M. Schader, editors, *Data Highways and Information Flooding, a Challenge for Classification and Data Analysis*. Springer-Verlag, 1997.

[96] Charles B. Owen and Fillia Makedon. Multiple media stream data analysis: Theory and applications (extended version). Technical Report PCS-TR97-321, Dartmouth College, 1997.

[97] Charles B. Owen and Fillia Makedon. Cross-modal retrieval of scripted speech audio. In *Proceedings of SPIE Multimedia Computing and Networking, 1998*, San Jose, CA, 1998. To appear.

[98] Charles B. Owen and Fillia Makedon. *The Handbook of Multimedia Computing*, chapter Cross-Modal Information Retrieval. CRC Press, Boca Raton, FL, 1998. To appear.

[99] Michael Papathomas, Christian Breiteneder, Simon Gibbs, and Vicki de Mey. Synchronization in virtual worlds. In Dennis Tsichritzis, editor, *Visual Objects*, pages 69–86. Centre Universitaire d'Informatique, Geneva, Switzerland, 1993.

[100] Sarvar Patel. A lower-complexity Viterbi algorithm. In *Proceedings of ICASSP'95, Volume I*, pages 592–595, Detroit, Michigan, 1995.

[101] John G. Proakis. *Digital Communications*. McGraw-Hill Book Company, New York, second edition, 1989.

[102] Lawrence Rabiner and Biing-Hwang Juang. *Fundamentals of Speech Recognition*. Signal Processing Series. PTR Prentice Hall, Englewood Cliffs, NJ, 1993.

[103] Ram R. Rao and Tsuhan Chen. Cross-modal prediction in audio-visual communication. In *ICASSP'96*, volume IV, pages 2056–2060, Atlanta, GA, 1996. IEEE.

[104] Mosur K. Ravishankar. Efficient algorithms for speech recognition. Technical Report CMU-CS-96-143, Carnegie Mellon University, 1996.

[105] Darrell R. Raymond and Frank Wm. Tompa. Markup reconsidered. In *The First International Workshop on Principles of Document Processing*, Washington, DC, 1992.

[106] Samuel A. Rebelsky, James Ford, Kenneth Harker, Fillia Makedon, P. Takis Metaxas, and Charles Owen. Interactive multimedia conference proceedings. In *Chi'95 Mosaic of Creativity*, volume 2, pages 13–14, Denver, CO, 1995.

[107] Samuel A. Rebelsky, Fillia Makedon, James Ford, Charles Owen, Peter A. Gloor, and P. Taxis Metaxas. The roles of video in the design, use, and construction of interactive electronic conference proceedings. *Journal of Universal Computer Science*, 1998. In submission.

[108] German Rigau and Eneko Agirre. Disambiguating bilingual nominal entries against WordNet. In *Proceedings of the Workshop on the Computational Lexicon, ESSLLI'95*, 1995.

[109] Gary D. Robson. *Inside Captioning*. CyberDawg Publishing, Castro Valley, CA, 1997.

[110] Matthew S. Ryan and Graham R. Nudd. The Viterbi algorithm. Technical Report CS-RR-238, Department of Computer Science, University of Warwick, Coventry, UK, 1993.

[111] Gerard Salton. *Introduction to modern information retrieval*. McGraw-Hill Computer Science Series. McGraw-Hill, New York, 1982.

[112] Johan Schalkwyk and Mark Fanty. *The CSLU-C Toolkit for Automatic Speech Recognition*. Oregon Graduate Institute Center for Spoken Language Understanding, 1996.

[113] Peter Schäuble and Martin Wechsler. First experiencies with a system for content based retrieval of information from speech recordings. In *IJCAI Workshop: Intelligent Multimedia Information Retrieval*, 1995.

[114] Jianbo Shi and Carlo Tomasi. Good features to track. Technical Report CS-TR-93-1399, Stanford University, 1993.

[115] David K. Smith. *Dynamic Programming, A Practical Introduction*. Ellis Horwood, New York, 1991.

[116] Joan M. Smith. *SGML and Related Standards: Document Description and Processing Languages*. Ellis Horwood, New York, 1992.

[117] John R. Smith. Quad-tree segmentation for texture-based image query. In *ACM Multimedia'94*, pages 279–286, San Francisco, CA, 1994. ACM Press.

[118] Michael A. Smith and Takeo Kanade. Video skimming for quick browsing based on audio and image characterization. Technical Report CMU-CS-95-186, Carnegie Mellon University, 1995.

[119] S. M. Smith and J. M. Brady. SUSAN – a new approach to low level image processing. Technical Report TR95SMS1c, The Oxford Centre for Functional Magnetic Resonance Imaging of the Brain, 1995.

[120] Institute of Neurology Short Course 1996: Statistical Parametric Mapping and Functional Neuroimaging, Functional Imaging Laboratory, London, UK.

[121] Richard Szeliski and James Coughlan. Spline-based image registration. Technical report, Digital Equipment Corporation, Cambridge Research Lab, 1994.

[122] Laura Teodosio and Walter Bender. Salient video stills: Content and context preserved. In P. Venkat Rangan, editor, *ACM Multimedia '93*, pages 39–46, Anaheim, California, 1993. ACM Press.

[123] Ari Trachtenberg. Computational methods in coding theory. Masters thesis, The University of Illinois at Urbana-Champaign, 1994.

[124] Pim van der Eijk. Comparative discourse analysis of parallel texts. http://xxx.lanl.gov/abs/cmp-lg/9407022, 1994.

[125] A. Verstermans and J. P. Martens. Automatic labeling of corpora for speech synthesis development. In *Proceedings of IEEE ProRisc-94*, pages 261–266, 1994.

[126] Minh Tue Vo, Ricky Houghton, Jie Yang, Udo Bub, Uwe Meier, Alex Waibel, and Paul Duchnowski. Multimodal learning interfaces. In *Proceedings of ARPA Spoken Language Technology Workshop*, Austin, TX, 1995.

[127] Alex Waibel, Minh Tue Vo, Paul Duchnowski, and Stefan Manke. Multimodal interfaces. *Artificial Intelligence Review*, 10(3/4):299–319, 1996.

[128] H. Joseph Weaver. *Theory of Discrete and Continuous Fourier Analysis*. John Wiley and Sons, New York, 1989.

[129] Hongjiang Zhang, Chien Yong Low, and Stephen W. Smoliar. Video parsing and browsing using compressed data. *Multimedia Tools and Applications*, 1:89–111, 1995.

[130] Victor W. Zue and Stephanie Seneff. Transcription and alignment of the TIMIT database. In *The Second Symposium on Advanced Man-Machine Interface through Spoken Language*, Oahu, Hawaii, 1988.

Index